Robert Lindsey

A True Story of Blood and Money

IRRESISTIBLE
IMPULSE

SIMON & SCHUSTER

NEW YORK   LONDON   TORONTO   SYDNEY   TOKYO   SINGAPORE

SIMON & SCHUSTER
SIMON & SCHUSTER BUILDING
ROCKEFELLER CENTER
1230 AVENUE OF THE AMERICAS
NEW YORK, NEW YORK 10020

DESIGNED BY LEVAVI & LEVAVI
PHOTO RESEARCH BY NATALIE GOLDSTEIN
MANUFACTURED IN THE UNITED STATES OF AMERICA

1   3   5   7   9   10   8   6   4   2

LIBRARY OF CONGRESS CATALOGING-IN-PUBLICATION DATA

LINDSEY, ROBERT.
IRRESISTIBLE IMPULSE: A TRUE STORY OF BLOOD AND MONEY / ROBERT
LINDSEY,
P.   CM.
1. TELLING, MICHAEL.   2. ZUMSTEG, MONIKA, 1956–1983.
3. MURDER—ENGLAND—CASE STUDIES. I. TITLE.
HV6535.G42E543
364.1′523′0942595—DC20   92-27668
ISBN: 0-671-68069-2   CIP

Picture Credits

Syndicational International 1, 26
Private Collection 2, 3, 4, 25
© Phillip Knightley 5, 6
Ron Bell/Press Association 7
Robert Lindsey 8, 22, 23
Devon News 9, 10, 11, 12, 18, 21
Press Association 13, 14, 17
Torbay News Agency 15, 16, 19, 20, 24

To SANDRA,
STILL MY STAFF OF LIFE

WHAT FOLLOWS IS A TRUE STORY.

He loaded the fishing tackle, tent, sleeping bag, pitchfork, spade, and ax along with his cargo into the van. He closed the door, started the engine, and with Mandy beside him, drove away in the darkness.

After an hour, he stopped for coffee, then drove on.

At the edge of the forest, he turned off the highway and stopped beside a gate. On the horizon, lights from the city illuminated the sky in a brilliant aurora. In the distance, he could see the rays of the summer moon reflected on the river. The only sound was the murmur of the wind pummeling the trees above him, an overture to a tempestuous storm.

He pushed the gate and it opened.

Beside a grotto in the woods, he parked the van and unloaded his cargo, raised the ax and let it fall.

As he drove home, he hoped he hadn't forgotten anything.

I

The child is father of the man.

WILLIAM WORDSWORTH

1.

Sausalito,
Autumn 1980

It began with a Harley-Davidson, on a Sunday morning in California. One man traveled north across the Golden Gate Bridge, the other south through the freshly harvested vineyards of the Sonoma Valley. They approached on converging paths, random blips in intersecting tides of traffic, beneath a fiery autumn sun. Neither was aware of what lay ahead of him. If either had known, he would have turned back.

On San Francisco Bay, the sails of weekend yachtsmen were already a blur of snowy triangles rhythmically rising and tumbling on a choppy sea, and the first boats of the Bay's dwindling fishing fleet, after trolling outside the Gate since before dawn, were headed for home at Fisherman's Wharf.

On shore, shoppers and tourists were starting to crowd the narrow sidewalks of Sausalito, the emerald village that plunges down a procession of forested hills into San Francisco Bay a few hundred yards north of the Golden Gate. In the marina, the engines of salt-dusted cabin cruisers roared to life after a week of silence. At the Alta Mira, Ondine, and The Spinnaker, brunchers hesitated over steaming platters of Eggs Benedict and omelettes stuffed with Dungeness crab to admire the distant profile of San Francisco, which loomed over the Bay like a far-off Oriental mirage, all white and parapeted.

At the edge of town, a traffic signal switched from green to yellow, and a man brought his motorcycle to a stop with a squeeze of his wrist.

Lou Zumsteg's passion for motorcycling amused some of the Oldsmobile-driving executives and union leaders with whom he did business. But contrary to their expectations, his decision at the age of forty-five to buy a motorcycle did not prove to be an impulsive whim soon abandoned for another toy. For Lou Zumsteg, what began as a hobby in mid-life had become a passion. Few things gave him more joy than kick-starting one of his bikes, squeezing the throttle, and speeding down a highway with a rocket between his legs. He was an introspective man, and the saddle of a motorcycle gave him peace, a place to think, and, when he needed it, a refuge from the demons that still tried to destroy him.

"A motorcycle is a strange thing," he said. "People either hate them or love 'em. I think most people probably hate 'em. But to me a bike is like a best friend who never expresses doubt in you. I never feel lonely on a bike. A motorcycle demands your full-time attention. You don't have a *conditional* relationship with a motorcycle."

On the morning of October 12, 1980, he owned eight motorcycles. In an affectionate joke, he had given each a name. Today, he rode south on Highway 101 from his home in Santa Rosa on a Yamaha named Genghis. His wife, Elsa, was seated on the bike behind him. Like many visitors to Sausalito that morning, they had been lured out of their home by the warmth of an Indian summer.

As he waited for the signal to change, Lou felt—before he heard—another motorcycle engine throbbing nearby. He glanced to his right and saw a glittering Harley-Davidson in the lane next to him.

He did not share the affection approaching idolatry that many bikers lavished on a Harley. He preferred faster, more agile Japanese bikes. But he understood the emotions a Harley could stir in other men and respected it for what it was, a unique American icon. Once, more than a hundred companies built motorcycles in America, but they had all vanished except one. The Harley-Davidson was the last motorcycle made in America.

Even fervent admirers conceded that Harleys were technologically inferior to the best motorcycles from overseas: the engine was loud, the gearbox noisy, the clutch stiff, the acceleration stodgy. Oil could dribble from crevices and orifices like steam through a sieve. But such imperfections mattered little to those who owned or lusted for a Harley: indeed, transportation was the least important reason for buying one.

A Harley embodied its admirers' vision of themselves: a Harley hog made the ground shake, the air tremble. It symbolized muscle, freedom, *masculinity*.

"Nice-looking bike," Lou said to the dark-haired stranger on the Harley. He was about thirty, perhaps younger, and dressed in the universal uniform of bikers: blue jeans, T-shirt, boots, and leather jacket.

He responded with a smile, and a "Thanks" whose accent, Lou thought, came from the British Isles.

"Where you from?"

"England."

When the light turned green, he asked Lou where he could park his motorcycle while he toured Sausalito.

"Follow us," Lou said and gunned the Yamaha to a parking lot several blocks away.

They dismounted and the stranger introduced himself. He said that his name was Michael Telling and he had come to California only a few days before, expressly to buy the Harley from the Dudley Perkins agency in San Francisco.

Lou knew the dealership. It was a legend among Harley fanatics. The Perkins family had been selling Harleys since 1914.

As they talked, he admired the lacquered all-black low rider. It was a limited-edition FXB Sturgis, which Harley-Davidson had recently developed to compete with an invasion of heavier bikes from Japan. A fluid sculpture in chrome, steel, and rubber with glistening forks and a long black saddle, it sparkled under the sharp rays of the sun that were bouncing off the Bay.

While Lou admired the motorcycle, Elsa Zumsteg studied the stranger: He was husky and good-looking and had a round face, blue eyes, a nice smile, and the faintest wisp of a mustache. He seemed cocky, like most of Lou's motorcycle friends, but there was a sweetness in his personality she found appealing. He was polite, well spoken, and deferential. Beneath his masculine airs, she suspected there was a shyness—a quality she seldom saw any more; underneath the biker getup, she decided, there was probably a young man from a good family. Except for his accent, he might have been a member of one of the better families of Santa Rosa.

Lou also liked the soft-spoken tourist, and when he inquired what sights he should see during his visit to Sausalito, Lou invited him to join them on their tour of the village. For the next two hours they strolled along the waterfront and browsed in the shops. Afterward, Lou invited him to join them for lunch.

When it was time to separate, he said: "Michael, if you run out of things to do before you go home, why don't you ride up to Santa Rosa? We'll show you around."

———

It was simple enough: an impulsive invitation to a friendly stranger.

Lou and Elsa didn't expect Michael to take them up on it.

But he did—and it changed their lives forever.

2.

When the telephone rang Friday afternoon, Elsa recognized Michael's accent immediately.

"Hi," he said. "I'm in Santa Rosa."

"Wonderful," Elsa said. "Would you like to come over now?"

"Love to."

She gave him directions. A few minutes later, she heard his Harley climb the driveway to the Zumstegs' two-story home, which was perched on the brow of a hill near the edge of Santa Rosa, where tree-shaded residential neighborhoods began to give way to farms, pastures, and vineyards.

Lou and Elsa had emigrated to Santa Rosa from the San Francisco Peninsula, seventy miles south of the Sonoma Valley, four years earlier, after Lou took a job as director of employee relations for a manufacturer. When it shifted operations to Chicago a year later, they decided not to leave California, and he soon prospered as a self-employed industrial-relations consultant—an itinerant hired gun for corporations facing a strike or an unwelcome employee union-organizing campaign.

Elsa showed Michael to the guest room, introducing him as they climbed the stairs to her eighteen-year-old twins, Erika and Mark. They had another daughter, she said, who lived on her own in Sacramento. When Lou arrived home from his office, he was delighted to see Michael. He led him first to the garage and showed him his motorcycle collection, introducing each bike by name—Hazel, Tony, Rocket, Gertrude, The Shark, and their siblings. Michael laughed at each introduction and suggested he should name his new Harley. Since their meeting, he'd wrapped a sheepskin over the seat, and he said: "How about *Wolf*—a wolf in sheep's clothing?" Then the two men climbed on motorcycles and Lou took Michael on a tour of the back roads of the Sonoma Valley. It was the first of several that weekend. Lou enjoyed spending time with someone who loved biking as much as he did, and their friendship deepened as the weekend passed.

After dinner Sunday evening, Lou and Elsa expected Michael to pack his bag and return to the St. Francis Hotel in San Francisco, where he was staying. But he said nothing about leaving and spent the night in the guest room. In the morning, Lou had to leave on a business trip. Since it was apparent Michael wasn't planning to leave yet, Lou suggested to Elsa that she take him to one or two Sonoma Valley wineries, sample some wines, and perhaps drive over to the Napa Valley, which was only a few miles away on the other side of a shallow mountain range east of their home.

After Lou left, Michael told Elsa he was a diabetic and needed insulin and hypodermic needles and her family doctor replenished his supply. He said he wanted to buy some gifts and souvenirs and also a police uniform: he collected uniforms and wanted one from California. In the telephone directory, Elsa found a store that served local law-enforcement officers, and on his second visit to the shop, Michael bought the full uniform—complete with helmet and handcuffs—of a California highway patrolman. At other stores in Santa Rosa, he shopped for gifts; when Elsa mentioned that Charles Schulz, the cartoonist who drew "Peanuts," lived in Santa Rosa, he bought a huge assortment of dishes engraved with the likeness of "Snoopy" and had them shipped to England—a gift, he said, for the three-year-old son of a friend. Using his American Express card, he bought many other gifts, seldom asking the price beforehand. Lou had speculated it must have taken Michael several years to save for his Harley—he'd paid $7,565 cash for it. But after observing how casually he used his credit card, Elsa began to suspect he was better off than Lou thought. Once, before leaving the house, Michael said he wanted to leave his wallet behind in a safe place. As she put it in a drawer, Elsa noticed it was filled with $500 traveler's checks.

By Thursday morning, Michael was still in the guest room and had said nothing yet about leaving. Because she thought it was impolite to ask when he intended to go, Elsa said nothing, either. It was as if Michael had moved into their lives, discovered he enjoyed it, and was in no hurry to leave.

Elsa thought there was something vaguely secretive and *mysterious* about him. Although he was full of questions about her family, he said little about himself. She intercepted a few clues: he had served in Vietnam as a medic for the Australian army; he had paid for the Harley by selling stock he inherited; and he implied he was on a leave of absence from his job. But he didn't identify the job.

Moments occurred during their conversations when it seemed natural for him to volunteer more about himself, but he usually steered the discussion to a different topic. Elsa suspected he might work for the British government, because once he said he had to call his boss in London to ask for an extension of his leave and he mentioned "Whitehall," which she knew was the headquarters of the British civil service. After that, he said nothing more about it. Elsa didn't pry beyond what he offered: she had once lived in England and knew Brits were slower to reveal things about themselves than Americans.

On Thursday afternoon, Elsa answered the telephone and heard an accented voice:

"Hello, this is the Australian Consulate in San Francisco. We're trying to reach Mr. Michael Telling. . . ."

The man's voice had a timbre of authority, and the call sounded official.

When Michael picked up the telephone, he smiled at Elsa but didn't speak. She interpreted his silence as an indication he wanted privacy. As she left the room, she heard him speak softly and wondered if the call had anything to do with his job.

When Lou returned home from his business trip Friday afternoon, Elsa told him Michael had still said nothing about leaving. He was a pleasant, undemanding guest, she said, but she was running out of places to show him: they had shopped, and toured most of the local wineries and several in the Napa Valley; there was nothing left to do. "I know it's impolite to ask when he's going to leave, but what should I do? He doesn't seem to have any plans to go. You know, Lou, it's not very easy for a middle-aged woman to entertain a young man for so long."

Aware that in two days Lou would have to leave on another business trip, she said: "Maybe we should ask Monika if she would show him around Sacramento."

"That's a good idea," Lou said. "Why don't you call Monika?"

3.

Oakland,
Spring 1955

As the car climbed higher into the Oakland hills and the long green gorge of San Francisco Bay grew smaller behind her, Elsa Aschwanden knew she had been right in the first place: not once, but twice, she had said *no* when the tall man dressed in an air-force uniform asked her for a date.

No, she had said, she didn't go out with customers. Then Otto, the lanky, broad-shouldered Viennese who presided nights over the long mahogany bar of the Hofbrau House, intervened: Lou Zumsteg, he said, was a decent man; give him a chance. Only then had she consented. Now, as they climbed deeper into the woodlands above the Bay, she knew she had been right in the first place. Her wariness was grounded in experience: just a few weeks before, her only other date in America—a blind date—had ended abruptly when her escort's hands persisted in exploring places she did not want them to go and she had been forced to extinguish his ardor with the tip of her cigarette on the back of his hand.

On this April evening in 1955, Elsa suspected she would have to do it again. It was supposed to be a dinner date followed by a movie, *Cinerama Holiday*. She was new in America, new in Oakland, but she already knew there were no restaurants or movie theaters in the Oakland hills—only forests of oak and eucalyptus trees, a few houses, and, beyond them, isolated lovers' lanes.

When the car suddenly turned a corner and began to slow, her sense of alarm increased. A moment later, Lou stopped in front of a large white house and said: "This is where my parents live. We're having dinner with them."

A few minutes later, he took his mother aside in the kitchen and said: "This is the girl I'm going to marry."

At twenty-five, Elsa Aschwanden was slender and full-busted, and her face was an oval of smooth alabaster skin fringed by clouds of dark-blond curls. Lou hadn't been the first customer at the Hofbrau House to be bowled over by her beauty and her dusky voice, which Otto compared to Marlene Dietrich's. But he was the first to crack the shell she had built around herself after arriving in America less than a year before. Born in 1930 in a small village in Switzerland, she had emigrated at eighteen to England, studied English, worked as an au pair, and dreamed of going to America. Her dream was fulfilled in October 1954. Arriving as an immigrant in Oakland, she took a bus to the Hofbrau House, a landmark locally famous for dark beer, dark beams, and fat sausages, and convinced the proprietor that he needed a German-speaking waitress. Waiting tables in a rathskeller hadn't been part of the dream that propelled her to America, but jobs were hard to find and, with tips, she was soon able to rent an apartment and start a new life.

Louis and Isabella Zumsteg were impressed by the young woman Lou brought home to dinner: she was intelligent, unworldly, Catholic, very pretty. Their eldest son was nearly twenty-five. They believed it was time he married. As they dined on the steaks she had prepared, Lou's mother mentioned a collection of antique Chinese figurines Elsa had admired before dinner and said: "I've promised Lou that when he gets married *those pieces are his*." Elsa blushed, and her knife slipped out of her fingers and made a loud scrape on her plate. After dinner, Lou drove her down the hill to Oakland and they saw *Cinerama Holiday*. Warned by Otto that she was wary of overly amorous American men, Lou didn't try to kiss her that night, nor did he several days later, when he took her to see Yosemite National Park.

Elsa was attracted to the good-looking, well-spoken American, and when he kissed her, on their third date, she responded enthusiastically.

Three weeks later, he asked her to marry him. She said she needed time to think it over, but the next day Lou brought an engagement ring and she accepted it. Six months later—October 30, 1955—at a resort north of San Francisco, they were married by a Roman Catholic priest.

Elsa knew Lou liked to drink—most of her customers did. But she had never seen any of them as drunk as Lou was several days before the wedding. When he knocked at her apartment, he could hardly stand. "Lou," she said, "you're not an alcoholic, are you? If you are, I don't want to marry you."

But Lou said he had only been out with his buddies to a bachelor party, and Elsa forgave him.

They spent their wedding night in Reno, then went to Palm Springs and later to Los Angeles, to catch a flight to Mazatlán, a resort on the west coast of Mexico. A few hours after they arrived, Lou found a bar and began drinking. Elsa spent the rest of her honeymoon in their room, alone.

4.

What demons conspire to decide that one man becomes an alcoholic—and another, drinking from the same well of whiskey or gin, does not? Is it genetically preordained? Is an aberrant chromosome responsible? Does a sinister and unexplained collaboration of biochemical, psychological, and cultural forces turn ordinary men and women into chronic drunks? Or is it simply bad luck? Those who claim expert knowledge on the topic have argued these questions for centuries without agreeing. But if Lou Zumsteg—and, because of experience, he considered himself an expert on alcoholism—was asked to define the most common cause of the disease, his answer was: "A lack of self-esteem."

He was born in Oakland on November 24, 1930. As far back as members of his family could recall, he had been considered precocious. His teachers agreed he was a child of extraordinary intelligence and predicted he would succeed at any career he chose to undertake. But somewhere on the path from infancy to adulthood, he failed to achieve the same degree of confidence in himself that his family and teachers had. From childhood, he emerged with a sense of inadequacy that he tried to anesthetize with a flood of alcohol.

When he was older, Lou said he could not recall a single moment in his childhood when his father had praised him. On the contrary, he remembered criticism. "He was a very critical man," Lou said. "And I guess I became the same way with my own kids."

In Lou's young life, his father and grandfathers were giant figures—hard-driving, successful businessmen who presided over their families in an authoritarian, Old World fashion. Lou's younger brother, Edward, said: "Any male in our family had a tough act to follow. All the older men we looked up to were strong and dominant—hardworking and successful self-made men. Any male growing up in our family who didn't have a lot of basic strength would have trouble establishing his own identity."

Until the outbreak of World War II, Lou and his father were close: they often camped and hiked together in the hills above Oakland, and Lou considered him his closest friend. But the war changed things: for almost four years, his father worked six and seven days a week at Oakland's Todd Shipyards, helping turn out a gray tide of liberty ships, and he had less time for his sons. After the war, it was never the same. A tension developed between Lou and his father, and by the time Lou was a teenager, they were almost strangers. He had his father's name and was told he was expected to live up to it, but he did not have the flair for deal-making that was considered a birthright of male Zumstegs. And after it became apparent his younger brother *did* have the personality and self-confidence of their father and grandfathers—a *salesman's* personality—Lou began to feel isolated, even supplanted in his family.

Lou's mother believed her husband worshiped Lou, but she saw the tension between them. The chemistry just wasn't right. Both were strong-willed, opinionated, and hot-tempered. "I could get to Lou," she said, "but his father never could, and it broke his heart, because he loved Lou very much."

It was not as if father and son did not try to get along. Lou's father was a mechanical wizard. He could fix a motorcycle or a car, or pick up the pieces of a broken gadget he had never seen and make it work. As a toddler, Lou adoringly watched him tinker for hours with a moribund engine, swear at it when things didn't go right, then give a yelp when it suddenly fired up. As a teenager, Lou bought a motor scooter financed in part by profits from a rare-stamp business he established to demonstrate his skill as a businessman. His mother hoped it would make them close again. But their collaborations on the scooter usually ended in acrimony and silence. The silence never ended—nor did Lou's efforts to prove himself to his father.

In his freshman year at St. Mary's Roman Catholic High School, he was elected class president and made the honor role, but he still felt inadequate. Nearsighted, introverted, and slightly built, he preferred collecting stamps, studying archaeology, and playing his accordion to sports, where other boys made their mark; he loved writing, journalism, languages, especially Latin and Greek. To mask his sense of inadequacy, he put a shell around himself that some of his acquaintances thought of as arrogance and aloofness. During his senior year, he decided to become a priest and was accepted at St. Albert's, the local Dominican seminary. But his father, a Methodist who had converted unenthusiastically to Catholicism for his bride, insisted he go to college and prepare for a position in the business world instead.

Dutifully, Lou enrolled at the University of California, a few miles from his home. During his freshman year, he was introduced to a campus tradition, the beer bust, and discovered alcohol could grant him temporary psychic relief from his sense of inadequacy. Then the Korean War started, and, as wars are wont to do, it changed the course of his life: his Air National Guard unit was mobilized and sent to Japan, where booze was even cheaper and more plentiful than in Berkeley. When he got back from Japan in 1953, two years later, he was an alcoholic. Instead of re-entering the university, he enrolled in an Oakland business college and accepted a full-time administrative job with his Air National Guard unit.

Two years later, Lou and Elsa married, joining a large, optimistic generation of American newlyweds, the progenitors of the Baby Boom. Most of its members shared an identical dream, rooted in a hunger for stability after years of war and depression: get a good job—a *secure* job; get married, buy a house, have children, live the good life.

Thirteen months after they were married—on November 24, 1956—Lou and Elsa's first child was born. They named her Monika.

It was sometimes *eerie*, friends said, how much the daughter who was born on Lou's twenty-fifth birthday resembled him. Like Lou, she demonstrated the power of a precocious mind during her first months, and her IQ was later measured at almost 140. Like Lou, she was an articulate bookworm, facile with words, ideas, and languages. Like Lou, she was introspective, stubborn, opinionated.

Later on, perhaps it was the similarities in their personalities and talents that made father and daughter so close, yet made them collide so often—and kept Monika loyal to him long after he had a right to expect it.

5.

When Lou Zumsteg decided, after the Korean War, that he wasn't going back to the University of California, his parents warned him he was forfeiting whatever chance he ever had of becoming a professional man. In the postwar world, they said, a college degree was essential for success. But he proved them wrong. His specialty in the Air National Guard was personnel management—meshing airmen's talents with job billets—and it brought him a job offer from the personnel department of Schlage Lock Company in South San Francisco three years after he married Elsa. The trainee's job started him on a career in industrial relations and personnel management that would take his family across the country, from California to Seattle, New Orleans, and Denver.

In 1965, Schlage offered him the job of managing the department in South San Francisco, where he had started as a trainee seven years before, and the family returned to California. More professional success followed: because of programs and innovations he introduced at Schlage, Lou's reputation spread and he was elected national vice-president of the American Society of Personnel Administrators, the largest professional organization in his field, and chairman of its labor-relations committee. Other companies asked him to advise them on their labor problems, and he was invited to speak at national conferences of his peers. His career flourished and his reputation grew, despite Elsa's belief that he was determined to demolish both.

For more than a decade, Lou's addiction to alcohol overshadowed everything else in the life of his family and nearly destroyed it. During the mid-sixties and early seventies, he sometimes disappeared for days at a time and couldn't remember where he had been when he returned. He was a sullen, angry, and sometimes violent man. In a bar, the focus of his hostility might be a stranger; at home, it was Elsa or the children. He abused his family terribly—sometimes physically, but the worst abuse was emotional. Like many alcoholics, he could use his tongue against his family like a rapier. Monika was the pride of his life, but when he was drunk she was often the first target of his abuse: he ridiculed and humiliated her, demeaned the way she looked, the clothes she wore, the ideas she expressed. To compensate for his own emotional insecurity, he assaulted the strength of those who most needed his love and approval.

The family tried to protect his secret. For a long time, Elsa denied, even to herself, that her husband was an alcoholic. She accepted Lou's defensive rationalization that he was a *social* drinker who occasionally lost control. It was less painful than the truth. And she became an expert at making excuses for him: his father was hard on him; his mother didn't love him as much as she did his brother; *she* was partly to blame for his drinking. "If you'd go to a bar with me like other wives," he told her, "I wouldn't have a problem." But neither denial nor excuses could pull her family out of its tailspin. As alcohol tightened its grip on Lou, Elsa began to lie awake at night and dream of escape. "I didn't know what to do or where to go," she said later. "I couldn't tell anybody how bad it was. I had nobody to talk to. I was standing in a desert crying for help and no one could hear me."

But someone did hear her: as wives of alcoholics sometimes do, she turned for help to her eldest child, and at seven or eight, Monika accepted the responsibility to end the pain and chaos around her.

She promised Elsa she would help make her father stop drinking. She became her mother's companion, ally, and coconspirator and was tenacious at it. When Monika and Lou argued, Elsa thought, it was sometimes like watching the same mind at war with itself. Physically, they were so different: she was a tiny, even frail, myopic child who looked out at the world through half-inch-thick glasses; he towered over her like a teetering derrick. But they were so *alike* when they argued: both were stubborn, dogmatic, capable of viciousness with their tongues, astonishingly articulate with words. When Monika shouted at Lou and said he'd broken another promise, or he'd lied again to the family, Elsa usually saw the storm clouds rising and tried to head off the storm. She shot a warning glance at Monika: "*Girl, get out of here before it's too late—leave while you're still ahead of the game or you're going to get hit.*" But Monika stood her ground. She refused to retreat and continued to speak her mind.

Elsa knew that despite everything—despite Lou's violence, withering criticism, and abuse, despite the sorrow and pain he brought to their home—Monika was devoted to her father. As children—even abused children—usually do, she offered her love to him unconditionally.

One night in 1971, after a bitter argument over his drinking, Elsa finally gave up. After Lou passed out, she got out of bed, roused the children, and led them to the garage. She said they were leaving. The twins climbed sleepily into the back seat, but Monika stood next to the car as rigid as marble.

"Monika, hurry up, get in," Elsa whispered. "We've got to get going."

"No. I can't leave Dad," Monika said. "He needs us. You go, I *can't.*"

Elsa stared at Monika, then the car. Realizing she was beaten, she lifted the twins out of the back seat, and they all went back to bed.

———

In elementary school, Monika was a competitive and compulsive child who hated failure more than anything: a B+ instead of an A was a humiliating defeat. By the time she entered high school, she was even more of a perfectionist and workaholic, still driven by a compulsion to prove to her father that she was worthy of his love. She made the honor roll, worked twenty hours a week in a convalescent hospital, and still found enough time to volunteer several hours a week to a group that delivered hot meals to the elderly. She was a reporter on the school newspaper, competed in gymnastics, played the piano at student assemblies, and became skilled enough as a figure skater to dream of trying out for the Olympics. But ultimately her adolescent ambitions settled not on sports or music, but on words: poetry and journalism.

When she graduated from Half Moon Bay High School on the western edge of the San Francisco Peninsula in June 1974, classmates expected her to join them at Berkeley or another university. But she enrolled instead at the College of San Mateo, a tuition-free community college near home. After two years, she said she would transfer to the College of Notre Dame, a four-year institution farther up the Peninsula. In her freshman year, she wrote articles for student publications and made the dean's list, but she decided journalism wasn't as challenging as she expected. In June, she took a summer job as a computer-terminal operator, and discovered a new goal. Unlike co-workers who thought computers were intimidating, she found them easy to use and was quickly promoted to a supervisory position. At the end of the summer, she decided not to give up the job, as she'd planned, and continued working full-time in addition to resuming her studies. Her paycheck enabled her to leave home and rent an apartment near the college. The following June, she earned an associate-of-arts degree in journalism from the College of San Mateo, then enrolled on schedule at the College of Notre Dame. But instead of becoming a poet or journalist, her ambition was now to become an executive in the computer industry.

At Notre Dame, she found it more difficult to combine a full schedule of classes with a full-time job. After she began to fall behind, she cut back on her class load; the alternative would have been quitting the job, but having tasted financial independence, she didn't want to give it up. Earning her bachelor's degree would take longer than she had thought, she said, but she would get it. Her parents didn't doubt her: she had matured into a tenacious young woman who didn't easily abandon a goal.

At twenty, Monika was also a strikingly pretty young woman: slender and petite, she had long auburn hair highlighted by flashes of red, her mother's oval face and porcelain complexion, and luminous green eyes whose beauty was revealed only after she exchanged the thick spectacles of her childhood for contact lenses. She was a member of the first generation of Americans who passed into adulthood after the 1960s and 1970s had changed nearly everything about growing up in America. She was part of the generation that first sampled previously taboo pleasures en masse, from drugs to casual sex, the first with easy access to the Pill. But she was not among those in her generation who turned their backs on materialism or the work ethic: she was determined to become a success in the business world.

Once she finished college, she said her goal was to be among the first women in senior management positions at a major computer company like IBM. Acquaintances in the industry advised her that, while she was finishing college, nothing would prepare her more for a management career than spending a year or two in the field as a computer service representative: tech reps learned the practical, everyday problems of business and how computers can help solve them. She applied to Reynolds & Reynolds, an Ohio company that produced specialized computing systems for automobile dealerships. In April 1979, after two months' training in Dayton, she was granted her request to be assigned to its San Francisco Peninsula office. As a field-service rep, Monika installed computers at car dealerships and trained employees to use them for monitoring parts inventories and service records and keeping general accounting records. She enjoyed it, and after several months began pressing for a promotion to a supervisory job. Before her first anniversary on the job, the company offered her a transfer to its Sacramento office. If she accepted, she would have to give up her studies at the College of Notre Dame, with barely a year to go before getting her bachelor's degree, but it would put her in line for promotion to a job as regional service coordinator—a management job no woman had ever held in the company.

After confirming she could continue her studies at a state college in Sacramento, Monika accepted the transfer and moved to the capital of California in April 1980.

———

Six months later in Santa Rosa, Michael Telling finished packing his bag to leave for Sacramento. He went to the garage and strapped it to his new Harley, then returned to the living room and told Lou he wanted to tell him something in confidence.

He said he was sorry he hadn't explained more about himself to him and Elsa. He suspected they were curious about the houseguest they were sending to visit their daughter.

Like Elsa, Lou *had* been puzzled by Michael's shy reluctance to talk about himself. But as they sat together on the living-room sofa, he was not prepared for the secret Michael revealed.

"I'm sorry I can't go into all the details," he said, "because my job is covered by the Official Secrets Act at home." But he said it was only fair that Lou and Elsa knew *something* about him.

He said he lived in Devon, on the southwestern coast of England, in a seaside town called Torquay, where he shared a cottage with two commandos in the British Royal Marines, although they all traveled so much they seldom saw each other.

He said he worked for the government in a sensitive position that often took him on short notice to places around the world.

"So that's what the calls from the Australian Consulate were all about?" Lou asked.

"The Australian High Command was trying to reach me," Michael said.

He said he had recently been involved in an intelligence operation in Iran. Though he couldn't discuss it because of the Official Secrets Act, he implied that something had gone awry and he had had a close call and his superiors had told him to take a special leave of absence. That was when he decided to come to San Francisco and buy the Harley, he said.

When Michael finished his story, Lou realized why the stranger they had met on a Sunday morning in Sausalito had been so secretive: he was a British intelligence agent on an American holiday.

6.

Sitting on the sheepskin-clad saddle of the new Harley, Michael was waiting outside their duplex when Monika and Samantha Hynes returned home from work, one behind the other in identical Chevrolet Malibus.

A Reynolds & Reynolds tech rep one month younger than Monika, Sammye had arrived in Sacramento from Lubbock, Texas, a few weeks before her roommate. The only women in the office, they decided to share expenses and rent a three-bedroom duplex. In matching leased cars, they commuted to automobile dealerships scattered across California's agricultural heartland, the lush, table-flat Central Valley. Some evenings, they didn't arrive back at the duplex until long after dark, but today they arrived home in time for dinner, because they were expecting a guest.

The previous day, Elsa had telephoned Monika. "Your dad and I met a very nice tourist from England when we were in Sausalito the other day, and he came up to spend a few days with us." After a pause, she added: "We're running out of things to show him in Santa Rosa and thought you might like to give him a tour of Sacramento—maybe take him to Lake Tahoe. Would you mind if we sent him up to see you?"

When Elsa heard Monika's reply, she smiled. It was the same question she would have asked when she was Monika's age: "What's he look like?"

"He's good-looking—about thirty—taller than you but not too tall—very nice. I think you'll like him. He's on vacation and has time on his hands and wants to see more of California."

"Okay, Mother, send him up."

Exactly when Michael fell in love with Monika is not known, although it was probably within twenty-four hours of his arrival in Sacramento. Monika took several days more to admit she loved Michael. On the first night, he took her and Sammye out to dinner. Afterward, while he was bedding down in the spare room, Monika told Sammye she thought her mother was right: he was an unusual, engaging young man. The next morning, she left the duplex briefly to resuscitate a client's balky computer, and Michael asked Sammye to drive him to a florist. When he walked out of the shop, all she could see of him were his legs: the rest of him was hidden by armfuls of long-stemmed roses and carnations.

The roses were for Monika, he told Sammye, and the carnations were for her. When Sammye started to protest, he said: "You can't buy a lady flowers and not give some to her flat-mate!"

The next morning, Michael and Monika left for Lake Tahoe. She had won an all-expense getaway for two at Harvey's, a gambling resort on the south shore of the mile-high alpine lake ninety minutes east of Sacramento. That night, in their room several floors above the casino, they became lovers.

Monika liked the way Michael treated her. Flowers were delivered to their room each day; he never let her open a door; he was affectionate, sophisticated, and well traveled; he didn't have the blustering overconfidence of many of the men she knew. He knew about fine wines and good food. Moreover—unlike a lot of the men she knew—he agreed with her enthusiastically that women were entitled to equality in the business world.

If anything troubled Monika, it was Michael's generosity. Before they headed back to Sacramento, he suggested a stop at a boutique to buy her a new outfit. She refused, but he continued to offer her expensive gifts, and the day after they returned to Sacramento, she came home from work and discovered a large new color TV set he'd purchased to replace her broken black-and-white set.

"Michael, why did you do that?" she asked unhappily. "I don't need you to buy things like that for me."

The gift embarrassed her, especially because, as she had often boasted to Sammye, she was proud of her independence and wanted to pay her own way. Apparently surprised by the sharpness of her rebuke, Michael promised not to surprise her with more expensive gifts.

That evening, Monika told Sammye she thought she might be falling in love with him. It troubled her, because it didn't fit in with her plans.

———

Since adolescence, boys and then men had been drawn to Monika like butterflies to a copse of lilacs. The number and variety of men attracted to her and who passed in and out of her life amazed Sammye. A dentist they had selected at random from a telephone directory began calling her several times a day after her first appointment for a teeth-cleaning. An old flame from San Francisco, a doctor, pleaded with her to marry him. She was pursued by an instructor from Sacramento State University, the owner of an Italian restaurant where they occasionally bought pizza, a sergeant from a local air-force base, and a succession of men she met at Mills Station, a country-western bar on the outskirts of Sacramento where Monika and Sammye often went for a drink after work.

Although Monika fully exercised the sexual liberties of her generation, she told all of the men she went out with that she wasn't interested in marriage or other commitments: her career came first, then marriage and children. Unlike the women in her mother's generation, she told Sammye, she was determined not to be dependent on a man. She could and would earn her own way.

To Sammye, however, it also seemed that Monika was determined to bring home every wounded male in Sacramento. Whether they were truck drivers or emergency-room physicians, she gravitated to men with problems. Reliable men who led ordinary lives appealed less to her: they were less exciting. "Why do you waste your time on guys like that?" Sammye asked after she had taken on the case of still another man who fit the mold: men who couldn't find themselves— men who said their wives didn't understand them—men who drank too much—men who needed the kind of ambition Monika possessed in abundance—boys in men's bodies who hadn't decided what they wanted to do when they grew up—moody, unpredictable men who sometimes treated her badly. "I think he has a lot of *potential*," she answered. "He just needs a push."

When Monika and Sammye invited a colleague from the office and his wife for dinner, these friends were as taken with their houseguest as they were, and as interested in his descriptions of life in England and Australia, where he said he'd spent part of his youth.

"What do you do for a living?" Monika's colleague asked.

Michael colored and let a moment pass before answering: "I work for the government—government work."

"That sounds interesting," the dinner guest said. "Generally, what kind of government work?"

Michael flushed again and explained, as he had to Lou, that he had a sensitive job in the intelligence field that was covered by Britain's Official Secrets Act, so, legally, he couldn't discuss it. But he explained he was on a special leave of absence after a recent assignment involving Iran and the U.S. hostages in Teheran that, he implied, had been unsuccessful. Several minutes later, while Monika and Sammye were clearing the dishes, he showed the guests a large black revolver that he said he used in his work.

After the weekend at Lake Tahoe, Michael made several overseas telephone calls from the duplex. Each time, he asked for privacy, citing his job. When he suggested to Monika that they fly to Bermuda for a week, she thought he was joking. Then he produced a first-class airline ticket with her name on it, along with a ticket for himself.

They left two days later, after Monika got permission to take a week off. In a restaurant overlooking the Atlantic, Michael proposed. She said she needed time to think it over—marriage wasn't in her plans. The following day, they went to a duty-free store in Hamilton and he bought her a $5,000 diamond-and-emerald ring. He said he would keep it until she said yes.

Michael and Monika interrupted the return trip to Sacramento with an overnight stop in San Francisco, where she offered to show him some of her favorite landmarks. While they were driving through a neighborhood of freshly restored Victorian homes—big, gaily painted turn-of-the-century houses embellished with ornate gingerbread, gables, and towers, which San Franciscans call "Painted Ladies"—she said one of her dreams was to own a similar house. Since moving to Sacramento, she said, she had discovered a passion for anything Victorian. It began during expeditions to California's former Gold Rush country, east of Sacramento, where old mining ghost towns were coming to life again and hundreds of antique shops had opened. The Victorian settee and a huge armoire in the duplex's living room, she said, were bargains from the Gold Country.

"If you want one, I'll buy one for you," Michael said.

Monika said the houses were a lot more expensive than he thought—at least $150,000, maybe much more. "I'll take two," she joked.

No, Michael said, he meant it: If you marry me, I'll buy one for you.

"You're English," Monika said. "How could you live in San Francisco?"

Michael said he would live anyplace in the world Monika wanted to live.

After the sightseeing tour, Michael left her in their hotel room and said he was going to visit friends at the Dudley Perkins Harley agency. When he returned, he gave her a silver-and-gold Rolex wristwatch—a gift, he said, that was meant to show her how much he loved her.

When they got back to Sacramento, Michael moved into Monika's bedroom. She called her mother.

"Mom, are you sitting down?"

"Why?"

"Michael asked me to marry him."

"What are you going to do? You hardly know him."

"I don't know."

"Are you in love?"

"I think so."

The next day, Monika's life became more complicated. She went back to work and was told she had won the promotion she had been campaigning for: she had been named the company's first female regional service coordinator and was scheduled to report to the Reynolds & Reynolds office in southern California in less than a month.

Michael encouraged her to accept the promotion. He said he could probably extend his leave several months, perhaps longer, although, if they did get married, sooner or later they would have to move to England.

"How can I get married?" she asked Sammye that evening. "What about my family? What about my job?" Then she added, as if she were conducting a dialogue with herself: "I don't know if I have a choice. I can't change the way I feel."

7.

"Are you sure you know what you're doing?" Elsa asked when Monika called and said she had decided to accept Michael's proposal. "You've known him less than three weeks."

"I know, but I love him. We had an incredible time in Bermuda. We're coming to Santa Rosa for Thanksgiving, and Michael's going to ask Dad formally if he can marry me. You're not supposed to know it. He—we—want to do it the old-fashioned way."

They arrived in Santa Rosa Thanksgiving morning in a new red Fiat convertible Monika had bought to replace her leased Chevrolet, a fringe benefit she surrendered with her field-rep job. In a three-piece suit, Michael barely resembled the biker in blue jeans and leather jacket whom Elsa had met in Sausalito. With his dark good looks, she thought he was as handsome as a movie star; she understood why Michael had swept her daughter off her feet. Elsa followed them to the garage, where Lou was on the floor working on a motorcycle. She stood close to Monika as Michael made his pitch:

"Lou . . . I would like to ask your permission to marry Monika."

Elsa had already confided to him that the relationship had escalated into something beyond tourist and tour guide.

"Well, what does Monika have to say about it?" Lou asked.

"I love Michael and want to marry him," she interjected before Michael could reply. She grabbed his arm and clung to him.

Lou knew his daughter well. He knew she was in love. He couldn't change her mind if he tried. He straightened up, hugged her and his future son-in-law, and said he was delighted.

Indeed, he *was* happy: he had already begun to think of Michael as the second son he had always wanted.

"What about your new job?" Elsa asked Monika when they were alone. "You worked so hard for your promotion."

Like Lou, she was fond of Michael. But she knew nothing mattered more to Monika than being promoted to a management job. For months, it seemed, it had been all she had talked about.

"I'll go to L.A. and see how things work out. Who knows what will happen?"

The position was vacant and the company needed her in a hurry, Monika said; she couldn't let them down, especially after fighting so hard for the promotion. "Whatever happens—even if I quit later on—it will look good on my résumé."

"When do you want to get married?" Elsa asked.

"This summer or fall," Monika said. She wanted a big wedding, with six or seven attendants, in St. Eugene's Cathedral.

"But Michael's not Catholic," Elsa said.

No, but he was Church of England, and one of his cousins had recently married a Catholic. Michael was sure they could overcome whatever religious obstacles they encountered: he had promised her to raise their children as Catholics, and that's all the church really cared about.

"You know, Monika," Elsa said, "you're going to be asking a lot from Dad and me: you're going to southern California and will be leaving all the work to us. I think we'd better settle some things now, while you and Michael are here. You should go down to St. Eugene's and see a priest and get things started."

The next day, Monika and Michael met with a priest and reserved Santa Rosa's Roman Catholic cathedral for a 2:00 P.M. wedding Saturday, September 12. Monika told Elsa afterward the priest had said Michael would have to sign a few documents, but they could marry in the cathedral. Although Michael did promise to sign the papers, he had become very upset with the priest. "He asked a lot of questions about Michael's background and attitude about religion, birth control, and so forth, and he didn't like it. He said his church doesn't pry into personal matters like that."

With their date set, the betrothed couple had to separate—Michael had to leave for a meeting in England, then was flying to Australia to spend Christmas with his mother and stepfather; Monika had to leave for Los Angeles to start her new job.

Although Elsa shared Lou's affection for Michael, she was more curious about the stranger who had entered their lives so suddenly than he was.

"You know, Lou, when you think about it, we don't know very much about him or his family."

"He's a good kid and they're going to be very happy together," Lou said.

Not long after Monika moved to southern California, Lou stopped drinking.

During the years she was in college and starting her career, he had remained in the grip of his addiction, despite futile searches for a cure at drying-out sanitariums and a flirtation with Alcoholics Anonymous. They all failed until a few months after he and Elsa met Michael in Sausalito. One evening when he was on an out-of-town business trip, he went, as he usually did, to a bar; as alcohol began to course through his body, it began to make him feel better about himself. Then he looked across the dance floor and saw a man who was very drunk. He had never seen him before, but he recognized and hated him: "In a moment of clarity, I knew *why* I hated him. He was *me*."

The image of the man was still with him several days later, when he was riding through the High Sierras on a motorcycle and the vision suddenly made him want to kill himself. Uncontrollably, his wrist began responding to an urge to accelerate the bike and propel it over a cliff. It went faster and faster while he fought his hand to keep from becoming airborne. Suddenly he began to cry, and once he started he couldn't stop. Tears streamed down his face. At the brink of a cliff, he stopped the motorcycle, laid it down on its side, and threw himself on top of it, crying so loudly he could hear his sobs echoing through the trees around him. Seeing the image of the dancing man made him realize he was powerless over alcohol, and in a cathedral of pine trees, he found the strength to admit it—and commit his trust to the force Alcoholics Anonymous calls "a Power greater than ourselves." In that moment, he took the First Step to becoming a recovering alcoholic.

8.

As regional service coordinator for Reynolds & Reynolds, Monika supervised its field operations throughout the West. From the first day, she loved it. A telephone headset became a semipermanent fixture around her frosted hair: one minute, she was on a line to Oregon pacifying an angry client; the next, she was helping a frustrated field rep in San Diego debug a misbehaving computer. A warm and easygoing style, her ability to express herself, and the knowledge of computers she had gleaned during the previous five years enabled her to help others cope with the mysterious, sometimes obstinate machines. The job was everything she had worked for—although much of the time it was Michael, not the job, that was on her mind.

Not long after starting the new job, she told Sammye she was beginning to have doubts about her decision to marry Michael. It wasn't only the job. She was reluctant to leave California; she didn't want to move so far from her family. "I don't know what to do."

Sammye realized she had been crying, and this surprised her. Monika had always been on top of things; she'd always known what she wanted. She was always in control. She had written the script for her life and had followed it faithfully: college and a career before marriage.

Now she was unsure and vulnerable and seemed disappointed with herself. She wasn't finishing something she had started.

Monika said the prospect of moving to England terrified her. "I keep going back and forth all day, trying to decide what to do, it's terrible."

"You'll do what's right," Sammye reassured her.

"But what if I don't like England? What if his family doesn't like me? What if I don't fit in? I won't have any friends over there."

She was only twenty-four; wasn't she a fool to give up a good job she had fought for and move thousands of miles to another country, where she would be a stranger?

"For God's sake, Monika," Sammye said, "if you love the guy and he loves you, you'll fit in. You're marrying *him*, not England. You fit in with him, and that's what counts."

"I don't know what to do," Monika repeated.

A few days later, on a Friday evening in early January, there was a knock at the hotel room where she was staying until she could move into the apartment she had rented. When Monika opened the door, she saw Michael smiling at her with his broad boyish grin, a suitcase in his hand. He dropped the bag, hugged her, and said he missed her so much he had decided to fly back and surprise her.

As Monika felt his arms around her, she later told Sammye, she realized her decision had already been made: her destiny was intertwined with Michael's, wherever it took her.

Michael said that when he was in London his boss had agreed to extend his leave, although he might be called away from time to time if assignments came up. It was even possible he could remain in California until the wedding.

When Monika drove him to the apartment building where she had placed a deposit, he said, "You can't live here."

It was on the fringe of one of the older neighborhoods in the San Fernando Valley, the monotonous amalgamation of look-alike housing tracts, shopping malls, and freeways carpeting the chasm between the Hollywood Hills and the Tehachapi Mountains. After World War II, the neighborhood had welcomed a generation of ex-GIs and their brides, along with their dreams of a better life. Most had since left for bigger dream houses, and the wooden houses they left behind were the beachhead for immigrants from Mexico and Central America.

"You can't live here," Michael repeated. "There's no security. A woman alone wouldn't be safe. I won't allow it."

"What do you mean?, *you won't allow it?*" It was all she could afford—and it suited her fine.

If she lived there, Michael said, he couldn't stop worrying about her when he was gone. He said he wanted to pay her rent at an apartment with better security.

Until they were married, Monika insisted, she would pay her own rent. With her promotion, she'd gotten a good raise and could pay her own way; accepting Michael's offer would diminish what she accomplished. Ultimately, however, she capitulated, though on her own terms: she agreed to live in an apartment he approved of, in a building with doorman and electric gates, but they would split the rent. Her share was the amount she had agreed to pay for the original apartment, and he would pay the difference. Since he would be sharing the apartment when he was in Los Angeles, she said, the arrangement was fair to both of them. A deal was struck, and during the first week of February—more than seven months before their wedding date— Michael Henry Maxwell Telling and Monika Elizabeth Zumsteg began living as man and wife.

Shortly after that, Michael confided in Monika the details of his secret life.

When he said he was a member of the "SAS," it meant nothing to her at first. Then he described the history and mission of Britain's Special Air Services Regiment.

The SAS, he explained, was a secret British military unit with origins in World War II, when teams of commandos were sent behind German lines on clandestine sabotage missions. Reconstituted after the war, it became an irregular arm of British foreign policy abroad—in the Middle East, Malaya, Kenya, Cyprus, and elsewhere. The regiment's motto was: "Who Dares Wins." Admission was extremely competitive. In wartime, its principal missions were sabotage and reconnaissance behind enemy lines; during peacetime, SAS troopers underwent rigorous, almost continuous training to sharpen their skills against terrorism, and went abroad on undercover missions to collect intelligence, sometimes working with agents of MI-6, the British Secret Intelligence Service. When he said his job took him to Iran and Northern Ireland, Monika asked if this meant he was in danger. Michael said there were elements of risk to his job, but he enjoyed it, and the training SAS men received was the best in the world. The size and membership of SAS, he continued, were secret; the names of its members were classified and protected by the Official Secrets Act, and it was even forbidden to photograph them unless their faces were unrecognizable. Most Britons, he said, had hardly known the SAS existed until a few months before he met Monika, when his regiment rescued hostages trapped in the Iranian Embassy in London.

Now that he had told her what he did for a living, Michael instructed her never to repeat the secret to anyone. She was now as bound as he was by the Official Secrets Act.

Except for Michael's Harley, there was little to distinguish the newcomers from other young couples in the high-security apartment complex in Van Nuys, the San Fernando Valley suburb where her office was located. Weekday mornings, she left in her new Fiat, and, not long afterward, Michael left on his Harley. Weekends were devoted to shopping and decorating the apartment. Although they often dined out, Michael encouraged Monika—who didn't enjoy cooking—to experiment in the kitchen. One evening, she came home to find only a carton of milk and a lump of cheese in the refrigerator, and produced, with a few additional ingredients, a cheese soup Michael pronounced a culinary triumph.

Financial concerns—balancing their checkbooks, saving for next month's rent, estimating how big a car payment they could afford— were seldom far from the minds of most of Monika's friends, but Michael had a different attitude about money. Before buying something, he rarely looked at the price tag. He spent money as if his wallet were bottomless and, despite her objections, continued offering her expensive gifts she didn't need. One evening, he presented her a strand of large, perfectly matched pearls. She suspected they were very expensive and said she couldn't accept them, but retreated after Michael—who had discovered she had a weakness for jewelry—said they were a gift from his mother for their engagement.

9.

Elsa was alone in Santa Rosa when the telephone rang in the middle of February. "Michael's in the hospital," her daughter said tearfully. "When I came home from work last night, he was in a coma. I don't know how long he'd been out, but he was lying naked on the floor of the bathroom."

Elsa suspected what had happened: Michael was a diabetic, and it sounded as if he had forgotten his insulin, eaten the wrong food, or drunk too much. She remembered that Monika had been trained to deal with medical emergencies when she worked at the nursing home.

"What did you do?"

"I slapped him hard, but it didn't do any good. I tried to lift him up, but I couldn't move him, so I ran next door and neighbors helped me get him into the car and I took him to the hospital. The doctor said, if I hadn't come home when I did, he could have died."

Monika had told Elsa all the details of the near-calamity except one. She did not tell her that, two days before, she and Michael had had a stormy argument and in the heat of battle she had threatened to call off the wedding.

Michael had invited over a friend—an ex-marine he had met in Los Angeles and brought to the apartment several times before—for drinks and to swap stories about Vietnam. Monika noticed that Michael looked forward to his visits eagerly and seemed to light up when they talked about the war, guns, uniforms, or soldiers of fortune. It did not surprise her, because that was his profession, but sometimes, she thought, he misled his friend. Michael had told her he had been forced to leave Vietnam prematurely by his diabetes, but he didn't admit it to his friend, and she thought he exaggerated some of his wartime exploits to impress him. And when Michael boasted that he belonged to an important family in England, it seemed unlike him; but she suspected she knew why he did it: male pride. The Official Secrets Act prohibited him from discussing his work, so he embroidered his war stories to avoid being overshadowed by his friend. She understood it, but it annoyed her that Michael felt a need to court the approval of this bearded former marine who was out of a job and apparently not in a hurry to get another one.

Then she was stunned when Michael suddenly took off his Rolex watch and handed it to their guest.

"Michael, are you *crazy?*" she said after the ex-marine was gone. "That was a $3,000 watch."

As a child, Monika had learned how to express herself with telling effect; as an adult, she was even more forceful, opinionated, and outspoken.

"What's the matter with you? People don't do things like that!"

Trying to defend himself, Michael said his friend was "a good mate." Besides, he could afford another watch.

Monika didn't like what she had seen: Michael's "friend" had flattered and manipulated him and hinted he liked his watch. Their dispute escalated into a shouting match, and she said she might call off the wedding.

The next day, she found Michael unconscious on the bathroom floor.

"Did he forget to take his insulin?" Elsa asked.

"That's what the doctor thinks. They said he'll be all right, but he has to stay in Intensive Care for a few days."

"Don't you think you should call his mother and tell her what happened and that he's okay?" Elsa said. Monika agreed she should.

When she arrived at the hospital, a nurse told her Michael had regained consciousness, and joked that the nurses in ICU would probably be happier if he was still comatose. As soon as he was awake, she said, he had insisted on leaving the hospital, and insulted and swore at them. When Monika reached his bedside, she could see he was still in a surly mood: Michael was cursing a nurse who was trying to put a hospital smock on him. Naked under the blankets, he refused to wear it.

Michael refused to speak to Monika, even after she said her threat to call off the wedding had been impulsive and she didn't mean it. She realized she was conducting a monologue: Michael's eyes were closed tightly, and he wouldn't respond to her. She had seen him pout before, and ordered him to look at her. But he said nothing until she suggested: "I think we'd better call your mother in Australia and tell her what happened."

Michael suddenly unsealed his eyes and erupted into a rage. "No. My mother doesn't give a damn about me. She's a bitch."

"What do you mean?"

When he was a child, Michael said, his mother had never cared about him, and wouldn't care now.

Monika said she was sure his mother loved him and would want to know that he was all right after he'd come so close to dying.

"No, she doesn't care anything about me. I don't want you to call her."

When Monika returned to the hospital the next day, Michael told her he wanted to leave immediately, because he had to be in London as soon as possible. "They won't release you yet," she said. "They told me you're not ready to go."

Michael insisted he was going to leave and asked her to go to the apartment and get his passport. He couldn't explain why, but it was urgent for him to return to England; it involved government business, and if he didn't return, he might get in serious trouble.

At the apartment, Monika collected his passport and packed his bag, then returned to the hospital, where she was intercepted outside Michael's room by the nursing supervisor: not only was the patient not ready to leave, she said, he *couldn't* leave, because he hadn't settled his bill, which totaled almost $10,000.

Michael, fully dressed, suddenly appeared outside his room and said he was ready to leave. When the nurse protested, he promised the bill would be paid, but refused to say by whom. Then he turned his back on her and left the hospital, with Monika trailing behind him. She drove him to the Los Angeles International Airport, and he boarded a flight to London.

Three days later, Michael called and said his boss had refused to extend his leave any longer, and he asked Monika to come to England: he missed her desperately. She said it didn't make sense to move to England yet, because there was so much to do before the wedding; besides, she wanted to keep her job as long as she could, to save some money to bring to England with her. But Michael was persistent: he telephoned every day begging her to come. When he called, the first thing she often heard was the recorded voice of Tony Bennett singing "I Left My Heart in San Francisco." Then Michael joined in a duet. He reinforced his telephone appeals with letters. In one he enclosed an airline ticket and said he was looking for a house for them to rent near London.

Early in March, Monika finally surrendered: she resigned her job at Reynolds & Reynolds and left for England and all the uncertainty she knew it would bring her.

10.

When he met Monika at Heathrow Airport, Michael told her he had
rented a furnished house in Royal Tunbridge Wells, a city in Kent, an
hour's drive southeast from London. They would live there until they
bought their own home.

Monika got her first glimpse of England on a route that had been
traveled by British royalty for more than three centuries, since an
iron-rich mineral spring discovered at Tunbridge Wells in 1606 was
proclaimed capable of prolonging life, increasing sexual potency, and
mitigating the discomfort of overindulgence in food and drink. When
she arrived there in the spring of 1981, Tun Wells—as locals called
it—was evolving rapidly into a bedroom community for London com-
muters. Although parts of the old royal spa had the tired look of
past-their-prime resorts the world over, the center of Tun Wells was
graced with elegantly restored colonnaded eighteenth-century buildings—many with boutiques and antique shops—and architectural
landmarks from a later era, huge Victorian brick buildings festooned
with chimneys, towers, and cupolas.

Monika's first letters home conveyed her sense of discovery: "I didn't
realize I had so much to learn about English history. . . . There's a lot
to see and I'm trying to learn as much as I can." She said she loved the

bucolic British countryside: "It's breath taking," she wrote to her mother. "Spring is beautiful here. Everyone has a garden. You can leave the city and five minutes later be surrounded by gorgeous scenery." She said she was also surprised by the level of poverty she saw in parts of England. Like most of the world, it was mired in a stubborn recession, and even though this was momentarily overshadowed by national euphoria over the upcoming marriage of the Prince of Wales and Lady Diana Spencer, the effects were apparent in Tunbridge Wells. "You'd be amazed at the housing some of the people here have," she wrote. The recession, Monika said, would probably make it hard for her to get a job, but she would find one as soon as possible; she was reading the help-wanted columns every day.

Shortly after Monika arrived, Michael said his superiors had informed him he must resume a full schedule of training to catch up with classes he'd missed during his leave of absence. It meant he would probably have to be gone from home occasionally. Operational missions would also come up on short notice from time to time, he said, and he wouldn't be able to discuss them with her.

Michael left for London each morning on his motorcycle, and occasionally remained overnight, while Monika tackled the challenge of turning their rented house into a home. The house at 12 Poona Road was spacious, but not opulent by California standards. It was a row house, one link in a chain of identical sandstone-and-brick, slate-roofed homes that stood shoulder to shoulder like a rank of sentries in one of Tun Wells's lesser neighborhoods. The furnishings were functional but not stylish, and Monika decided to redecorate it in the Victorian style she'd learned to love in California. Michael said he'd arrange for the SAS to ship her furniture to England. Bringing Victorian antiques from the California Gold Country to England, she admitted, was a little like carrying coals to Newcastle, but that's what she wanted. Since he was gone so much, she also had time to hunt for bargains at local antique shops, and in letters home boasted of bargains she had found for a fraction of their value in America. With no job to go to yet, she also had plenty of time to read—books on English history, architecture, and antiques and Agatha Christie mysteries.

On one of his days off, Michael urged her to ride with him into London on the back of his Harley. After bruising her elbow on a car as he darted in and out of traffic, she proclaimed this was the last time she would accept such an invitation, but it was an adventure she talked about for months. They lunched at the Hyde Park Hotel, across from the great urban forest in the center of London, and visited Trafalgar Square, Westminster Abbey, Piccadilly Circus, and the Tower of London, from which she sent a postcard to her friends at the Reynolds & Reynolds office in Sacramento:

> Dear Sammye, Roger, Chappie, Barbara and all:
> Just thought I'd let you know I haven't disappeared off the face of the earth. Hope all is well with you. London is a wonderful place when it comes to entertainment and food and history, as you'll notice by the card. Miss you all.
>
> Love
> Monika.

On nights when Michael was home, they usually went out for drinks and a meal at the pub, where it was generally Monika, not Michael, who spoke first to strangers. More a spectator than a participant, he tended to be reticent among strangers, but Monika was a compulsive maker of friends: she easily struck up conversations with other customers, often to their surprise, for many were as standoffish as Michael. From California, she had brought a directness that was uncommon in England. She spoke her mind and offered her friendship with a quickness and warmth many found disarming. In this, her British friends agreed, she had an unusual gift: she was easy to like.

When Michael was gone, Monika often went shopping with friends she had made in the neighborhood and the pubs. If any asked about his job, she said simply, "He works for the government," and that satisfied them.

11.

Returning home after a shopping trip, Monika opened the front door and laid her purse and packages down on an antique table she had bought for a few pounds at a local flea market. As she expected, the house was empty. Michael was away on an overnight assignment.

She put away her groceries and walked to the bedroom. It was chaos: the dresser drawers were open, blankets were torn from the bed, the mattress askew. Quickly, she made a mental inventory: Michael's CB-radio equipment was safe; none of their clothes were gone, nor the ornate Victorian clock she had recently purchased. Then she remembered the pearls Michael's mother had given her. She went to the drawer where she kept them and discovered they were gone. "All I could think of," she later told Elsa, "was, *What am I going to say to Michael's mother?*"

A police constable said the burglar appeared to have entered the house through an unlocked window. Detectives from the local CID— the Criminal Investigation Division—would try to determine if the necklace was being offered for sale by any of the local fences, but he suspected a string of pearls as valuable as Monika's would probably have already been fenced in London. He gave her little hope they would ever be recovered. Indeed, he talked as if the pearls had already disappeared into the British underworld.

———

In Santa Rosa, Elsa ordered wedding invitations and reserved a band, photographer, and banquet room for the reception. In letters and transatlantic telephone calls, she kept Monika and Michael informed of what she was accomplishing and pressed them to agree on a guest list for the wedding. "Please ask Michael to give me all the addresses and mail the papers back to the church in Santa Rosa (please print addresses so I can read them)," she wrote in early May, "and tell Michael to learn a few dance steps. Love to you both . . ."

With Monika's coaching, Michael learned several dance steps, but he was less obliging about preparing the guest list. He said his family were scattered all over the world and he needed time to assemble their addresses.

In July, almost three months after Monika's first trip across the Atlantic, she and Michael returned to California to complete their wedding plans. Monika confided to Elsa that their sex life had lost intensity since its peak at Lake Tahoe and Bermuda, and she was very homesick for California, but she was happy nevertheless. She endorsed Elsa's choices for the reception and wedding cake, and they decided on simple Victorian sack dresses for her bridesmaids and Sammye Hynes, her maid of honor. For her own gown, Monika selected a lush white brocade design modeled on the dress of a pretty Victorian bride whose picture she'd seen hanging on the wall of a Tunbridge Wells antique shop. A dressmaker in Tun Wells promised to copy it exactly, using fabric from America. After ordering the brocade for her dress, Monika bought a gun—a .357-magnum Colt Python—for Michael. He needed it for his job, he said, but as a British subject he couldn't buy it himself. Monika told the proprietor of the sporting-goods store that she lived alone and needed the gun for security, and it was registered in her name.

When Elsa pressed Michael again for the addresses of his relatives, he said he still didn't have them. Alone with Elsa, Monika warned her: "I don't think Michael is going to give you his mother's address. He calls her a 'bitch' and says he doesn't want her at the wedding."

"I think out of common courtesy we *have* to invite her," Elsa said. "She's his mother. We can't be that rude."

Monika promised to work on Michael, but she was learning he

could be very stubborn; he didn't like to do what he didn't want to do.

Michael and Monika returned to England after less than a week. Monika promised to come back in six weeks or so to help Elsa with the final preparations before the September 12 wedding.

The night before they left, Michael told Lou he wanted to apologize again for not being more forthcoming about his job because of the Official Secrets Act. "It's okay, I understand it," Lou assured him. Michael said there was something else he hadn't told Lou about himself: his family, he said, was rather important and prominent in England.

Lou wondered if he was trying to hint that he expected resistance from his family to his decision to marry Monika and if that explained why he was so reluctant to give Elsa a list of his relatives. He asked Michael: "Is your family unhappy you're going to marry an American?"

"Oh, no," Michael answered. "There's a long tradition of men in my family marrying Americans."

Monika's suitcase was as tidy as her house: blouses, skirts, and sweaters were as neatly stacked as those behind the counter of a Regent Street boutique. As she removed her clothing from the bag after the trip to California, her fingers felt a hard lump at the bottom. She reached in and pulled out a pistol. It was the revolver she had bought for Michael in California.

She was furious.

"Michael! Why did you make *me* bring your gun through Customs?" She could have been arrested if her bag had been X-rayed. "If you're going to smuggle a goddamn gun into England, smuggle it in your own suitcase."

Since it was registered in her name, Michael said he thought it best to carry the gun in her suitcase. But Monika was not placated—and this argument was not the only one after the trip to California.

After four months of living together, strains were starting to appear in their relationship, changes occurring in its balance and symmetry. Such a process perhaps takes place in all conjugal associations: with time, shifts occur in the balance of power between two people; roles change, shaped by their daily emotional transactions, the intimacy of the marriage bed, the interplay of their respective strengths and weaknesses, and the unmasking of emotional disguises. Monika was more

verbal than Michael, quicker-witted, more determined to control events
around her—traits she had carried with her from childhood. She had
started to assert herself as the dominant member of the partnership. And
she began to discover a side of Michael she'd only glimpsed in California: In England, he often became moody, tense, and truculent; a
week or more might pass when he was as even-tempered and good-
natured as ever, but his mood could change in a moment to sullenness
or petulance, as if he were a spoiled child. One evening, for instance,
they accepted an invitation to the home of a couple they had met at the
Grange Public House—Christine Percy, who worked at a Tun Wells
bank, and her boyfriend, David Wallis, a salesman—for a game of low-
stakes backgammon. After losing a few shillings, Michael suddenly
turned quiet, then surly. He got up, threw the dice on the table, and
said: "This is a stupid game. I'm going home."

After an uncomfortable silence, Monika said: "*Michael, come on, sit
down and play.*"

When he refused, she said: "Michael, please, you're making a fool
of yourself. *Sit down!*"

She reminded Christine of a mother admonishing a misbehaving
child. Michael returned to the table but brooded for the rest of the
evening.

Monika made excuses for Michael; she attributed his moodiness to
his diabetes, the pressures of his job, and, in part, her own behavior:
because she was homesick, she was drinking too much in England.
Sometimes it made her cranky.

She continued to make excuses for Michael even after discovering a
still darker side to his personality—a side she decided not to tell her
parents about.

———————

As a child, Michael said, he had been close to an aunt who lived in
London—his mother's sister—and her children. At Monika's urging,
he arranged a night out for them with one of his cousins in London.
Before leaving Tun Wells, he asked her not to mention they had set
the date for their wedding, because he didn't want his mother to know
about it yet.

They met for dinner at the Hyde Park Hotel, where they had
lunched during Monika's first visit to London. His cousin Christopher
was three years older than Michael and a barrister, or trial lawyer.
Monika immediately liked him and his wife. After dinner, the two

women were absorbed in conversation when Monika overheard Christopher ask Michael a question:

"Have you seen Alison and Matthew lately?"

Monika wondered whom he was referring to and listened for Michael's answer. He saw her sideways glance and responded with silence. Suddenly the four-way conversation came to a halt, as if a curtain had descended.

Michael's cousin looked at Michael, then Monika.

"Michael, doesn't Monika know about Alison?" he asked.

Michael was still silent.

"Michael, don't you think you should tell her? I think you better tell her parents, too."

12.

"Mother, Michael and I are flying home tomorrow."

Startled by the call early on a Saturday morning, and even more so by the anxiety in Monika's voice, Elsa said: "What is it, dear? What in the world is wrong?" Monika hadn't been planning to return to Santa Rosa for at least another month.

"Michael and I don't want to discuss it on the phone," Monika said. "We'll be there tomorrow night and talk about it then."

After calling her mother, Monika telephoned Sammye Hynes in Sacramento and said: "The wedding's off. The son of a bitch has been lying to me. He's already married."

"You're kidding," Sammye said.

"That's only half of it."

———

Not until Monika and Michael arrived in Santa Rosa did they tell Lou and Elsa that Michael was married and the father of a two-year-old son.

Three years before, Michael said, while he was living in Australia, he married an eighteen-year-old English girl after a whirlwind court-ship. Although he quickly realized it was a mistake, she was pregnant within a few weeks and it became impossible to leave her. They moved to England, where their son, Matthew, was born, and settled in Torquay. Lou remembered Michael had once told him he lived in Torquay, but had said his roommates were Royal Marines. Michael explained that he hadn't told them before about the marriage for several reasons. When they met in Sausalito and later, during his first visit to Santa Rosa, it didn't seem appropriate to discuss a failed marriage with people he had only just met. To him, the marriage was dead, emotionally if not legally, and he never expected to fall in love with their daughter. When he went to Sacramento, at first he didn't mention it to Monika, for the same reason; and once he fell in love with her, he was afraid that, if he admitted he hadn't been truthful with her from the beginning, he would lose her. One lie led to another. As soon as Monika accepted his proposal, he flew to Australia to ask his wife, Alison, for a divorce, and she agreed to it. That was why he had gone to Australia after Monika accepted his ring: Alison had been visiting his mother and stepfather in Sydney at the time.

Monika interrupted: "The reason Michael got so upset when we went to St. Eugene's was that the monsignor was asking him so many questions and he was afraid he'd get caught right there."

Keeping the secret had been tough on him emotionally, Michael said. It made him moody and grouchy, and there were times in Tunbridge Wells when he hadn't treated Monika nicely. The pressure had been too much.

Lou listened to Michael sympathetically: from his own experience, he knew how one lie could lead to another.

Seated next to Michael on the sofa, Monika looked weary. It had been a long flight, quickly arranged, and instead of her contact lenses she was wearing her big wide-rimmed glasses, which made her eyes look even larger than they were. She seemed a little disoriented; sometimes she slurred her words.

"Tell them the rest, Michael," Monika said.

Michael said there were two additional things he wanted to tell Lou and Elsa about himself.

The first involved his family.

He reminded Lou that he had once told him he was from an important family in England.

"Have you ever heard of the Vesteys?"

"No," Lou said, "I don't think we have."

"No," Elsa agreed.

If Lou and Elsa had been in London instead of Sausalito on the
Sunday morning in October when Michael Henry Maxwell Telling
rode into their lives on a new limited-edition Harley-Davidson, their
answer might have been different. That morning, an article about
Michael's family had filled much of the front page of the Sunday
Times. Part of a series that continued for a month of Sundays, it began:

RICHEST FAMILY IN HUGE TAX-DODGE
THEY MADE £2.3m IN PROFITS . . . THEY PAID
JUST £10 TAX

WHY?

The Treasury is losing millions of pounds a year in unpaid income
tax and surtax because of a major loophole in the tax law. The loophole's existence has been revealed in a sensational but virtually unre-
ported tax case in the House of Lords involving the Vesteys, Britain's
richest family. During the case it emerged that the Vesteys—peers of the
realm, old Etonians, friends of the royal family, polo-players, deputy
lieutenants of their county, pillars of the British establishment—have
been exploiting this and other loopholes to avoid paying enormous
amounts of income tax for more than 60 years.

The Vesteys, headed by Lord 'Sam' Vestey, 39, and his cousin Edmund, 48, run a worldwide empire in shipping, clothing, insurance,
shops and meat—the Dewhurst chain of butcher shops is theirs. Inland
Revenue decided that six members of the family, including Lord Vestey
himself, were, over a four-year period, liable for income tax on £4.3
million and surtax on £7.3 million. But the Law Lords ruled—as they
have done in the past in other Vestey cases—that the family need not
pay a penny. In the taxation world, the shock of this decision was,
according to the British Tax Review, 'like an atom bomb.'

It was not surprising that Lou and Elsa didn't recognize the name.
Until that Sunday morning, few Britons knew the name of England's
wealthiest family after the royals, either; for most of a century, the
Vesteys had obsessively tried to keep their affairs private.

13.

Chicago,
Summer 1876

Even after making many trips to Chicago—even after he made his fortune there—William Vestey hated the stench of the Union Stock Yards, the stinking square mile of pigsties, slaughterhouses, and cattle pens Upton Sinclair called *The Jungle*. The odors exhaled by the blood-smeared meat-packing plants—a "ghastly odor of all the dead things of the universe," Sinclair wrote—so permeated the Near South Side of Chicago that men and women who worked in the malodorous killing zone could never escape it. It lingered in their clothes and the strands of their hair, followed them home, pursued them wherever they went. Michael Telling's great-grandfather hated the smell. But when opportunity presented itself to him in the stockyards of Chicago, he knew how to respond to it.

William Vestey was seventeen and on a mission for his father when he arrived in Chicago in 1876, the year General George Custer died in the Battle of Little Big Horn and Alexander Graham Bell patented the telephone. Time was closing in on the American frontier, and a nation still nursing the wounds of civil war was beginning to flex its industrial might—and nothing, until Henry Ford invented the automobile assembly line a few years later, so demonstrated the genius of American enterprise on a grand scale than the Union Stock Yards.

Every day, trains of a dozen railroads rolled into Chicago bearing thousands of sheep and swine and lowing cattle for slaughter, and when the executioners in the stinking brick buildings were finished, the trains hauled their carcasses back to the dinner tables of America.

In Victorian England, meanwhile, the industrial revolution was in full bloom, and the country was celebrating a new secular religion, enterprise and empire-building. A generation of hard-working commoners—merchants, industrialists, and entrepreneurs—were amassing fortunes and beginning to push their way into an aristocracy that had long been based on blood, pedigree, and primogeniture.

William Vestey's father, Samuel, was a prosperous Liverpool food broker whose ancestry was rooted in the poor backwaters of rural Yorkshire. He sent his eldest son to Chicago to buy foodstuffs that he could resell to shopkeepers and captains of the ships that sailed into Liverpool Bay. The Lancashire teenager was amazed at the waste he discovered in Chicago. Every week, the assembly-line butcheries discarded enough pork and beef scraps to feed thousands of Britons—and he wondered how he could package and sell the stuff profitably at home. With his own enterprise and his father's capital, he established a packing plant to can the flotsam and jetsam of the slaughterhouses, which he could buy cheaply because Americans didn't want it. In so doing, he helped invent a product that, generations later, would give his descendants a nickname: "Lord Spam." His contributions to the invention of a forerunner of the tinned meat later known as Spam made William Vestey a multimillionaire in his early twenties. In his early thirties, he retired to a splendid country home near the Irish Sea and turned over management of the Chicago operation to his younger brother, Edmund. But, burdened with an overpowering work ethic instilled by their father, he was restless as a country squire, and months after retiring boarded a ship for South America, to satisfy a professional curiosity about reports of meat-canning operations on a huge scale by Armour, Swift, and other American companies. When he landed in Argentina in 1889, he was awed by the vast panoramas of cattle herds on the pampas—and more so by the meager prices ranchers were willing to sell them for. Steers were being slaughtered for their hides alone, their peeled carcasses left to rot on the treeless grassland. William wondered—as he once had in Chicago—how he could package the Argentine beef and sell it profitably in England—not in tin cans, but as *fresh* meat.

In an experiment, he decided to test the British market for frozen partridges, which were nearly as plentiful as cattle in Argentina. Although the fundamentals of mechanical refrigeration had been patented in 1834, entrepreneurs had not yet applied the principle to transporting chilled foods great distances over the sea. William bought and froze several hundred partridges and shipped them to England in ships outfitted with iced compartments. After they arrived safely, he and Edmund erected a cold-storage plant in Argentina and another in Liverpool, and sent a cargo of frozen beef carcasses to England; they were able to sell the beef for substantially less than the cost of domestic beef and still make a profit. After further experiments, they commissioned the building of a ship specially designed with refrigerated compartments and began a regular beef trade to England. Before long, they built more ships, and the Vestey brothers had made their second fortune.

They did not stop there. Living frugally, they invested their profits to expand the business—to build more ships and cold-storage plants and search the world for new markets. In China and Russia, they discovered huge quantities of cheap eggs, chickens, and other commodities, and an appetite for British manufactured goods; soon they made their third and biggest fortune.

To supply the growing markets for cheaper food they were creating in England, they bought farms and ranches, sheep and cattle stations in many countries. They built packing plants and cold-storage facilities wherever they went and usually established such a dominant position in the local markets that they could regulate not only supply and demand but the price they paid for the ranchers' and peasants' food. They also diversified. Why let others profit from selling the beef they imported from Argentina? They opened more than three thousand retail meat stores in England; their Dewhurst butcher shops became fixtures in virtually every city and village in the country. Why enrich shipping companies with fees for transporting their products across the ocean? The Vesteys built one of the world's premier shipping companies, the Blue Star Line. They became one of the world's largest producers of leather and knitted wool: why let others profit from tanning and hides and processing the wool of their animals?

In 1913, William Vestey was honored by the British government with a baronetcy—Britain's highest-ranking title short of a peerage—

for helping make cheaper food more available to ordinary Britons. The outbreak of World War I a year later gave the brothers another opportunity to serve their country—and to make an additional fortune. Their flagship company, Union Cold Storage Ltd. of Liverpool, became the largest supplier of rations to British doughboys in France and helped fill stomachs throughout Europe.

The war, however, had a two-edged impact on the fortunes of the Vestey brothers.

In 1915, Parliament overhauled the nation's tax laws to raise money for the war, and among the changes was one William Vestey considered a direct assault on the global enterprise he had created. Before, no income taxes had been levied on the profits of British-owned companies earned abroad unless the earnings were brought into England. The new law broadened the net of British tax collectors to include *all* earnings of British companies.

Until then, the brothers had been able to invest their profits tax-free and continue their relentless campaign of expansion. The new law was unfair, they told the Royal Commission on Taxation in 1915, if for no other reason than that their competitors in the U.S. meat-packing industry could sell meat to Britons while paying no taxes in either America or Britain. It penalized them simply because they were English: if allowed to stand, it would destroy their ability to survive, and they wouldn't stand for it. "If I kill a beast in the Argentine and sell the product of that beast in Spain, this country can get no tax on that business," William told the Royal Commission. "You may do what you like, but you cannot have it." Their protests were to no avail. The law stood. As a result, in November 1915, at the peak of the war, William and Edmund took their families to live in Argentina. Under a scheme drafted by their American lawyers and William's secretary and financial adviser, Edward Brown, the brothers moved their company's headquarters to America—first to Chicago, then to New York— and assigned control of its assets to a new American company. None of their profits ever entered the United States, so no U.S. taxes were due; the earnings flowed tax-free to the brothers in Buenos Aires, and since Argentina did not impose an income tax, it was theirs to keep or invest in further expansion. During the war, they doubled their fleet of refrigerated ships, bought more farms and ranches, and gained a foothold in half a dozen new nations. Still, for the Vestey brothers, one thing was wrong with the arrangement: they missed England. "I was born in the good old town of Liverpool and I want to die in this country," William had told the Royal Commission.

When the war was over, they returned to England in triumph—thanks to a series of legal maneuvers that left British tax attorneys in awe for generations, kept their fortune inviolate, and helped the Vesteys complete the passage from a family of Liverpool butchers into the British aristocracy.

Soon after Armistice Day, rumors circulated in London that Prime Minister David Lloyd George was offering knighthoods and other titles in exchange for contributions to his Liberal Party. According to the rumors, the price of a peerage was £20,000.

Twice a year, the Prime Minister submitted a list of honors to the King, who was required under Britain's unwritten constitution to confer them. In 1922, his honors list included the name of William Vestey to be a *baron*—a peer of the realm and full-fledged member of the British nobility, with a title he could pass to his descendants. Almost sixty years later, in a series of articles about the Vestey family published in October and November 1980, the *Sunday Times* reported that behind the investiture of Baron William Vestey there was a scandal that reached into Buckingham Palace. In an uncommon breach of parliamentary etiquette, the newspaper reported, several Members of Parliament, outraged by the brothers' wartime desertion to Argentina, publicly denounced the honor, and one peer in the House of Lords demanded to his face that William reply to charges that he had purchased his title—a challenge to which the new peer did not respond. After learning about this exchange, King George V reviewed William's wartime comments before the Royal Commission on Taxation, in which he had boasted: "The present position of affairs suits me admirably. I am abroad; I pay nothing." According to Phillip Knightley, author of the *Times* series, the King then sent "to Lloyd George a letter (now filed in the House of Lords' Record Office) that in its tone and content must rank among the most critical a British monarch has ever sent his prime minister." Dated July 3, 1922, it began:

My Dear Prime Minister:
I cannot conceal from you my profound concern at the very disagreeable situation which has arisen on the question of honours. The peerages which I was advised to confer upon . . . Sir William Vestey have

brought things rather to a climax; though for some time there have been evident signs of growing public dissatisfaction on account of the excessive number of honours conferred, the personality of some of the recipients and the questionable circumstances under which the honours in certain instances have been granted. . . . In recent years there have been instances in which honours have been bestowed where subsequent information has betrayed a lack of care in the enquiries made as to the fitness of the persons selected for recognition. . . . I do appeal most strongly for the establishment of some efficient and trustworthy procedure in order to protect the Crown and the government from the possibility of similar painful if not humiliating incidents, the recurrence of which must inevitably constitute an evil, dangerous to the social and political well being of the state.

In reply, the Prime Minister defended his methods for choosing peers but conceded he had been uninformed of Baron Vestey's tax-avoidance schemes and wartime desertion to Argentina; if he had known, he implied, he would not have nominated him to be a baron. But it was too late: despite the royal protest and ministerial regret, the school dropout from Liverpool who had founded his fortune in Chicago's Union Stock Yards could call himself Baron Vestey of Kingswood, County Surrey. He bought a gold coronet, commissioned the creation of a family coat of arms featuring three eggs balanced on an iceberg—in homage to the origins of his wealth—and chose a family motto: "*E Labore Stabilitas*," "From Labor, Stability."

Meanwhile, the Vestey brothers and their lawyers quietly devised a new financial plan—one that allowed the brothers to live again in England and still pay no income tax.

The heart of the new scheme was the establishment in 1921 of two family trusts in France, one for each brother. Nominal control of their business was transferred to the French trusts, which were administered by loyal family retainers. They collected the earnings of the brothers' worldwide enterprises in Paris and sent the money to them in England. Under prevailing British law, their lawyers discovered, they did not have to pay taxes on income from trusts domiciled abroad. William and Edmund could move back to England, live off the income from the trusts, pay no tax on it, and watch their pile grow.

In 1924, William's wife of forty-one years, the mother of his four sons, died. A year later, at sixty-five, he married Evelyn Brodstone of Superior, Nebraska, the daughter of an immigrant Norwegian farmer, in New York City. She had been hired as a $12-a-week typist in the Vesteys' Chicago office shortly before the war, beginning a career that would make her one of the most successful female business executives in England or America during an era when women seldom saw the inside of an executive suite without a steno pad in their hands. Demonstrating the kind of industriousness and enterprise William revered, she rose to a powerful position as the company's senior financial executive, her future husband's alter ego, and finally his wife—as driven as he was to enlarge the company and make it more profitable.

In choosing an American for his second wife, William followed a pattern set by his brother, Edmund, who in 1887 had married a girl from Passaic, New Jersey. After *he* became engaged to an American, one of William's great-grandsons, Michael Henry Maxwell Telling, would say he had done the same thing as they: he fell in love with an American girl who had a good head for business.

The Vestey brothers' fortune continued to multiply after World War I, despite the Depression and several efforts by Parliament and British tax collectors to close the loophole they employed to avoid taxes. In 1936, Parliament ruled that Britons had to pay taxes on income they received from foreign trusts over which they exercised control. The Vesteys' lawyers soon found another loophole: according to their interpretation of the law, taxes could be levied *only* on the income received by the *original creators* of foreign trusts, not "passive beneficiaries," including their sons, daughters, and other descendants.

On the eve of World War II, the family sold an estimated 70 percent of the meat consumed in Great Britain. It owned businesses and vast acreage in Argentina, Australia, Brazil, France, Madagascar, New Zealand, Paraguay, Portugal, South Africa, Spain, the United States, and Venezuela. World War II brought it even more wealth. One measure of its role was the size of its casualty list: the Vestey companies lost twenty-nine ships to enemy action during the war.

Shortly before German troops marched into Paris, the family trusts were moved from France to neutral Uruguay. Profits continued to accumulate tax-free overseas while their trustees made "occasional and discretionary" payments to family members in England. To assure that his descendants shared in the fruits of his success, Baron Vestey, before his death in 1940, directed his heirs "to extend good offices and render pecuniary and other assistance to the other members [of the family] according to their merits and needs."

Britain's tax-collection agency, Inland Revenue, wasn't finished with the Vesteys, however. In 1948, complaining that in the postwar years many wealthy families were emulating the Vesteys by establishing offshore trusts to evade taxes, it persuaded Britain's supreme court, the Law Lords, to review the Parliamentary Act of 1936. The court accepted Inland Revenue's position that, contrary to the Vesteys' claim, Parliament intended to tax *all* income from foreign trusts, not only amounts received by the creators of the trust. Inland Revenue— which had been trying since the 1920s to break the Vesteys' tax-avoidance schemes—interpreted its victory very broadly, claiming that it now had the right to tax William's and Edmund's heirs not only on income they actually received from the trusts, but on any money retained by the trust abroad. It also claimed a right to levy taxes on *potential* beneficiaries, including infants and children or anyone it decided had future claims on the fortune. However, in a conciliatory gesture that eventually brought its undoing, the tax-collection agency said it would not exercise its authority fully; instead, it would tax only a portion of the trust's total income and apportion it among family members based on a formula devised by its staff.

The Vesteys' lawyers went back to court and continued their legal war with Inland Revenue for another thirty years. In 1979, the case reached the highest court in the land again. This time, the Vesteys prevailed.

Reversing the court's 1948 decision, the Law Lords ruled that the family was right: as written, the Parliamentary Act of 1936 was meant to tax only the income from foreign trusts received by creators of the trusts, not their descendants. It also ruled that Inland Revenue's formula for apportioning income among members of the family was unconstitutional, because only Parliament—not an administrative agency of government—had the legal authority to fix tax rates.

It was a complete victory for the Vesteys. The decision meant members of the family could once again collect income from the foreign trusts free of taxes, no matter where they lived.

The conglomerate founded by William and Edmund Vestey, who died in 1953, was now the largest privately owned multinational company in the world, Britain's last great merchant empire. Valued at more than $4 billion, it employed seventy thousand people and embraced more than 250 companies in twenty-seven countries. It was a textbook example of a vertically integrated conglomerate with a global reach—a hoof-to-market meat empire rigidly controlled from top to bottom: one of the world's largest retailers of meat, the world's largest producer of leather used in the manufacture of clothing, and one of the world's largest producers of textiles.

And, after more than a century, everything was still all in the family.

Not only was the Vestey fortune intact, but it had multiplied many times, while the fortunes of many of England's wealthiest families had been depleted by death duties and the progressive income tax. Except for the Windsors—the royal family—the Vesteys were England's richest family, and they had scaled the cliffs of British society to an aerie very near the top.

Their offspring attended Eton and Harrow, Cambridge and Oxford; they were invited to join the best clubs and the Scots Guards, the country's most elite military regiment. They socialized with the royal family, took their seats in the rooms where power was exercised in Great Britain. They lived in almost feudal isolation on huge estates and paid virtually no income tax—thanks to the perfectly legal strategies of William and Edmund.

At William's death in 1940, his title passed to his eldest son, Samuel. In the normal course of events, his firstborn son, Captain William Howarth Vestey of the Scots Guards, would have inherited the title. But in 1944, he was fatally wounded in Italy, and the title passed instead to *his* son—Samuel George Armstrong Vestey—in 1954, at the age of thirteen. Although his title as the third baron was now "Lord Vestey," playmates called him "Lord Spam."

Until the Sunday *Times* articles in October 1980, the Vestey family, for all its wealth, power, and status, was largely unknown beyond the upper reaches of British society and London's financial community. It controlled its global business empire privately, while its privileged members lived out their lives far from the public eye, and that was exactly how the family wanted it. As the third baron told the *Financial Times* in 1972, "For more than eighty years, we have maintained a total silence about our affairs. We are, after all, a very private business."

II

Like William and Edmund, the present generation of Vesteys lead a life apart from the mainstream of British society, able—or obliged—to do so because of their immense wealth.

PHILLIP KNIGHTLEY, *The Vestey Affair*

14.

After revealing he was an heir to one of the world's great fortunes, Michael told Lou and Elsa more about himself and his family.

The first baron, Lord William Vestey, had four sons, he said, one of whom was Michael's grandfather Captain Leonard Vestey, who in turn had two daughters. Michael's mother was the eldest. His branch of the family was headed by his second cousin, the third baron, Lord Samuel Vestey, who was nine years older than he was. As the lineal descendant of his great-grandfather's firstborn son, Samuel had inherited not only the title but the largest share of the family wealth—*too large* a share, Michael implied.

The trusts established by his great-grandfather were worth billions. As a beneficiary, he received a monthly income, and the trust paid all his bills. Each month, he sent the bills to the family offices in London, where an accountant named Mr. Brown paid them. Once he and Monika were married, he said, Mr. Brown would buy them a house.

Elsa remembered that Michael had mentioned there was a third matter he wanted to explain about himself. Monika brought it up before she did: "Michael doesn't have a job. He lied to us."

Contrary to what they believed, Michael continued, he was not in British intelligence or the SAS; he had implied that he was, during his first visit to Santa Rosa, because he'd needed privacy during telephone calls to Alison—to arrange the meeting with her in Australia to discuss a divorce. The calls from the Australian Consulate, he said, had nothing to do with intelligence work, and the Charlie Brown dinnerware he'd bought was for Matthew.

He said he hadn't told Monika about his family or its wealth—or that he didn't have a job—because he didn't want to lose her. He didn't want this to affect how she felt about him. In the past, some of his friends had been "sunny-weather friends" who played up to him after discovering he was wealthy.

Monika interrupted: "He got up every morning and went to work, and I never suspected anything. I just thought it was 'top secret' and he couldn't talk about it. We had the money for the rent and everything, so I naturally figured it came from his job. I never suspected. I can't believe he let it go this far: he let us set the wedding date, let Mom order the invitations, and never said anything."

As his web of lies grew and the family accepted him as a secret agent, Michael continued, it had become a convenient story to conceal his marriage, account for his income, and explain his absences from Tunbridge Wells.

In London, he pressed his solicitors to expedite the divorce so he and Monika could be married in September as planned, but it took longer than they'd expected. Now, he said, all he could do was ask Lou and Elsa to forgive him and help him persuade Monika she should still marry him.

Under Monika's prodding, Michael said there was one more thing he wanted to clear up: it was not true he had served in the Vietnam War.

He had made up the story, he said. As a little boy, he'd idolized his ancestors who had gone to war. It had been his childhood dream to enter the service, but his diabetes kept him out of a uniform. Embarrassed, he had made up the stories about Vietnam.

Monika said she was very angry but was still willing to marry Michael. If Lou and Elsa knew more about his childhood, she said, they would understand.

His mother, Michael explained, was a very wealthy woman who lived on a five-hundred-thousand-acre ranch in Australia. When he was growing up, she had paid little attention to him, sending him to a boarding school when he was very young; he had rarely seen his father after his parents divorced.

No one was more moved by his story than Monika. Even though she had heard it before, it made her cry. Growing up the daughter of an alcoholic hadn't been easy, but she always knew that Lou and Elsa loved her. Michael seemed to have grown up without love, and needed it now.

After two weeks, their visit to Santa Rosa ended on an emotional high: with Michael's confession complete, Lou and Elsa felt more affection for him than ever, and Monika said she loved him more than ever. He repeatedly apologized for his deceptions and promised never to lie again. As a wedding gift—or perhaps a peace offering—he bought Monika a Pontiac Firebird sports coupe and had it shipped to England.

Lou had been moved by the courage it took him to confess. He had unloaded everything. He had been honest and direct and made a plausible case: if Monika had known everything, she probably wouldn't have promised to marry him and he might have lost her. Men had done worse in the pursuit of women they loved.

Elsa knew that, since Monika's childhood, she had dreamed of a big church wedding. Now they both knew it was out of the question. She called St. Eugene's and canceled the wedding, and told Monika: "After his divorce is final, if you still want to marry Michael, why don't you just have a small civil ceremony in England and we'll fly over for it."

Everyone agreed it was the best plan now. On the night before they flew back to England, Elsa offered some motherly advice to Monika: "Don't be in a hurry, now. Take your time and be sure. Don't get married unless you're sure."

Monika promised she'd remember this.

15.

Michael and Monika returned to Tunbridge Wells in time for the loveliest weeks of the year in Kent. The pastures of the Kentish Weald were green and lush, the orchards heavy with apples and cherries. On the drive from Heathrow, they passed stone manor houses perched atop craggy hillsides, and half-timbered cottages with straw roofs and thatchers hurrying to make repairs before autumn. Everywhere, the English countryside was beautiful. During her brief residency in Britain, Monika had taken up English history with a passion. Every book she read, every ride she took was an opportunity to discover more about her adopted country and its history. As they rode home from the airport, she pointed out landmarks she suspected Michael might not know about—the ruins of old Roman walls, the homes of Charles Dickens and William Makepeace Thackeray, the country home of Winston Churchill, and locales featured in the works of Dickens, Trollope, Agatha Christie, Arthur Conan Doyle, and William Wordsworth, her favorite poet. When she telephoned Elsa to tell her they had arrived safely in England, she exclaimed at how beautiful the summer was and said it felt good to be home.

Michael went to London several days later, and came back to say his solicitors had told him the divorce proceedings were well under way and they could probably be married by Christmas. Before the wedding, however, the solicitors wanted Monika to sign a prenuptial agreement forfeiting any claim on his share of the family trust or the house the family intended to buy for them. The solicitors and trustees, he complained, were upset because they hadn't asked Alison to sign a similar agreement, and as a result the family had had to give her the house in Devon and a lifetime income. Monika said she didn't object: she didn't expect anything from Michael's family.

When Monika began monitoring the London newspapers for job opportunities again, she learned more about the family she was about to join. The Sunday *Times* articles published the previous autumn had stimulated additional journalistic scrutiny of the Vesteys, not all of it flattering. Although a few Britons came to the family's defense—everyone had a right to exploit every legal tax loophole, they argued—the disclosures had embarrassed the Thatcher government, and the Prime Minister responded with legislation designed to close the largest of the tax loopholes used by Michael's family. Phillip Knightley, author of the Sunday *Times* articles, wrote a book, *The Vestey Affair*, that added more embarrassing details about the family's past, and Fleet Street's tabloids, which catered profitably to the appetites of working-class readers for revelations about the upper crust, focused on the social and business lives of the family. They reported that the Vestey business empire was directed from a skyscraper in London by the contemporary heads of the two main branches of the family—Michael's second cousin, Lord Samuel "Spam" Vestey, and Samuel's first cousin, Edmund Hoyle Vestey, a forty-nine-year-old graduate of Eton, former high sheriff and deputy lord lieutenant of Essex, former lieutenant of the City of London Yeomanry, chairman of the Blue Star Line, joint master of the Pickeridge and Thurlow Foxhounds, and squire of a 150-square-mile domain in the Highlands of Scotland. "Lord Spam"—his title was "Baron Samuel George Armstrong Vestey of Kingswood, County Surrey"—was also an old Etonian and, like his late father, an officer in the Scots Guards. He divided his time between a London townhouse and a sixty-five-room seventeenth-century mansion at Stowell Park, a seven-square-mile wooded estate in the Cotswolds. The tabloids reported he was divorcing his wife of eleven years and remarrying, in part because his first wife had not given him a male heir. Polo, it was reported, was his passion. With a brother, he ran two of Britain's most successful polo teams, commuting to matches in a helicopter. Among his teammates and close friends was the Prince of Wales.

Michael told Monika that many members of his family were passionate about equestrian sports—polo, show jumping, fox hunting, and thoroughbred racing—although he preferred motorcycles himself. A few days later, during a drive through the Kent woodlands, they happened upon a local hunt. From their car, they saw a pack of hounds, chased by a troop of red-jacketed riders, bounding over a meadow near the road, pursuing a fox neither of them ever saw, then disappearing into the mists of a foggy morning.

The image remained with Monika, and when she asked Michael if he thought they could buy a horse, he said he would buy her anything in the world she wanted—starting with the house of her choice, wherever she wanted to live.

London was too crowded, Monika said. She preferred a country village. Even Tunbridge Wells, with its stoplights and shopping centers, was too big. She wanted an old house in the country with room for a horse.

By telephone, Monika kept Sammye Hynes informed of what she was learning about her new family and said the prospect of becoming part of it terrified her. "I'm just a simple girl from California," she said during one call. "Their wealth is *incredible*. I don't know how I'm going to fit in."

"You'll love it once you get used to it," Sammye assured her.

"Don't count on it," Monika said.

After the call, it occurred to Sammye that her best friend was living a fantasy—perhaps every girl's fantasy. "She was like Cinderella," she remembered years later. "In the middle of California she meets a guy—an ordinary tourist who's recommended to her by her parents— and falls head over heels in love with him; then she discovers he's one of the richest men in England. It was straight out of the storybooks. They could travel, go anywhere, have no financial worries; he could give her anything she wanted. It was a fairy tale, and I thought Monika had found her real Prince Charming."

16.

"How old are you, Miss Zumsteg?"

That was the first question Mr. Brown asked. He was smiling at Monika.

Michael had taken her to the seat of power of the Vestey family, an eight-story building that filled most of a full city block in Smithfield, London's meat-market district. She was invited to meet the men who controlled the purse strings of the Vestey Settlement.

First there was Lord Spam himself, who said cheerily he would be delighted to have her in the family. Then she was introduced to a retinue of family retainers who quickly got down to business. Edward Brown, Jr., a tall, gray-faced man in his early sixties, was a second-generation financial counsel to the Vestey family. Almost sixty years before, his father had helped William and Edmund Vestey create the formidable moat of overseas trusts surrounding the family fortune. The son was an exemplar, in a three-piece suit, of the loyal and financially astute acolytes wealthy families often place at their sides, as committed as their employers to keeping the families' affairs private and profitable. During the 1970s, the junior Mr. Brown helped orchestrate the family's successful response to Inland Revenue's assault on its overseas trusts. His father had erected the fortress; he had successfully defended

it. Now, among his other duties, Mr. Brown—and apparently no one
except Lord Spam or his wife called him anything but that—controlled
disbursements to the beneficiaries of the Vestey Settlement at the
direction of its trustees.

"Twenty-four," Monika answered. "I'll be twenty-five in November."

It is not recorded what Mr. Brown thought of the young American
who sat across his desk as a nominee for access to the Vestey fortune.
But Monika told her mother afterward that she thought she had made
a good impression on him. "I think," she said, "he thinks Alison was
too young for Michael and he needs a wife with more maturity."

Next Monika met the family solicitors—including Kenneth Dimmick, a man dressed, like Mr. Brown, in a dark suit and bowler, the
uniform of his class and calling, and signed a prenuptial agreement,
after her rights under the contract were explained to her.

The Vestey Settlement, she was told, was a trust benefiting the
descendants of Baron William Vestey that disbursed payments at
the discretion of the present Lord Vestey and other trustees. In signing
the agreement, she would be surrendering any claim she might otherwise have as Michael's wife to his share of the fortune or to the house
the trust intended to buy for them. But, it was emphasized, she and
Michael would not be destitute: once they were married, Monika, like
Michael, would receive a monthly allowance for out-of-pocket expenses, and if it proved insufficient, she should bring this to the attention of the trustees. At the end of each month, she and Michael
were to mail their credit-card statements and other bills to Mr. Brown,
using special envelopes he would provide them, or, under certain
circumstances, bills could be sent directly to his office for payment.
When they wanted to travel, Monika was to call a family firm—the
Blue Star Travel Agency—and first-class tickets would be sent.

They could begin looking for a house as soon as they wanted, Mr.
Brown said. He offered no explicit guidance regarding how much they
could or should spend for the house, but, in a comment Monika later
compared to a counselor's advice to a new girl on her first day in camp,
he mentioned some of the traditions of Michael's family. It found
ostentation repugnant, he said. Since the days of William and Edmund, the Vestey way was to live inconspicuously—to live on interest,
not principal—to ride in conservative motorcars, not flashy ones—to
spend money with moderation, not extravagance.

He gave them the name of a firm of real-estate agents with whom the family did business and said someone would contact them shortly to help them select a house. After an interview to determine their interests, the agent would submit a list of properties he thought they might find suitable in one or more areas outside London. Once they narrowed their choice to three prospective homes, he would open negotiations, determine a price, and submit the figures to Mr. Brown. An appraiser would inspect the properties in Monika and Michael's order of preference, and if the negotiated price was agreeable, the house would be purchased, although it would be owned legally by the Vestey Settlement. Once their choice was final, Mr. Brown added, they could select furniture.

When they shopped, Monika inquired, were they supposed to adhere to a particular budget?

No, not really, Mr. Brown said. But they should be prudent: it was the Vestey Way.

After the meetings with the lawyers and accountants, Michael took Monika to visit his favorite aunt.

Aunty Liz, his mother's younger sister, was approaching sixty and lived alone—except for several cats—in a large nineteenth-century house in the Royal Borough of Kensington and Chelsea. When he was a boy, Michael said, she had often looked after him and made him feel like her third son.

Like Lord Vestey, Aunty Liz enthusiastically welcomed Monika into the family. But Monika later told Lou and Elsa she had a curious feeling during her meeting with her—just as she had during her meetings with Messrs. Brown and Dimmick; she felt Michael's aunt was appraising her closely, like a specimen under glass. It was natural enough for a prospective bride to be scrutinized by members of her new family, she said, but Michael's aunt and the others seemed to be taking her measure to determine what she could do for Michael, beyond simply being his wife.

While Snoggers, one of the cats, slumbered in her lap and a fat ginger named Asquith balanced himself behind her on her Windsor chair, Aunty Liz poured tea for her guests and said: "Has Michael told you much about his childhood?"

Monika nodded sympathetically, thinking of his lonely assignment to a boarding school as a child. She'd since learned that many wealthy British families dispatched their sons to boarding schools at seven, and she thought the custom was cruel.

"He's had some bad luck," Aunty Liz agreed.

"Yes," Monika replied.

Perhaps Monika could help him find a tutor and make up for some of the deficiencies in his education. None of his schools had done a very good job, Aunty Liz said.

She turned to Michael and asked if he was seeing his psychiatrist regularly.

"Yes," Michael said, lying.

Near the door, when they were ready to leave, her hostess spoke quietly to Monika. "Make sure he keeps his appointments with his doctor."

Monika said that until she'd mentioned it, she hadn't realized Michael was seeing a psychiatrist.

Aunty Liz said he was scheduled for weekly visits with one of London's best Harley Street psychiatrists, but he often missed his appointments, and Monika should do her best to make sure he didn't miss any more.

On the way back to Tunbridge Wells, Monika scolded Michael for not telling her about the doctor. But he said that Aunty Liz was wrong: there was no reason he should see a psychiatrist.

17.

Monika and Michael discovered their dream house in Buckinghamshire, near the village of West Wycombe. Michael's family never
confirmed the story, but some of their friends later said they found
West Wycombe by accident. They had asked the estate agents to look
for a house in West Wickham, a village in Kent not far from Tunbridge Wells, on the southern edge of Greater London, but he mis-
understood and went instead to West Wycombe, forty miles to the
north. Whether it was truth or legend, when Monika and Michael saw
Lambourn House, they decided this eighteenth-century home on a
country lane a mile from the village was where they wanted to live.

West Wycombe was one of only a few British villages that were
owned and managed entirely by the National Trust, the organization
whose major mission was to preserve the historic houses of Great
Britain. The people of the nation, through subscription, bought the
village during the 1930s to preserve its historical character. It was as
close as they were likely to find so near London, Monika said, to the
kind of country village she dreamed of and read about in the Agatha
Christie novels she devoured.

In one of the guidebooks she bought to educate herself about England, a writer described West Wycombe:

Snuggled in the Chiltern Hills thirty miles west of London, the village
of West Wycombe still has an atmosphere of the early 18th century.
The thatched roofs have been replaced with tiles, and some of the
buildings have been removed or replaced, but the village is still two
centuries removed from the present day.

For centuries, Lambourn House and the village itself had been part
of a vast private fiefdom, the West Wycombe Estate. Early in the
eighteenth century, Sir Francis Dashwood, a wealthy silk trader, began
assembling land for a country estate two hours by coach from London.
When he died in 1724, his sixteen-year-old son, also named Francis,
continued the project but abandoned the original plan for a large brick
mansion and created instead a spectacular colonnaded house strongly
influenced by the architects of Rome and Greece. Behind his vision,
West Wycombe House became one of England's foremost examples of
Palladian architecture, with a portico copied from the temple of Bac-
chus in the Greek city of Teos. Perhaps it was fitting that the house
paid homage to the god of wine, for Sir Francis was to secure his place
in history less for the grandeur of his home or forty-year career in
Parliament than for the rituals of a club he founded at West Wycombe
House, the Knights of St. Francis of Wycombe, better known as the
Hell Fire Club. Dressed as monks and drinking wine from silver chal-
ices shaped like women's breasts, the members met in caves near the
house and at an ancient abbey nearby with women who were
garbed—at least upon arrival—in the habits of Catholic nuns and
committed to vows to act "as the lawful wives of the brethren during
their stay within the monastic walls." The club's abbot presided over
mock religious services and was accorded first choice of the women.
Founded in 1748, the Hell Fire Club, whose roster included some of
the most prominent men in England, thrived for more than twenty
years, until a falling out among the brethren brought embarrassing
publicity and its demise.

———

Lambourn House was what British architects call a "conversion," a
polite way of saying it was once a barn. The sprawling house had been
created by connecting several eighteenth-century buildings that were
once part of a tenant farm on the estate that the Dashwood family sold
during one of the recurring periods when it needed cash. Weathered
by almost two centuries of British winters, the house was built of brick

and stone, with a slate roof, half-timbered stucco walls, and crystal-paned French windows framed in white. Next to the house was a large courtyard.

To the north of the house were broad pastures bounded by dark hedgerows and brick walls, then a steep ridge crowned by thick stands of beech trees. Inside, its plastered white walls were slashed by broad, blackened oak timbers and, here and there, ruddy expanses of flint and brick. There were four bedrooms, including a large master suite. The kitchen and bathrooms were as modern as any in England. One out-building—local people called it the "summer house," Monika called it the "outhouse"—was still being modernized, and the estate agent warned Monika that workmen might be underfoot for months if they bought the house. But she was undeterred. Her verdict was sealed during a visit to the village, where she saw two notices on a community bulletin board: one announced an upcoming antiques fair, confirming an observation by the agent that antiquing was popular in the Chiltern Hills; the other promoted a riding academy at the West Wycombe Estate, an effort by its owners to subsidize the high cost of its operation. Lessons were offered in jumping, steeplechase riding, and hunting.

Lambourn House was perfect, Monika declared: a rustic, rambling country house near a postcard village with room for a horse, and close enough to London so they could get there by car or train in less than an hour.

In early October, she excitedly telephoned Elsa: "Mother, Michael's solicitor called and said we can get married next month. His divorce will be final then."

"Is there really such a rush now, Monika?" her mother said, thinking that everything seemed to be going so well. "Why such a hurry?"

Monika said she and Michael were anxious to get married. Besides, her visa permitted her to remain in England only six months, and it was running out; and once they were married, it would be easier for her to get a job.

"I'm going to keep my own name, 'Zumsteg-Telling,' after the wedding, and Michael's agreed," Monika said. "We're hoping to get married on the twenty-fourth of November. Michael's going to send tickets for you and Dad and the folks to fly over."

Elsa recognized the date—Lou and Monika's birthday.

18.

When Monika met them at Heathrow with a limousine and a liveried chauffeur named Alex, Lou and Elsa realized for the first time how much her life had been changed by their chance meeting with Michael in Sausalito thirteen months before. Together with Lou's parents, they had traveled to London via British Airways on first-class tickets that cost the Vestey Settlement more than $8,000.

At Lambourn House, Monika introduced them to her new pet, a nervous white cockatoo called Cocky she had already taught to say "Hello" and "Piss off." Unfortunately, it was a neurotic and jealous bird: if Michael or another man approached Monika in its presence, it flared its wings angrily and let out a scream, and if it wasn't caged, it sometimes went after the intruder with beak and claws.

Exhausted by the flight and still attuned to California clocks, Lou and Elsa and Lou's father decided to take a nap, but Monika's grandmother said she was anxious to hear about her new life in England. Monika gave her a glass of wine and poured herself a Coke, or so it appeared; while the others slept, they chatted almost two hours.

Monika explained who the Vesteys were, how they made their money, and how Mr. Brown paid for anything she and Michael wanted. The house had cost about $300,000 and there were few restrictions on how much they could spend, although anything that drew attention to the family was frowned upon. In a small way, she had already experienced the family's disapproval in this regard: when she and Michael ordered a hot tub from California, she detected a sigh of disapproval from Mr. Brown.

Monika told her grandmother about her decision to take riding lessons and buy a horse and said that, when she was skilled enough, she was going to join Michael's family in riding to hounds. The prospect was very exciting to her, she said. Except for Michael, the whole family was crazy about horses.

Like Lou and Elsa, Monika's grandmother had no idea of Michael's wealth until she arrived in England. She was happy for her granddaughter, but not because of the money: she was impressed by how affectionate and protective Michael was. "You know, Monika, you're very lucky. Michael's so kind. You're fortunate to have a husband who's so gentle and warm. . . ."

By now, Isabella Zumsteg had realized Monika was not drinking only Coca-Cola. She had watched her refill her glass several times from a bottle of dark rum, and it had loosened her tongue, as alcohol always did to her.

Monika brushed back a lock of hair that had fallen over her forehead, took another sip from her glass, and gave her grandmother a guilty smile.

"Grandma, he's nice most of the time, but he's not always that way. He sometimes has temper tantrums, like a child. I'll give you an example. . . ."

Then she told her grandmother a story she hadn't told anyone else in the family yet.

When they were living in Tunbridge Wells, they had invited their friends David and Christine—"You'll meet them at the wedding"— over for drinks one night. It was a Tuesday, when Michael was supposed to see his doctor in London. She learned he had lied about keeping his appointment, and they had an argument; Michael was still pouting when their guests arrived, and continued to sulk. She asked him upstairs and said his pouting was embarrassing her. After more scolding, Michael suddenly exploded into a violent tantrum.

"He became a crazy man; I'd never seen him like that," Monika said. "It was as if he were in a trance." Glassy-eyed, he pushed past her and grabbed the banister on their staircase and began shaking it violently. It cracked, and he threw pieces of the handrail down the stairs;

then he uprooted the wooden uprights one by one and hurled them while Christine and David watched from below.

Monika said she had shaken Michael and said: *"Stop it. Stop it!"* After a moment, his eyes regained their focus. He came out of the trance and his fury subsided. When she showed him the ruined banister, he said, "Don't worry, I can afford to fix it. . . ."

"What caused him to do that?" Monika's grandmother asked, mystified, even amazed by the story.

Monika said the rage may have been touched off by his diabetes—he might have had too much to drink or eaten the wrong food. Since then, he'd had other, similar tantrums. And it wasn't the only thing she had learned about him since moving to England. "Grandma, Michael is sweet, you're right. But he's very spoiled and is used to getting his own way, and if he doesn't, he gets very moody. He had an awful childhood."

"What happened?"

Monika told her about Michael's being sent to a boarding school when he was only seven, in accordance with custom among the rich families in England. "Michael says, if it's the last thing he does, he won't send our children to a boarding school. As it was, he didn't even get a very good education at the boarding school, and now his family wants me to find a tutor for him." She said he was a poor speller and his handwriting was often barely legible.

His relatives, she said, were also putting great pressure on her to make sure he saw his London psychiatrist each Tuesday, something he'd asked her not to mention to her family. Monika said Michael was not living up to his potential but she thought she could change him.

Monika's grandmother was in her seventies and thought she knew a few things about life. Long skeptical about Monika's interest in helping wounded animals, human and otherwise, she said what was on her mind: "You know, Monika, in life you really can't change anybody. The only person you can change is yourself."

———

Michael's final divorce decree was delayed briefly, adding a few days to the family's visit and making a wedding on Lou and Monika's birthday impossible. Alex, the chauffeur retained by Michael's family, drove the family to London for a day of sightseeing, then took them for a tour of the Thames Valley and Oxford, where Monika revealed that she had submitted her application for admission. If Oxford accepted some of her credits from California, she said she could probably earn her degree in two or three years.

———————

The night before the wedding, Lou had a few moments alone with Monika in a restaurant overlooking the Thames. She told him how Michael had destroyed the banister in Tunbridge Wells, and about his having kept from her that he had seen a psychiatrist off and on since childhood. Despite his promises to be truthful, she said, he still lied and bragged to strangers about fictional exploits in the British secret service and invented other stories about himself.

Like many young women on the eve of their weddings, Lou thought, Monika was having doubts about the man she was committed to marry. It didn't surprise him; he'd seen it before.

"Do you think I should marry him?" she asked.

Instead of raising a flag of parental caution, Lou responded with a question: "How do *you* feel about him?"

"I love him," she said.

"Well," he said, "then you have your answer. If I were you, I'd follow my conscience."

19.

Michael and Monika were married at the High Wycombe Registry Office on the afternoon of November 27, 1981, one day after Michael's divorce became final. The civil ceremony, lasting less than ten minutes, gave Monika a kind of immortality, the entry of her name after that of her husband in *Debrett's Peerage*, the roster of Britain's noble families.

The wedding couple and their guests assembled at Lambourn House at three o'clock. Then Alex drove Michael and Monika to High Wycombe, a city fifteen minutes from West Wycombe. Their guests followed the red Mercedes in a caravan beneath a gray sky.

Several hours earlier, while she was making breakfast, Elsa had taken a sip from a glass of orange juice that Monika had rested on the sink. "Monika!" she said. "This is *spiked*. Why did you put liquor in your orange juice?"

Monika said she was merely starting her wedding celebration early.

———

Christine Percy was Monika's maid of honor. Michael's cousin Christopher was best man. The other guests included more cousins and several friends from Tunbridge Wells. Michael's mother sent regrets, saying it was impossible for her to leave Australia because her husband was bound to a wheelchair by rheumatoid arthritis. Michael's father was missing, too. In a note signed "Sam," Lord Vestey apologized for his absence and said he had to be in Hong Kong on Michael's wedding day. To represent him, he sent Mr. Brown.

Along with a check, Aunty Liz also sent a note with her regrets. Snoggers, she said, had had another operation, "so I don't like to go too far away from home. . . ."

When Elsa saw the note, it reminded her of one of Monika's observations about the British: "To some people here, Mother, animals are more important than people." The day before, she'd seen further evidence of this during a TV report about Michael's second cousin Lord Spam. It said his future wife was such a devoted horsewoman that she sometimes invited her favorite horse indoors for afternoon snacks. Something else impressed Elsa about Michael's family: after the expensive limousine rides and first-class tickets, she was surprised by the *ordinariness* of their wedding gifts to Michael and Monika. The Vesteys sent *nice* presents—linens and so forth—but none were lavish or especially expensive. She had seen fancier gifts at the weddings of friends' children in Santa Rosa. When she remarked on it, Monika said: "Mom, in Michael's family, gifts don't mean as much as they do to other people. People can go out and buy whatever they want. Everyone knows that, and they think it's bad manners to flaunt your money or be ostentatious."

Monika decorated the Registry Office with roses and other flowers, softening its icy bureaucratic aspect. Nevertheless, it was still a far different place from the cathedral in which she had dreamed of being married. After the ceremony, presided over by a gaunt, sober, and businesslike civil servant, the caravan returned to Lambourn House for champagne, cake, and a catered supper. Michael and Monika returned with Alex, who later drove them to the Hyde Park Hotel for an overnight honeymoon. Michael's cousin Christopher and his wife invited Lou and Elsa to ride with them to Lambourn House.

On the trip to West Wycombe, Christopher said he couldn't be happier for Michael: "I think Monika's going to be very good for him."

"You do know about Michael's background, don't you?" he asked cautiously.

Lou thought he detected an edge in his voice.

Yes, he answered: "Monika and Michael have told us he had some emotional problems as a child."

A troubled expression flashed in Christopher's eyes as if to say: "Is that *all* he said?"

He turned around in the driver's seat of the Jaguar and stared for a moment at Lou. He seemed about to say something more, but then he looked back at the road and was silent for the rest of the short trip to Lambourn House.

III

A story better left untold
A heart to which
misfortune was sold

Death prepared the parting blow
The illness of grief
A pain spread much too slow

But love reacquainted by soul
Overcame the physical being
Sorrow lost to its toll

MONIKA ZUMSTEG
March 20, 1974

1

Monika Zumsteg-Telling

2

3

Monika Zumsteg dreamed of a
career in the computer industry
but revised her plans after falling
in love with Michael Telling, a
handsome British tourist who rode
into her life aboard a
Harley-Davidson motorcycle. On
their wedding day a year later,
Monika and Michael posed for
pictures outside Lambourn House,
the country estate Michael's
family bought for them in the
Chiltern Hills north of London.

4

In England, Monika learned
Michael was an heir to the
enormous fortune left by the
Vestey brothers—William, at
the left in the front row of this
group photo taken about 1905,
and his brother, Edmund, at
the far right. Between them is
William's second wife, the
former Evelyn Brodstone of
Superior, Nebraska.

5

6

7

Michael's branch of the family was led by Lord
Samuel Vestey, whom the tabloids called "Lord
Spam," a polo-playing pal of Prince Charles and
friend of the Royal Family. Though Michael and
Monika lived in a lovely country home, it was
meager compared to Lord Vestey's Stowell Park, a
sprawling estate in the Cotswolds of which
Michael was increasingly envious.

At The Boot, a pub in rural Buckinghamshire, Monika and Michael
started a friendship with Richard and Cheryl Richardson.

In the southwest of England more than one hundred miles away, a call of
nature led to a discovery near a clearing in the woods in Exeter
Forest. . . .

11

12

. . . and Cheryl's phone call brought the police to Lambourn House (BELOW). Presiding over the ensuing trial was Sir John Gervase Sheldon of Kensington (ABOVE). Appearing for the prosecution was Alan Rawley Q.C. (TOP RIGHT), and for the defense, George Carman Q.C. (RIGHT), one of Britain's most celebrated barristers.

13

14

15

16

18

17

Among the witnesses at the trial were, clockwise from top left, Linda Blackstock and Susan Bright, two of Michael's former girlfriends; Julie Chamberlain, an acquaintance of Monika's; and Alison Ruth Telling, Michael's first wife.

19

20

Dr. John Hamilton (LEFT, TOP)
testified for the prosecution.
Opposing him were two
defense psychiatrists, Drs.
Robert Bluglass (ABOVE) and
Paul Bowden (LEFT).

21

For Detective Superintendent Brian Rundle (LEFT, BOTTOM) and Detective
Inspector Jeffrey Henthorne of the Devon and Cornwall Constabulary, the
investigation that began in Exeter Forest was the biggest case of their careers.

22

23

24

For years after his chance meeting in Sausalito with Michael Telling, Lou Zumsteg continued to visit a grassy hillside near his home in California to think about Monika and consider what might have been. His wife, Elsa, never forgave Michael, nor the British legal system.

25

26

20.

West Wycombe,
Winter 1981–82

England did not extend a warm welcome to the bride from California. The winter after Monika married Michael was one of the coldest of the century in Great Britain. Storms gathering off the North Sea hammered the ridges and bottoms of the Chiltern Hills again and again, depositing mountains of snow that frequently cut off Lambourn House from the village. The storms made the narrow lanes of West Wycombe so hazardous that Monika was often afraid to leave the house in her new Pontiac. After enrolling in a computer-programming class in High Wycombe, to make use of her time until she heard from Oxford, she missed the first meeting because of the slippery roads. For the second meeting, she got Alex to drive her to class in the limousine that was on call for members of Michael's family. She was learning to enjoy the perquisites of wealth.

Shortly after the wedding, the erratic swings in Michael's moods resumed, and he began to complain, sometimes angrily, about not being granted immediate access to his full share of the family trust. It annoyed him that, when he wanted to buy something especially expensive—another car or motorcycle, for example—he had to arrange it in advance through Mr. Brown, who occasionally tried to talk him out of it, reminding him that it was the Vestey Way to spend money conservatively. The advice from his family's hired hand made him bristle: if that were true, he asked Monika, then why did Lord Vestey live in a mansion with thirty-eight bedrooms while his relatives had to grovel for their fair share of the estate? If it hadn't been for bad luck, *he*—not his cousin—would own the title, and Monika would be Lady Vestey. When she repeated the remark to Elsa, Monika said she wasn't sure but suspected Michael thought only a quirk of fate had deprived him of the title and more wealth.

Though the storms often made Michael and Monika prisoners of Lambourn House, they began to reach out and make friends. In Australia, Michael had taken up the hobby of Citizens Band radio, using inexpensive transmitter-receivers to talk to other, similarly equipped enthusiasts, many of them strangers. He installed his equipment and a more powerful long-range ham-radio rig in a spare bedroom at Lambourn House he christened the "Radio Shack."

Before long, rumors were spreading in the CB fraternity that a wealthy newcomer had moved into Buckinghamshire—"Bucks," as residents of the county called it. The rumor, however, had not yet reached a house a few miles from Radnage Lane in the village of Lane End, where Richard Richardson was hunched over his set one evening and heard an unfamiliar voice:

"Has anybody seen my kangaroo? I've lost my kangaroo."

"One just passed my window a few minutes ago," Richardson replied, "but what did *your* kangaroo look like?"

Michael answered:

"He's an odd looker, tall and slim."

"No, the one I saw was fat and short—looked like a rabbit. It's not *your* kangaroo," Richardson responded.

After several minutes of bantering about kangaroos, Michael signed off with a closing other Wycombe CB'ers were already emulating:

"Beers and cheers and look out for the queers."

When Richard Richardson switched off his radio, he told his wife, Cheryl: "The bloke I just talked to is as nutty as I am."

Richardson was a short, wiry man who was born in India in 1942, the son of a British civil servant's daughter and a British infantryman who was killed at Singapore shortly after Richard's birth. After being evacuated from India, he spent the war in a displaced-persons camp in South Africa, then was repatriated to a refugee camp in Scotland, where he spent his adolescence. Unable to find work in Scotland as a mechanic and an engineer, he moved to Bucks, where he met Cheryl, a transplanted Londoner who had also migrated to Bucks during the lean postwar years to find a better life.

After more friendly exchanges on the CB, Richard and Michael decided to meet face to face with their wives at The Boot at Bledlow Ridge, a village straddling a long saddle of the Chiltern Hills three miles from Lambourn House. Outside the inn was a swaying sign with the likeness of a devil peeking out from the top of a boot, and beneath it a more prosaic invitation: "Good Food." The Boot was the principal social center for the two hundred or so residents of Bledlow Ridge and surrounding valleys. Most of the regulars came from local working-class families, although a growing proportion were well-to-do exurbanites, like Monika and Michael, who had moved to Buckinghamshire because of its solitude and rural beauty.

The proprietor of The Boot presided at the center of a big U-shaped bar like the master of a ship on his bridge, while beneath him his wife prepared sandwiches, fish and chips, and occasionally more ambitious fare in a subterranean kitchen. To his left, the publican served a largely male clientele of locals whose families had known each other for generations. To his right, he served mostly couples and travelers in the saloon bar, which his wife had spruced up with wall prints of Buckinghamshire, chairs with padded seats, and tables topped with thick slabs of dark oak.

The moment Monika and Michael entered The Boot, Cheryl and Richard observed a curious tableau they never forgot: as if a clock had chimed, the room suddenly became quiet. Voices stilled, and virtually all movement stopped. Even the arm of a man who was taking aim at a dart board came to a halt in mid-throw when Monika walked in the door. Virtually every man turned to appraise her, preoccupied at first with her petite figure, then her smile, which did not flinch from the attention. Later on, Richard and Cheryl often observed Monika having this effect on men. She radiated sexual energy. It was a sensual force that filled every room she entered and reached out to every man she encountered. She acknowledged their glances, smiled, then looked away.

The second thing Cheryl and Richard noticed about Monika was that she was *wary* of them: when their drinks arrived, she fastened her eyes on Richard to see if he would offer to pay for them. Only after Richard, unaware of her scrutiny, tossed some coins on the table did she relax. Weeks later, she admitted to Cheryl she had been suspicious of them and explained why. She had not known Michael long before she realized strangers often tried to take advantage of him; once they learned he was rich, they toadied to him, flattered him, tried to exploit him. During the past year, he had already given away three expensive Rolex watches to people he hardly knew.

After the drinks, they ordered supper, split the bill, and agreed to meet at The Boot again in a few days. They had enjoyed each other's company, and a friendship was born. Monika had overheard Michael tell Richard he had a government job that he couldn't discuss because it was covered by the Official Secrets Act, but she didn't want to spoil the evening, and so said nothing.

Monika made two more friends, nearer home. A few days before the wedding, she had knocked at a neighboring house on Radnage Lane and asked to use the telephone, saying hers hadn't been installed yet. Chilled by a dampness she had never known in California, Monika dashed for the heater in the living room as she introduced herself.

Ettie Turner welcomed her to the village and offered her a cup of tea. Apologizing, Monika said she was an American and hadn't become a tea drinker yet and asked for coffee. After her first visit, Monika began to visit three or four times a week. Once she learned Monika could finish a pot at one sitting, Ettie always had coffee waiting for her.

Ettie and her husband, Alf, had bought a small farm near Oxford, twenty-five miles north of West Wycombe, after he retired from the Royal Air Force several years before, but they had recently given it up and moved to West Wycombe. Like the Tellings' more sumptuous house, their home had once been part of the West Wycombe Estate. Ettie had wanted to live near a city when they gave up the farm, but Alf preferred the country and he prevailed.

Like many Britons who encountered her, the Turners were at first put off by, then taken by, the quickness with which Monika offered her friendship. She had neither the British gift for understatement nor for pretense: uninhibited, quick to form an opinion, quick to express it, she said what was on her mind.

Ettie and Alf Turner were almost half a century older than she was, but if anything the gap in their ages hastened the growth of their friendship, and it grew very strong. Since childhood, Monika had had an affinity for older people, and before long the Turners had become much like surrogate grandparents. After Ettie said she felt guilty about leaving Alf alone when she attended meetings of the Over 60's Club, Monika began keeping him company, usually arriving with a tray of cookies for Ettie to take to the senior-citizens club; sometimes she prepared a casserole for their dinner. To celebrate the Turners' golden wedding anniversary, she invited neighbors to Lambourn House. But it was a two-way friendship. Clouds were beginning to form over Monika's life, and when the deluge began, Alf and Ettie Turner were nearby to offer a sympathetic ear.

21.

Since high school, Monika had been an occasional user of marijuana, but not hard drugs. Unable to find it easily in England, she bought a tiny marijuana plant and tried to nurture it indoors, under a bright light. It died after several weeks. During lulls between the storms, she shopped for bargains in the antique shops of Buckinghamshire and started to dream about opening a stall of her own at one of the local antique fairs. Until she found a job, she told Elsa, it would keep her busy and earn her a few dollars. Other than shopping and supervising the renovation work at Lambourn House, she hadn't found much to do in England.

It wasn't just the house Monika was remodeling. During the first few weeks of her marriage, she took on another rehabilitation project as well: Michael.

She took him shopping for new clothes, put him on a diet, persuaded him to change barbers, and urged him to look for a job he would enjoy. Michael alternately acquiesced to her campaign, resisted it, or pretended to comply with it. He promised to look for a job, but said none of the positions he inquired about interested him. For a few days, he drove a taxi, then gave it up. He enrolled in an electronics training program but quickly lost interest. He bought a new suit for job interviews, but seldom wore anything except jeans and T-shirts, of which he owned almost a hundred—more than two dozen printed with the Harley-Davidson logo.

One Tuesday, after he left the house without his customary objections to keeping his appointment in London, Monika called his doctor's office and discovered he not only had missed his appointment but had lied to her about others.

As the days passed, Michael's lies and reluctance to look for a job, to see his doctor regularly, or to meet with the tutor Monika had hired at his family's request began to cause tension, then bitter arguments.

Alf and Ettie Turner usually knew when there was another argument at Lambourn House. First they heard the roar of an engine, then the screech of tires. It was Michael riding off on one of his motorcycles, or Monika speeding past their home in her white Pontiac.

During her first winter in West Wycombe, Monika complained often of being homesick. She told Michael she would never give up her U.S. citizenship, never become a *real* Englishwoman, and listed for him the ways in which she disapproved of England: she didn't like the freezing weather, which cracked the pipes on the hot tub even before they had a chance to use it, then cracked the plumbing in the house and flooded it—she didn't like the pizza at British pizzerias—she didn't like having to ask for ice every time she ordered a drink in a pub—she didn't like the dampness—she didn't like the depressing clouds that descended over the Chilterns every afternoon and gave her another excuse to have a drink.

In Sacramento, according to friends, Monika had been a moderate drinker. But on her wedding day, she drank Benedictine and orange juice with breakfast; in the months that followed she turned more and more to alcohol. During telephone chats with Sammye Hynes, she blamed it partly on boredom: she and Michael had too much time on their hands; she couldn't find a good job, and the only things that interested him were his motorcycles and CB gear, his favorite football team, the Spurs—London's Tottenham Hotspurs—or partying with friends she didn't enjoy.

Sammye, who still envied her best friend's fairy-tale life, tried to cheer her up during one transatlantic call: "You guys are sitting pretty: you've got a house, you don't pay any rent, you've got no car payments, you don't have to work, you travel anywhere you want. It sounds pretty good to me."

"Yeah, but *there's nothing to do*," Monika said.

"What do you mean?"

"There's just nothing to do."

They had all the money they wanted, and she enjoyed going shopping, but "you can only shop so many hours a day." And she said Michael's family had been less than anxious about inviting them to join their social world.

At a party at the country home of Lord Vestey, she said, Michael's second cousin and his new wife were charming, but a Rothschild snubbed her. "There was too much phony English pretentious bullshit," she pronounced. Monika said she felt some of Michael's relatives didn't think much of his decision to marry an American, especially one without money or social standing. When she told one of his relatives at a party that she was taking riding lessons and planning to buy a horse and ride to hounds, the woman responded with a condescending smile, as if she thought Monika was plotting to invade a world in which she didn't belong.

"I say, to hell with 'em—they're never going to make a Britisher out of me," Monika said. She said she was beginning to suspect that Michael's relatives thought of him as a black sheep, and that they had been nice to her only because they thought she could keep him out of trouble, so he wouldn't embarrass them. They were constantly putting pressure on her to make Michael improve himself. They looked down on him: she knew it from the way they treated him—and this annoyed her. They asked him patronizing questions about his motorcycles when she knew they didn't care; it seemed to amuse them. Mr. Brown, who controlled the family purse strings, had even asked her to make Michael moderate his spending, which was impossible.

"I thought you guys got all the money you wanted from his family and could travel anyplace you want," Sammye said.

"We do, but if we want to go on a trip, we have to arrange it through his family's travel agency. It's like we're on a leash. We can't just pick up and go. Michael hates it. I'm trying to get him to become more independent from the family."

Money wasn't their problem. Buying anything she wanted was fun and she loved it, Monika added, but she missed the satisfaction of having a job.

"Why don't you just go get a job?" Sammye asked.

Monika said she was looking, but it was practically impossible for an American woman to get started on a management career in computing, especially in a recession; besides, Michael didn't want her to work.

"He says it would be embarrassing to the family if I did. I don't think he's even happy I applied at Oxford."

There were more invitations to Lord Spam's estate in the Cotswolds, Stowell Park, and the homes of other members of Michael's family. Monika told Sammye she always felt as if she was being appraised at the parties and never felt comfortable, but it didn't matter: after a while, the invitations became less frequent. She had tried to be accepted, she said, but her candor and openness—which went over in pubs—were not considered a social virtue among most of Michael's relatives and their aristocratic friends.

At an antique fair in Chinnor, a village a few miles north of West Wycombe, Monika introduced herself to several of the women presiding behind rows of wooden tables laden with silver, glassware, jewelry, and other merchandise and said she wanted to rent a stall. They encouraged her, and after buying a small inventory of Victorian rings, brooches, and other jewelry and several antique French clocks, she became a regular vendor at the monthly fair. The women were friendly, and Monika invited two of them to a party at Lambourn House. It was not a success, however; neither they nor their husbands—business executives who commuted from Bucks to London—found much to say to the guests Michael invited, leather-jacketed motorcycle enthusiasts with shaved heads who spent the night talking about Harley-Davidsons. The next time Monika invited them to a party, the women said they had other plans.

22.

On Christmas Day, less than a month after their wedding, Michael hit Monika for the first time. He slugged her during an argument, knocking her down and giving her a black eye. He said she had driven him to it: she drank too much, nagged him too much, and incessantly demanded more ice for her drinks—an intentional snub to him and England.

Several days later, with her eyelid still bruised, Monika flew to a ski resort in Austria with a friend from Tunbridge Wells, the wife of a solicitor. Michael followed the next day, apologized, gave her £100, and appealed to Monika to come home. Although they made love in her hotel room, she refused to leave, and Michael, after arguing with the solicitor's wife, left by himself.

After returning from Austria, Monika visited Michael's aunt in London and told her Michael had hit her during a tantrum. Aunty Liz confided several details about his past that the family had not told her previously.

"Has Michael told you that when he was a boy he spent some time in hospital?"

"No," Monika answered. She knew about his boarding school, but not a hospital.

Michael had been a problem child, Aunty Liz said, with serious problems that had required his confinement to a psychiatric institution for several years. That was why it was so important for Monika to make sure he saw his doctor regularly now.

Monika said she was trying, but Michael was obstinate. He objected to taking orders from her or anyone and hated especially to see his psychiatrist.

The family was counting on her, Aunty Liz reminded her.

Monika promised to do her best.

————

In January, Monika and Michael had another shoving match, which escalated into something more sinister than the one Christmas Day. For several months, Monika kept it from her parents, not wanting to spoil their opinion of Michael. Only later did she tell Elsa what had happened. They had been having an argument when Michael's face suddenly became twisted into the same glassy-eyed frenzy she'd seen the night he ripped out the banister in Tunbridge Wells. This time, he smashed a chair and several windows. "When I tried to stop him, he chased me outside with a gun and knocked me over and kept me on my knees in the snow for ten or fifteen minutes. He threatened to kill me. For some reason, Mother, all I could say, was: 'Mom, Mom . . . please help me. . . .' "

Afterward, she said, Michael apologized and blamed the tantrum on an imbalance in his blood sugar.

Several days later, on a Saturday in late January, they were invited to the wedding of one of Michael's cousins in Guildford, Surrey.

It was an elaborate, formal wedding with many attendants, the kind Monika had imagined for herself. At the reception, she remarked to Michael that she regretted not having a big wedding. This began an argument that grew more heated after Michael accused her of drinking too much and flirting with one of his relatives. Then he noticed that the wife of one of his cousins was wearing a fur coat. It set off a fuse: why did *she* have a fur coat when Monika didn't have one? He looked around for Mr. Brown and said he was going to complain about it on the spot, but Monika stopped him. When Michael said he was going home and ordered her to come with him, Monika said she was enjoying herself and refused to go: if he insisted on leaving, she would find her own way home to West Wycombe. Michael walked to the parking lot, got behind the wheel of his souped-up Mini Cooper, and waited.

When Monika subsequently left the reception with several other guests and got in a car owned by the husband of one of Michael's cousins, Michael started his engine and pressed his foot on the accelerator: the Mini leaped forward, smashing into the other car. He backed up, shifted gears, and rammed it again. Then, as Monika and the others screamed, he shifted back into reverse, hurtled forward, and crashed into the car one more time before speeding away.

As other guests poured out of the building, Monika found one of Michael's cousins and told him that several days before Michael had threatened to kill her. She was afraid to go home. He had a cache of guns hidden at Lambourn House; worse, he might return to the wedding with a gun.

Michael's relatives gathered around her and urged her to call the police. While she found a telephone, Michael raced toward West Wycombe in his orange Mini Cooper, the car he called "the best road Cooper in the world: 130 miles per hour, goes like a rocket . . . stops on a dime . . . handles like a good woman. . . ."

23.

Cheryl and Richard Richardson were startled by what they saw when they emerged from the hedgerow-lined, single-track country lane they used as a shortcut between Lane End and West Wycombe: in the gray shadows of twilight, a thick column of smoke was billowing out of a window at Lambourn House. They looked around for fire engines, but Radnage Lane was as deserted as usual. Save for an occasional day-tripper who got lost while searching for the caves of the Hell Fire Club, few people used the narrow road besides tradesmen and the few residents. As they raced toward the burning house, Richard saw a policeman standing near the garage and stopped beside him.

"Friends of ours live here," he said. "Is there anything we can do?"

Richard said he knew the layout of the house and could help the fire brigade, which he assumed was on its way.

"No, everything's being taken care of," the policeman replied.

Richard said he was worried about his friends: "Can I go in and see what I can do?"

No, the policeman said, everything was under control.

"All right, but you should know there's a cockatoo at the far end of the house, right in the corner, and if somebody doesn't get it out, it's going to suffocate."

"Everything's in hand," the policeman insisted, then glanced at the car. "This your car?"

"No, it belongs to a neighbor."

"Well, you'd better move along or I'll nick you because your side light is out."

Richard returned home and telephoned Lambourn House. The man who answered identified himself as a policeman. Richard explained he had seen the fire and was worried about his friends who owned the house.

The detective said the fire was out, the woman of the house was not at home, and her husband was safe.

"Can I have a word with him?" Richard asked.

"No, I'm sorry," the policeman said.

Only later did Richard learn that Michael was under arrest, and why. After leaving the wedding reception, he had returned to Lambourn House and set fire to some of Monika's mementos from California—family photographs, college papers, notes and letters from friends and family, commendations from former employers, and other keepsakes. The fire he set was extinguished before causing serious damage, thanks to policemen from the Thames Valley Constabulary, who went to the Lambourn House after receiving an urgent call from Surrey about a reported cache of illegal firearms there.

When they found the .357-magnum pistol Monika had bought for Michael in California, several other firearms, and almost two hundred rounds of ammunition, they accused him of being an Irish terrorist. The outlawed Irish Republican Army had recently stepped up its campaign of terror in England and was suspected of stockpiling weapons near London. Michael called his solicitor, Kenneth Dimmick, who informed the CID detectives their prisoner was a Vestey, hardly someone likely to be an Irish terrorist. The policemen were unconvinced, but he was released on bail pending a trial on firearms charges and for ramming the car at the wedding in Surrey.

Michael pleaded with Monika to stand by him—now, more than ever, he needed her; he didn't want to go to jail. Not wishing to worry her grandparents or undermine their affection for Michael, she did not mention the arrest on the Valentine she mailed a few days later:

Dear Grandma and Grandpa:
    Thank you for the Valentine cards for the two of us. Michael especially liked his.

So far we have gotten over two bouts of knee deep snow, the worst winter in 31 years or so. I shall probably be coming to visit in April, although it's not 100% definite yet. I'm currently taking a programming course once a week at the local college and am still waiting for Oxford University to process my application. And we are still working on converting the separate building we own (the one by our fishpond) and it's a slow process.

Happy Valentine's to both of you and please pass on the same to Aunt Bertha.

Love to both of you
Monika and Michael

On Valentine's Day, Monika gave Michael an electronic air purifier for the "Radio Shack," where his chain-smoking had left a permanent odor of soot, and he gave her another black eye. She had been drinking heavily, there was a bitter row, and she told Michael she was going to leave him. After she fell asleep, Michael swallowed a handful of sleeping pills, then wrote two notes before losing consciousness.

In one, he told Monika he had killed himself because he couldn't live without her. The second was addressed to Lou. He said he had hit Monika several times and regretted it, but "she keeps running with words and I cannot communicate with her." She was drinking too much and needed help. "She says she loves me, yet she is criticizing me all the time." If he touched her, he added, she threatened to call the police, and he couldn't stand spending any time in jail. The prospect terrified him. That's why he had decided to commit suicide. In a postscript, he said he still loved Monika and had loved her from the first day they met.

When Monika awoke several hours later, she found Michael in a coma and rushed him to a hospital in High Wycombe. She told a nurse she was afraid for her own life and begged them not to release him when he came to. If they did, he might hurt someone. By now, Michael was starting to come out of the coma. In the hospital records, Monika was described as an obnoxious and inebriated American with a black eye who sipped whiskey from a sterling silver flask while arguing with a semiconscious husband who insisted he didn't want to enter the hospital. Monika fled as the nurses struggled to put a gown on Michael. As she left, she said she was going to Devon for several days.

24.

It was a trip of nearly 140 miles from West Wycombe to Torquay in Devon. Alison Telling, Michael's first wife, lived with her son near the sea, in a house called Fir Tree Lodge that had been given to her by his family after their divorce. Monika telephoned ahead to invite herself: Michael, she said, was in the hospital, and she wanted to meet Alison and Matthew and talk about him.

The meeting between the two women who had been drawn into the turbulent orbit of Michael Henry Maxwell Telling was at first stiff. But after a few minutes, a curious intimacy emerged—even a friendship, one based on common experiences with a difficult man they both loved. They were an unmatched pair: one, a green-eyed American beauty fashionably dressed by Harrods who arrived at Fir Tree Lodge with a caged cockatoo; the other, an unsophisticated and plain woman of twenty-two from the British working class whose life after Michael abandoned her had centered almost exclusively on her four-year-old son. Still, Monika discovered that Alison's life with Michael had been in many ways very much like her own: a roller-coaster trip of shifting moods . . . happy times followed by periods of depression . . . sulking and sometimes violent tantrums when he didn't get his way . . . mysterious disappearances . . . fanciful stories of imaginary exploits . . . an obsession with guns, uniforms, and Harley-Davidsons.

Although they had always had enough money, Alison said, Michael was never satisfied. He was constantly upset that he didn't have immediate access to his entire share of the family fortune. That was familiar, too, but, for all the similarities, Monika realized there was one important difference in their lives: Alison hadn't tried to change Michael. She said she had merely tried to cope. Going along with Michael was easier than fighting him.

The first year of their marriage, she said, was pleasant, but then they began to drift apart, especially after Matthew was born. Michael resisted taking on the responsibilities of a family man, she said, and though he loved Matthew, he resented the attention she gave him. Soon he began to disappear for days at a time, and began lying more and more to avoid responsibility of any kind.

Monika discovered what had happened to the necklace that had disappeared from the house on Poona Road: Michael's mother had intended it as a gift for Alison; he gave it to Monika instead, then reclaimed the pearls by simulating a "burglary" after his mother discovered what happened.

It turned out that, when Michael had left Tunbridge Wells on what he said were secret missions for the SAS, he was sometimes meeting Alison and Matthew in Torquay or Bristol. And Monika learned other things about Michael that his family had kept from her.

Did you know, she asked Alison, that Michael spent several years in a mental institution when he was a youngster? Aunty Liz had told her that, she said.

Yes, Alison replied, she knew that.

Did *you* know, Alison said, that when Michael was a child he set fire to his boarding school and nearly killed all the other children? Or that he tried to kill his mother with a carving knife?

No, Monika said, no one had told her that.

Alison said she hadn't known it, either, until after she married Michael, when his mother told her.

Considering the problems in their marriage, Alison said she hadn't been surprised when Michael asked for a divorce after he met Monika. They had decided to break the news to his mother in Australia when they took Matthew to see her at Christmas, after Michael's trip to California to buy a new motorcycle. But shortly after they arrived in

Sydney, Michael disappeared: he said he was going to retrieve something from his car, then never came back. Instead, she learned later,
he flew to California to rejoin Monika, and it was left to Alison to tell
Michael's mother he had fallen in love with an American and wanted
a divorce. "He said he was very much in love with you," Alison said.

When it was again her turn to speak, Monika—between nips from
her flask—said Michael had hit her a number of times but she couldn't
help loving him, and she was determined to help him straighten out
his life. "He had a terrible childhood," she said.

Getting in the way of friendship between the two women was jealousy. It annoyed Alison that Monika kept agreeing with her that
Michael loved Monika very much and said he couldn't live without
her. To Alison, that felt like gloating.

When they awoke in the morning, Monika drank Drambuie with
breakfast while her cockatoo kept a watch over the dining table from its
cage. She told Alison she felt guilty about leaving Michael and asked
if she could use her telephone to call him at the hospital.

"I'm sorry, Mrs. Telling," a nurse at Wycombe General Hospital
told her. "Your husband isn't here."

"What?"

"He discharged himself yesterday."

Monika was furious: "You released him? *I told you not to let him go.
He's in no condition to go home.*"

"Mr. Telling discharged himself," the nurse said curtly.

Monika telephoned Lambourn House twice but got no response.

"Oh my God," she said, "I hope he hasn't done something foolish
again."

He had.

The previous day, there had been a pitched battle at the hospital:
Michael refused to let the nurses take a sample of his blood and, still
wearing his patient gown, he left the hospital, hailed a taxi, and
ordered the driver to take him to Lambourn House, where he said he
would get the fare from his wife. When his pounding on the door
elicited no response, he broke a window with a stone and unlatched a
lock to let himself in. After collecting his fare, the driver went straight
to the home of Alf and Ettie Turner, told them what had happened,
and suggested they call the police. But Alf recognized his description
of the passenger as Michael, and said that if a man wanted to break into
his own house it was his right.

As they talked, Michael was wandering through Lambourn House smashing everything he encountered, dismembering chairs and tables, breaking more windows, ripping kitchen-cabinet doors from their hinges. He upended the Victorian sofa Monika brought from California and hurled one of her antique French clocks against a wall, then collapsed in a coma.

After her second unanswered call to Lambourn House, Monika tried calling Cheryl and Richard Richardson but got no response. Next she called Frank Collier, a gardener and friend from Bledlow Ridge whom they had inherited from the previous residents of Lambourn House, and asked him if he would look in on Michael. "I'm afraid he may have done something silly. On Sunday, he took some pills and tried to commit suicide. I took him to the hospital, but they just told me he'd left and they didn't know where he is. I rang the house, but there's no answer."

When Collier knocked at the door, he was greeted by silence. Calling Michael's name, he let himself in, then walked from room to room, surveying the damage Michael had inflicted on his own home. Debris was everywhere: the furniture was smashed, drapery ripped from its rods; broken glass and dishes were all over. He found Michael unconscious in the master bedroom, called an ambulance and then Monika.

The doctors said that, when Michael discharged himself the previous day, his diabetic condition had not yet been stabilized after the suicide attempt; if Collier hadn't found him when he did—if Monika hadn't asked him to look in—Michael could have expired in a few hours.

After a hurried drive from Devon, Monika arrived at the High Wycombe hospital several hours later. She was tipsy and her eyes were red. "Please," she begged in a tearful telephone call to Mr. Brown, "Michael needs *help*." If somebody didn't do something, he would hurt himself or someone else. Then she called Michael's solicitor and Aunty Liz and pleaded to them with the same message: "I can't do it alone. Michael should be in a hospital where he can get psychiatric help."

A few days later, Alex drove her and Michael to Northampton, a city in the Midlands, about an hour's drive north of West Wycombe. The Mercedes entered a high, walled compound. They might have been arriving at a private country resort.

St. Andrew's Hospital was encircled by more than a hundred acres of lush woodland. For almost a century and a half, behind its guarded

walls it had provided discreet and expensive care for members of mon-
eyed British families afflicted by emotional and mental illness. Some
had lived out their lives in its comforting, exclusive private-club atmosphere; there was even a golf course.

After Michael was admitted to the hospital, Monika called Elsa and
said she was coming home. Alex took her to Heathrow, and she
boarded a jetliner for San Francisco, uncertain whether she would ever
return.

25.

Melinda Stevens didn't approve of alcohol—she was Born Again. But she did what she had to do: she refilled the glasses of her passengers in the first-class cabin of the TWA jet with a professional smile as it soared seven miles above the North Atlantic.

The daily flight between London and San Francisco via Boston was popular among TWA cabin-crew members, who competed for assignments to it based on seniority. A senior TWA flight attendant with almost fifteen years of flying experience, Melinda had seen many passengers get drunk. But she had never been so worried about one as she was about the young American woman on her flight from London late in February 1982.

When she boarded the plane at Heathrow, she had seemed disoriented and weary, as if she hadn't slept for days. She slurred her words and appeared to have been drinking. The rims of her eyes were bloated, her cheeks pale; as soon as she sat down, she requested a vodka on the rocks. Once they were in the air, she asked for another—then another.

After the meal, they began to talk. Monika said she had met a handsome British tourist in California, fallen in love with him, and moved to England to marry him. Now, she said, she was going home, the marriage a failure. Although she did not tell Melinda everything about the last several days, she said enough to suggest that the marriage had ended with an explosion.

When Monika asked for another drink, Melinda said: "I don't think it's a good idea." Monika didn't argue. A few moments later, Melinda saw her remove a bottle of pills from her purse and open it. Melinda suspected they were tranquilizers or sedatives and warned her against mixing medicine with alcohol at high altitudes. Monika lied and said she was taking medicine for a cold. By the time the plane began to descend over Nova Scotia and the captain locked on the Instrument Landing System at Boston's Logan International Airport, Monika was barely coherent.

Melinda forced her to drink a cup of coffee, but it had little effect. After landing, Melinda kept her in her seat while the other passengers deplaned, then propped her up and led her, stumbling, into the customs-and-immigration hall inside the airport. She urged Monika not to continue her trip to San Francisco until the next day and invited her to stay overnight at her apartment in Boston. Monika insisted she would be all right, but a few moments later Melinda heard Monika's screams echoing through the cavernous baggage-inspection center. In a blur, security men arrived and grabbed her. Melinda tried to intervene, but they quickly strapped her to a gurney and she disappeared into an ambulance.

It was Friday evening, and Lou and Elsa were waiting for Monika's call to let them know she had landed safely in San Francisco and would be renting a car for the ninety-minute drive to Santa Rosa. Instead, when the telephone rang, Elsa heard the voice of a stranger: "Mrs. Zumsteg?"

"Yes."

"My name is Melinda Stevens. I'm a TWA flight attendant, and I was on your daughter's flight from London today. Don't be worried— she's all right—but she's going to be delayed a little. She's in a hospital here in Boston."

"Oh my God, what happened?"

"When we landed, there were some problems at the airport and Monika became a little disoriented. I think she drank a little too much and took some pills, and I think the combination set her off. I'm a Born Again Christian, and I offered to let her stay overnight with me, but they took her to the hospital. She's going to be all right. I just wanted you to know, so you wouldn't worry."

The next morning, after the effect of her sedation wore off, Monika awoke in the psychiatric ward of a Boston hospital. She was lying on her back, unable to move, her arms and legs lashed to the bed. Her shouting summoned a doctor and a nurse.

"What am I doing here? Why am I strapped in like this? Please let me up; I've got to use the ladies' room."

When the physician told the nurse to take her to the bathroom, Monika protested: "Doctor, I'm not dangerous—I'm not going to hurt anybody. Please take these things off so I can go to the ladies' room by myself."

The doctor told her why she was in the hospital: she had hit a customs agent, then fought with airport security guards and ambulance attendants.

Whether Monika's threat to sue the hospital for unlawful imprisonment contributed to its decision to release her is not known, but a taxi was called, and TWA gave her a seat on its first flight to San Francisco. At the airport, she discovered she didn't have any money: she had been so desperate to get out of the hospital that she'd left her money, watch, and jewelry there. But she didn't wait to collect her things; she wanted to get home as fast as she could.

26.

A few hours later, Monika sat at her parents' dining room table with a cup of coffee in front of her and told Elsa how Michael had smashed up their house and then tried to commit suicide. She repeated what Aunty Liz and Alison had told her about his troubled childhood, including his setting fire to his boarding school.

They didn't like the same friends, she said—she wanted a career, he didn't—he wanted to spend everything they had, she wanted to save. If she mentioned leaving him, he threatened to kill himself. She now suspected he had induced the near-fatal coma when they were living in Van Nuys after she threatened to leave him. It was emotional blackmail.

Still, she said, she loved him very much—and she knew he loved and needed her. Usually he was fun to be with: he tried to please her and had a wonderful sense of humor. But living with him was like living over a land mine: she never knew when it would explode. The pressure was driving her to drink, as the incident in Boston proved. "For some reason, I just lost it, and they put me in a loony bin."

Lou had not been home when Monika arrived. He walked into the kitchen as she spoke these words.

"Hi, Dad."

"Monika, I think you've got a problem."

"Yes, Dad. I've got a problem."

"I think you need some professional help," he said, "and I think I know where you can get it."

The next day, they drove to Calistoga, a small town at the northern end of the Napa Valley, and split a pizza at an Italian restaurant; then Monika admitted herself to a residential alcohol-treatment center called Myrtledale. "If Michael calls," she told her parents, "please don't tell him where I am."

The main building at St. Andrew's Hospital was a huge Georgian manor house, the mansion of a long-dead squire. Scattered in the forest around it were newer buildings with single-room accommodations for short-stay patients. St. Andrew's was a pioneer in the treatment of patients with psychiatric problems that were considered receptive to therapies of a few weeks or months. Michael's lawyers had persuaded the police to allow him to enter the hospital until his trial, hoping this would help him avoid a prison sentence; they were worried that a judge would throw the book at him because of the IRA's mounting campaign of terrorism.

Two days after his admission, Michael wrote a letter to Lou and Elsa recounting the events of the previous week. He said he had no memory of discharging himself from Wycombe General Hospital or smashing Lambourn House. He said he was under observation in the main hospital but hoped to be transferred soon to a room of his own in one of the newer buildings. Despite everything, he said he hoped Monika would come back to him.

After Michael's admission to the hospital, a member of the staff wrote in his file:

1) Aggressive; has smashed his house up on two or three occasions, most recently when he discharged himself from hospital and before re-admission; 2) Beats his wife up when she has been drinking. She is very good with words and [he] says "I can't shut her up." 3) Pushed her to the ground . . . and hurt her quite badly; wife is very forceful, very driving [he says,] and if she was a man she would be running a company.

Michael's IQ was measured at 110—"high average," a psychologist noted. Other tests indicated there was nothing organically wrong with his brain—he did not suffer from any neurological disorders and was not schizophrenic—he was not manic-depressive or psychotic—he could understand reality and was not psychopathic. A psychiatrist noted Michael was "immature, inadequate, [and has] low self esteem." He said Michael was egocentric and felt little sense of obligation to conform to society's ordinary rules of behavior, because of his family's wealth and position; he expected immediate gratification of his desires and became frustrated when they were denied him. A treatment program was devised aimed at helping him raise his self-esteem, understand the roots of his problems, become more aware of society's expectations of him, and control his temper when things didn't go his way.

Several days after entering the hospital, Michael wrote to Monika, "I am OK and doing the things I am asked to do." He said he swam twice a week and might take judo or karate classes at the hospital. He was also losing weight, which would please Monika: "I am getting fit in body and mind. So if I keep it up I may surprise myself. . . . I have not spoken to the family at all yet. . . . I love you darling. . . ."

When he didn't receive a reply, Michael started to call Santa Rosa daily, first asking, then demanding to speak to Monika; next he sent boxes of long-stemmed roses to her each morning.

Since Lou was often out of town, Elsa usually answered his calls, and soon she dreaded them.

"Michael, I'm sorry, Monika isn't here right now, she's out shopping," she said. When he called again, she invented another excuse: Monika was visiting friends in Sacramento; she was staying overnight with high-school chums on the Peninsula; she was in San Francisco for the day.

After several days, Michael wrote again to Lou. He missed Monika, he said, but his treatment was progressing well and he felt better; he had already trimmed four inches off his waist. "The house is in one piece and beginning to get cleaned up. When Monika comes back we can start again. We have everything good to look forward to and I can be the man I should have been all the time. . . ."

Monika was discharged from Myrtledale after three weeks, dried out, sober, and a convert to Alcoholics Anonymous. Now Lou took over the stewardship of her recovery: it was a task he knew something about. After his epiphany of self-discovery during the motorcycle trip through the High Sierras, he no longer drank, and attended A.A. meetings several times a week. Like many men and women salvaged by Alcoholics Anonymous, he had accepted, with the zeal of a missionary, a commitment to help others make the same journey. He was available anytime, day or night, to newcomers, to help them resist an urge to drink again, following a basic tenet of Alcoholics Anonymous: "When anyone, anywhere, reaches out for help, I want the hand of A.A. always to be there. And for that I am responsible." Now the alcoholic to whom he extended a hand was his own daughter.

27.

Monika plunged into her campaign to stop drinking with the tenacity and stubborn will to succeed that had been her style since childhood. She also swore off marijuana. Several times a week, she attended A.A. meetings with Lou, and other evenings she went to meetings alone. Although she had been raised a Catholic, she had drifted away from the church since high school. Now she turned back to the spirituality of her childhood, bestowing her faith in the same "Higher Power" that had helped her father stop drinking.

Michael's calls from England became more frantic. He accused Elsa of lying to him and Monika of seeing other men. He said he felt abandoned, and threatened to kill himself if she didn't return to England.

"Monika," Elsa said finally, "I think you owe Michael an explanation. He's talking about committing suicide again. He's putting me under a lot of pressure. I can't lie to him any more. I think he has to know what you're doing."

Monika telephoned St. Andrew's and told him what had happened in Boston. She also told him about Myrtledale and A.A. and said she thought that, with God's help, she'd be able to stop drinking permanently. She admitted her drinking had been a source of some of their problems. Alcohol had sometimes made her mean and cross, she said. But she was optimistic now.

Michael said his doctor said *he* was making great progress, too, and when Monika returned, they could make a clean start.

Perhaps, if Michael's doctors had been eavesdropping on the call, they would have given a less optimistic view of his therapy at St. Andrew's. According to their records, Michael was "disruptive, aggressive and rude" and uncooperative with the staff. During group-therapy sessions, other patients said, he bragged constantly about his wealth, his adventures in the SAS, and his beautiful wife, and eventually he refused to attend the group sessions altogether.

After almost six weeks in California, Monika asked Lou to fly with her back to England to help her get started in A.A. Her Oxford interview was scheduled in a few weeks; she also wanted to support Michael at his trial. Now that she wasn't drinking and he was getting proper help, she felt they would make it—especially if they could both get good jobs and reduce their financial dependence on Michael's family, which she jokingly called "the British Mafia."

After Lou and Monika arrived at Heathrow, Alex drove them to St. Andrew's, where Michael smothered Monika with kisses, hugged Lou, and predicted everything would be fine now.

It troubled Lou that Michael did not seem to take his upcoming trial very seriously. Not only did he express no regrets about violating British gun laws; he insisted he hadn't done anything wrong. Indeed, he considered that the police had been wrong to confiscate his property. Why shouldn't someone in his position own a collection of firearms? he asked. It was evident Michael had a powerful fear of going to jail, but he predicted that, as soon as the judge learned who he was, all the charges would be dropped. He wouldn't go to jail, and the judge would probably release him with an apology—although he might have to pay a small fine for the sake of appearances.

Lou also thought Michael wasn't taking his therapy very seriously: when they were alone, he ridiculed the staff and said he had attended group-therapy sessions only because his solicitors said it would help at his trial. It seemed to Lou like a charade.

Lou asked his psychiatrist to explain to him the kind of problems

Michael was suffering from. But he was disappointed with the vague-
ness of the answer: Michael didn't suffer from any mental illness, the
doctor said, but was "emotionally immature." This problem couldn't
be solved during a short stay at St. Andrew's. It would probably require
years of counseling.

After promising to continue his therapy as an outpatient, Michael
was discharged from St. Andrew's April 21, 1982. He had been a
patient at the hospital nine weeks and said he hated the experience.
Lou decided to stay in England until after Michael's trial the following
month.

Each day, he went with Michael to the police station in High
Wycombe, where he signed a log confirming he had not taken flight
during the previous twenty-four hours. Meanwhile, each evening, two
new faces appeared at Alcoholics Anonymous meetings in Buckinghamshire.

First a man stood up and said: "My name is Lou and I'm an alcoholic. . . ." Then a petite women with sexy green eyes rose and faced
the same assembly of strangers and said: "Hi, my name is Monika . . .
and I'm an alcoholic."

At his trial, Michael's prediction turned out to be partly correct: he
didn't get an apology from the judge, but he was not sent to jail. With
Lou and Monika seated near him, his lawyers argued that, by com-
pleting a successful program of treatment at one of England's foremost
psychiatric hospitals, the defendant had proved he could deal maturely
with the problems that had led him, during an atypical moment of
aberrant behavior, to import prohibited firearms and 184 rounds of
ammunition and to smash three times into a car containing his wife.
He was fined £6,500 and given a conditional discharge: for two years,
he would be on probation; any serious violations could send him to
prison. The fine was paid—as were all expenses in his life—by the
Vestey Settlement.

Afterward, he told Lou: "In this country, you can get away with
almost anything if you have the money."

After taking a brief ride through the Chiltern Hills on one of Michael's
motorcycles, Lou returned to Lambourn House and found him in the

garage surrounded by a half-dozen young men and a bottle of Jack
Daniel's bourbon. The scalps of two were completely shaved; the
spiked hair on the others was dyed a variety of neon shades, mostly
pink and green. As he joined the group, Lou observed a side to
Michael's personality he hadn't seen before. In California, he had
been reticent, even embarrassed, about discussing his family wealth;
but holding court among the fawning skinheads and punkers, he
boasted about it: he could afford to buy any motorcycle he wanted,
anything he wanted. Then, he poured each of them more bourbon.

After they left, Lou said: "Michael, why do you hang around with
guys like that?"

"They're my friends," Michael replied.

"Are they really *friends*?"

Monika, Lou continued, had told him that Michael sometimes gave
away expensive gifts, including Rolex watches, to friends like them. "Is
that true?"

Michael admitted it was.

"Friends" who hint they want expensive watches aren't friends, Lou
suggested, but scavengers and predators.

Michael was annoyed: They were good mates.

"Michael, you may not be an alcoholic like I am, but I think you've
got some of the same problems I do. No alcoholic I ever met had any
self-esteem, so what do they do? They go in a bar and tell the bar-
tender: 'Buy everyone a drink.' When I did it, I got instant approval
and instant companions. You're the same way, and I think it's because
you've never had to earn a living. Somebody from your family has always taken care of everything, and I don't think it's been good for you."

Lou had worked in what he called "the people business" all his professional life. Before anything else, he knew, people had to like themselves. Outwardly, a man could radiate physical strength and a woman
could arouse the envy of other women because of her beauty; but inside,
either of them could have an ego as fragile as crystal that made them
miserable, magnified the smallest slight, and made them do irrational
things: hunger for praise while doubting the sincerity of it, want to destroy others' self-esteem to compensate for their own shortage of it.

Lou said Monika had told him she thought Michael should get a job
and he agreed with her—not because Michael needed more money,
but because a paycheck would give him more pride in himself, and he
wouldn't have to give away gold wristwatches to buy it.

If Michael didn't want a conventional job, Lou suggested, how about this idea: why didn't they start an export-import business? Each knew of first-rate motorcycle accessories that were available in his own country but not the other's. They could both choose some of the best examples and ship them back and forth across the Atlantic; it would be fun and profitable. Michael immediately embraced the proposal. A few days later, they negotiated a franchise to sell the products of a respected British maker of boots and motorcycle apparel in the United States: Michael would handle the British end of the business, Lou the American side.

Before flying home, Lou also gave Monika a lecture.

Michael had promised to behave himself, Lou said. "I think I convinced him we're all responsible for ourselves and we're all responsible for solving our own problems." But, he added, Monika had to do her part: Michael said she criticized him too much, and Lou agreed.

Monika admitted she was sometimes a nag. But she said Michael *needed* it: she was trying to make him stand up for himself, become more independent of his family. It was the only way she knew how to improve him and make him behave himself. Even the members of his family said they wanted her to be strong with him.

"You've got a sharp tongue, Monika," Lou said. Michael needed more praise, less criticism, he added. "You're an alcoholic, and he's like one. He's got a problem, and so do you: neither of you has enough self-esteem. I know because I'm the same way myself. I don't care if you're from a dysfunctional family or not. When you're young, you've got to have emotional security, and if you don't get it, you're not going to have enough self-esteem when you grow up."

When she felt like criticizing Michael, Lou said, she should remember that genuine love meant giving without expecting anything in return—and when she needed extra strength, she should seek help from her Higher Power and remember a piece of advice from A.A.: During your first year of sobriety, don't make any major decisions about your life.

Monika, as eager as ever for her father's approval, promised to do as he asked. When they saw him off at Heathrow, she and Michael were holding hands affectionately.

As he boarded the plane, Lou glanced back at them and decided his mission to England had been a success. In trying to repair the relationship of his daughter and son-in-law, he had advised them to follow principles of A.A.'s Twelve Step program: humble yourself, admit you are wrong, and make amends to those you have hurt.

IV

Behind the shadows darkly waiting
Lies a devil in man's soul
Cast a shadow on a corner
And the meek will change their role

Flaunting breeze across the moors
Breathing soft satanic plans
For in each there lies a devil
To possess the soul of man

Twisted branches of the trees
Twisted branches of the mind
The devil's always seeking . . .
For a misguided soul to find.

MONIKA ZUMSTEG
June 14, 1976

28.

West Wycombe,
Summer 1982

The frigid weather Monika and Michael had endured during their first winter in Lambourn House was followed by an unusually warm spring and summer. In many ways, the change in weather seemed a metaphor for their marriage. After Lou returned to California, the clouds over the marriage lifted: Monika was sober, supported by new friends at the A.A. meetings she attended as religiously as a convert who had discovered Zion. Michael attended meetings of Al-Anon, the support group for spouses of A.A. members, and pursued several job openings Monika pointed out to him in the newspaper. He also took an interest in the export-import business and signed up several orders for American-made helmet shields that he mailed to Santa Rosa. He was enthusiastic about Monika's proposal that he and Richard Richardson open a shop in High Wycombe to repair motorcycles and cars.

Monika, meanwhile, while she awaited word on her application to Oxford, bought and sold antiques two or three weekends a month and worked at temporary office jobs. She became an eccentric sight in Buckinghamshire: an office temp in designer clothes who sometimes arrived for work in a chauffeured Mercedes.

She told Elsa she had given up hope of a career in computers in England, and her new goal, after getting her degree from Oxford, was becoming a barrister, like Michael's cousin Christopher.

Keeping her promises to Lou, she massaged Michael's ego, praising him for his new willingness to look for a job and to attend Al-Anon meetings. And she persuaded him they should save a portion of their respective monthly allowances from the family, along with the profits from her antique business, in a special bank account earmarked for a down payment on an apartment building. Having something of their own, she said, would make them more independent of the British Mafia.

Although the antique business and occasional temp jobs filled some of her time, Monika was still bored. Everything now hinged on Oxford. To keep herself busier while her application was evaluated, she plunged into charity work—she modeled clothes at fund-raisers, donated several hours a week to a home for the elderly, and volunteered her time at the hostel for wayward boys where Cheryl Richardson worked. The remodeling continued, and a sauna was installed in the unused outhouse. They bought a duck named Daphne and a goose named Gilbert and gave them the run of the courtyard. Sending a signal that life had returned to normal at Lambourn House after her sabbatical in California, they invited their neighbors over for an American-style barbecue. While Monika sipped Cokes, Michael barbecued the steaks. Ettie Turner complimented him on the meat, and Monika joked: "We don't even get a discount from the Dewhursts."

They were happy days for Monika, and when a letter arrived from Oxford informing her that she had passed her entrance interview, she could have concluded that her new life in England—like the weather that spring—had taken a brighter turn. But she had already lived there long enough to know that she could wake up to a bright sun and by noon it could be raining.

Several weeks after Lou went back to California, she wrote to Elsa:

Dear Mom,
    Happy late Mother's Day! I didn't realize that England doesn't have Mother's Day on the same date, so I completely forgot what date it was in the States until someone in the program mentioned it (they were American, of course). Hope things are going well with you and Dad.
    I passed my interview at Oxford and now have to do two general

papers for admission. The head of the dept. waived the entrance exams in lieu of the papers, which was fortunate I guess. I don't think I've ever had a tougher exam in an interview before. She kept giving me hypothetical situations in psychology and asking me how would I go about proving this theory scientifically. I guess something was on my side. I still don't know how I answered them correctly, but I did.

I also have a stage exam in Drama on July 5. My instructor thinks I'm a natural! Maybe you're right. I should have been an actress—at any rate, it keeps me occupied. I've been working with Michael Bainbridge and his parents with their antique fairs and have picked up quite a few bargains. I also booked a stall at a fair on June 5th, so I might be able to sell some of the things I picked up and make a bit of extra money.

Michael is still going to Alanon and seems to be at a more even keel than before. Oh well, only time will tell I guess. I go to about 4 meetings a week roughly. I have a sponsor as of today. I picked an Australian woman named Janet. I think Dad has met her before. She looks like Elizabeth Taylor (that might jog Dad's memory).

My love to you both. Take care of yourself.

Love, Monika

In telephone calls to her mother, Monika said she suspected Michael's family was growing more disenchanted with her. Even though his cousins had urged her to call the police after he rammed the car at the wedding, other family members were unhappy. Informing on him was not the Vestey way—the family's dirty linen was to be washed in private.

That was probably why, she said, the family had vetoed her plan to buy a horse. Nobody ever told her they had done so, but she knew. After finishing her riding lessons and spending several weeks looking for a horse, she said, she found a handsome chestnut jumper and told Mr. Brown she wanted to buy it. Someone in his office said that a representative of the family would buy the horse, but several weeks later she learned it had been sold to someone else, and the owner said he had never heard from Michael's family. After that, she said, the family repeatedly found other reasons to stall and not buy a horse. "I think they just decided I wasn't in their class and I was cheeky to want a horse," she told Elsa.

The family's attitude toward her had changed in other ways since Michael's trial, she said. All the family seemed to care about, she said, was accommodating Michael and keeping pressure on her to see to it

he didn't embarrass them. Mr. Brown had asked her several times to
curb his spending: Michael was using his credit cards too recklessly.
Couldn't Monika take them away from him? When she said that was
impossible, he indicated the family was disappointed in her: they had
expected her to be a better influence on Michael. The family had been
pleased when they learned Monika had a strong, forceful personality.
Now, he implied, they felt she had let them down.

The optimistic spring did not last long: after three months, Michael
began to lose interest in the import-export business. He forgot the
proposed repair shop with Richard, neglected to see his psychiatrist,
stopped attending Al-Anon meetings, and quit looking for a job—even
after Richard, in a conspiracy with Monika, taught Cocky to chant
"Work! Work! Work! . . ." when Michael entered the room.

Monika reported to Elsa that Michael was retreating to his old ways
and preoccupations: hot cars, Harley-Davidsons, the Tottenham
Hotspur football team, his CB gear, and other toys. On a letter decorated with a caricature of a woodpecker, she wrote to Lou in August:

Dear Dad:
   Just thought I'd send you a picture of a little English pecker (wood,
of course!) Michael says to tell you he was too big to mail.
   I seem to be in a slump period right now. I had a job but I ended up
working for a not-so-dry alkie, it figures?! A pity. I was a promotions
manager for an int'l public relations firm for a month. Easy come, easy
go. I quit because my sobriety was wavering every time this guy came
near me. I really wish I was in Calif., but then I suppose my commitment is here. Michael still doesn't have a job or school lined up. Maybe
someday or year, right??
   Give my love to Mom.

                                                        Love, Monika

Several days later, Monika received a devastating disappointment.
The college at Oxford to which she had applied had reversed itself and
ordered her to take a written entrance examination. When her suspi-
cion she had done poorly was confirmed by the university, she telephoned Elsa and said: "I flunked it." She was crying, and Elsa knew
why: above all, Monika hated failure. The topic of the exam, she said,
had been English history and politics. "They didn't even tell me until
I got there that I had to take an exam. If I'd had some warning, I would

have boned up; all I had to do was go to a library. They know I'm an American. How could they do it to me?"

Monika said a dean at the college had encouraged her to take the exam again, but even if she passed, it was too late for the term starting in a few weeks. Now, she told Elsa, she would have to start all over and find something else to make herself feel useful.

29.

Shortly after Monika received the bad news from Oxford, Michael began to disappear again. And when he was home he began to descend more often into the dark, brooding moods she had first encountered in Tunbridge Wells. During a transatlantic phone chat, Monika told Sammye Hynes: "Sometimes it's crazy: I'll be talking to him, thinking he's in the next room, and I'll discover *he's not there*. He just walks out without saying a thing."

"Well, where does he say he's been when he gets back?" Sammye asked.

"He just says he wanted to get on his motorcycle and take a long ride."

Richard and Cheryl Richardson often knew why Michael had disappeared, but they decided not to tell Monika. Buckinghamshire's CB fraternity was like a large family that used a single party line: by switching channels, the members could listen to the conversations of all the other members. About three months after Monika had come back from California, Richard began to overhear Michael speaking late at night to young women—mostly divorcees and single mothers, one of whom bought her CB rig after hearing a rumor that a rich and generous Lothario was romancing women via the airwaves from West Wycombe.

From his "Radio Shack," sandwiched between the guest room and the attic at Lambourn House, he courted the women while Richard eavesdropped, sometimes using a makeshift code that was based on references to things Australian: kangaroos, koalas, wallabies, and cryptic phrases about Australia. He apparently thought other CB'ers couldn't decipher his messages, but Richard quickly did decode them and heard him inform the women he was single, a decorated veteran of the Vietnam War, and a member of the family that owned the Dewhurst butcher shops. He said he couldn't talk about his job because it was covered by the Official Secrets Act, but if he was off the air for an extended period of time, it meant he was gone on government business.

Richard overheard the working-class women flatter and flirt with Michael, thank him for sending them roses and other gifts, and refer to mutual pleasures they had shared. Monika knew nothing about the flirtations or about his meetings with the women, and Richard and Cheryl didn't tell her: they decided that, when a marriage between friends was in trouble, neutrality was the best policy. Michael made one mistake, however: he charged the florists' bills to his American Express card. Since Monika routinely reviewed the credit-card bills before mailing them to Mr. Brown, she asked about these charges. Michael said he had sent flowers to friends and relatives for birthdays and anniversaries, but after that he got to the mail before Monika did.

As Monika's first wedding anniversary approached, she began to awaken late at night and discover she was alone in bed.

She got up and searched the house. Sometimes she found no trace of Michael. At other times, she found him downstairs, talking quietly on the telephone in the dark, or she heard his voice speaking from behind the locked door of the Radio Shack. She told Cheryl she was beginning to suspect there were other women in Michael's life but couldn't prove it.

———————

Then, for a brief moment, there was a burst of joy in Monika's life. She called her mother and said: "How would you like to be a grandmother?"

"Are you serious?" Elsa said.

"Yes," Michael interrupted excitedly from an extension line.

Monika said her gynecologist had told her she was pregnant, "but don't tell Grandma yet. I'm only six weeks along. . . . Michael's hoping for a boy."

"The firstborn in our family is always a boy," Michael boasted.

"But we're *not* going to send him to a boarding school," Monika said.

"No," Michael agreed.

————————

Monika didn't tell Elsa that, after her return from California, she and Michael had had several bitter arguments over whether she should have a child: Michael wanted one immediately, she wanted to wait until she had graduated from Oxford. But after the university turned her down and Michael began to disappear again, she acquiesced. "When she decided to have the baby," Cheryl Richardson recalled later, "I think it was because she was so lonely and she and Michael were growing apart. Michael was gone a lot, and I think she thought it would bring them together. I think all Monika ever wanted was to have an ordinary life, and she couldn't with Michael."

Three weeks after the call to Santa Rosa, Monika called home again, this time alone on the phone and sobbing. The day before, she said, she had felt a stabbing pain in her womb and immediately went to bed, but in less than an hour, she had lost her baby in a painful miscarriage. Instead of giving her sympathy, Michael flew into a rage, blamed her for losing the child, stormed out of the house at midnight, and said he was going to Devon to visit Matthew. "I told him I was in horrible pain, but he just walked out on me." The next morning, still in pain and unable to drive, Monika tried to reach Alex, the chauffeur, but couldn't locate him; finally, a friend from the antique trade took her to her doctor, who performed an emergency procedure to end the pain.

When Michael returned home a week later, he bought Monika a fur coat and apologized. He said he had overreacted because of his disappointment; he badly wanted another son.

Once again, Monika forgave him.

A few days later, on the stationery of an Edinburgh hotel, she wrote to her parents:

Dear Mom & Dad:

Just arrived in Scotland today. We decided to take a trip up to get out of Bucks. for a few days. I've talked with Michael, and he's agreed that he's still a "practicing liar," addicted to the first deceit like I was to the first drink! I suppose he has to hit a rock bottom eventually. I hope it isn't far off for his sake. Within seven days of returning he's back to "minor" tempers and hiding the mail. Now it's finally dawned on me that he has the same problem I had as a "practicer"

I find myself praying for his release from the "lying addiction," but still keep in mind that in the long run, I have to do what's best for me and my gift of sobriety. After all, I feel now that if I continue to enable him (just like an alkie!) by taking him back in, then his bottom may never come. If my leaving is his "bottom" then my higher power will find a way of arranging it, as he arranged mine. Until then, I am going to see as much of Europe as possible, keep looking for a decent job and go to A.A. (not necessarily in that order!) I only have today and today Edinburgh is lovely and Scotland breathtaking. Thank God, to you and Dad for introducing me to A.A. and thank God for A.A. itself.

Happy Anniversary
Love, Monika

A month later, she called Elsa and said she wanted to come home for Christmas—alone. The situation was getting worse, she said. Since her miscarriage, Michael had taken her to Scotland, then Morocco, but he was continuing to lie and deceive her, and she wanted to spend a few days away from him. With the help of A.A., she was still sober, but the temptation to drink was growing worse every day because of the pressures she was under.

"Monika," Elsa said, "why don't you *both* come? I think it would be good for you to get away from England and stay in Santa Rosa for awhile. Michael's your husband, and it would be hard for you to be separated at Christmas. Dad and Michael can go on a bike ride, and maybe we can go to Reno for a couple of days."

"All right, Mom," Monika said with a reluctant sigh. "But you've got to promise me one thing: Santa Claus has to give me some real pizza for Christmas."

30.

They arrived five days before Christmas, and for two days did little but shop, although Monika's suitcase contained her most prized gift for Elsa: a blue-fox jacket like the one Michael had given *her* after the miscarriage. Two days before Christmas, he borrowed one of Lou's motorcycles for a visit in San Francisco with his friends at the Dudley Perkins agency. Afterward, he was invited for dinner at the home of a member of the Perkins family; for Michael this was like an invitation to Buckingham Palace.

After Michael left, Monika and Elsa headed east for a mother-daughter assault on the slot machines of Reno. Donner Pass, the main route over the Sierras, was clogged with cars and trucks because of a powerful, unexpected snowstorm. Heeding the advice of a friendly truck driver, they took a detour and went to Boomtown, a truck stop and casino only a few miles inside the Nevada border, and never made it to Reno.

It was nearly empty and the lights flickered on and off erratically because of the storm; finally, an emergency generator was activated, and it kept the flashing banks of neon-lit slot machines spinning through the night.

Elsa did nothing but win. Monika, after surrendering a few nickels to the machines, gave up and handed her remaining coins to Elsa, who immediately used one to win another jackpot.

Elsa saw that Monika had more on her mind than gambling. More pensive than Elsa had ever seen her, she was very jumpy and critical of Michael. To raise her spirits, Elsa said something complimentary about him: "You know, sometimes I think you're too hard on Michael."

"Mom, you and Dad don't know Michael the way I do. He's got a side of him you've never seen. He's like a chameleon. You always see his good side. But when we're alone, he can act like a spoiled child. Because of his family, he thinks he can get away with anything—he says you can get away with anything if you have enough money. How can I live with that?"

"Monika, that's a decision you alone have to make. Do you love him?"

"Yes."

She knew why he acted as he did: it was his awful childhood. But he was becoming harder and harder to live with, and sometimes she was afraid of him. Despite his promises, he still lied and hid the mail. Sometimes he showed up at her antique stall looking like a man from Mars, wearing his motorcycle helmet and visor and demanding—in front of her friends—that she come home immediately.

Monika said Lou had told her he believed Michael deserved another chance, and she was going to give it to him. Once again, he had promised to look for a job or go to school, and to see his psychiatrist. If he didn't, she'd be coming home.

"I still think, if he can get a job and become less dependent on the family, he'll—we'll—be all right. He's smart and can charm the pants off anybody. The problem with Michael is that you can't stay mad at him very long. He's got too much charm. People love him—like you and Dad."

"Well, if things don't work out, just pack up and come home," Elsa said. "I'm sure you can get your old job back."

"I'm almost two years behind now in computers, and it all changes so fast. . . ."

"You've always been able to do anything you set your heart to," Elsa said with honest, motherly pride. "You'll do it: just come home, finish college, and get back into computers."

"Maybe," Monika said.

The snowstorm kept them at Boomtown until after dawn, prolonging Elsa's winning streak. After the highways were cleared, they returned to Santa Rosa, where they all spent a pleasant Christmas Eve at home. Monika and Michael cuddled on the sofa, joking and kissing, and their grievances seemed to have been lost in a wave of holiday spirit.

Save for one incident, the rest of the visit was a success, too.

On Christmas Day, Michael and Monika showered the family with gifts—Elsa was momentarily speechless over her fur jacket—and they had to borrow a suitcase to carry home their gifts from the family and presents they had bought for themselves in Santa Rosa and San Francisco.

Save for that one incident—on New Year's Eve—everything was perfect.

Lou and Elsa talked it over and decided not to tell Monika about it. They didn't want to upset her.

31.

Monika and Sammye Hynes climbed the steep stairs clinging to the side of a wooden building on a country road north of Sacramento and entered Mills Station again. The first thing they noticed was that the bandstand was gone: in place of the small stage where a four-piece band had harmonized the melodies of Nashville stood a juke box.

It was the day after New Year's. Monika had driven to Sacramento to spend the night with Sammye while Lou and Michael went on a camping trip, and they decided to revisit the country-western bar where they had often gone for drinks after work when they were roommates. Monika ordered a Coke, and Sammye did, too, remembering that when she was on a diet Monika had never brought sweets to their duplex to tempt her. Monika was wearing a T-shirt ornamented with a camel. When Sammye asked about it, Monika said Michael had bought it for her in Morocco.

"What were you doing in Morocco?"

"Michael took me there after my miscarriage."

She told Sammye the whole story—how he had abandoned her on the night she miscarried, then came home with an apology and a fur coat and took her on a trip. Sammye had never seen Monika look so weary—or so blonde.

"For God's sake, what did you do to your hair?"

"Michael says all California girls should be blonde, and I'm a California girl, so I should be blonde."

For seven o'clock, there weren't many customers in the bar, but a few began to arrive: bearded men with leather vests, leather caps, black boots, and tattoos on their arms.

"God, this isn't a country-western bar any more," Sammye said. "They turned it into a biker bar. Let's get out of here."

They abandoned the Cokes and drove to Sammye's apartment, where they talked until midnight. Sammye brought Monika up to date on the gossip at Reynolds & Reynolds, and Monika told her about the problems in her marriage. It was the tension and constant arguments that had probably caused her to lose her baby, she said.

"Why don't you just come home?" Sammye asked.

Despite everything, Monika said, she loved Michael and he loved her. He depended on her—and she hated to give up, although she might have to.

A moment later, she said, "If I do leave, do you think I could move back in with you for a while until I get on my feet?"

"Hell, yes, Monika, don't ever worry about that. I'm sure you can get your old job back at Reynolds & Reynolds, and if you can't, you can damn sure get another one."

The next morning, Sammye thought, Monika still looked very tired. "Don't worry," she assured her friend. "If it doesn't work out, show up on my doorstep and we'll get you a job." As Monika drove away, a thought occurred to Sammye: The year before, Monika had seemed to be living every girl's fantasy. Now she no longer seemed like Cinderella. She was a sad, worried, uncertain young woman.

———

After Monika and Michael returned to England, she began to complain of excruciating headaches. Friends noticed she was losing weight. She used less makeup, wore her glasses more often and her contact lenses less. She was starting to let herself go, Cheryl thought. She continued to attend A.A. meetings religiously but started using marijuana again after finding she could buy it from someone who worked at a restaurant in High Wycombe.

In January and February—in less frequent calls to California—

Monika told Elsa about her headaches and said that Michael, despite his promises at Christmas, hadn't changed much: he was still lying and having tantrums, hiding the mail, not keeping his promises, and refusing to take any responsibility.

"Monica," her mother said, "you don't *owe* him anything. If things get any worse, why don't you go into London and rent an apartment?"

Monika said she couldn't afford it, and she didn't want to ask Mr. Brown for the rent because he might tell Michael where she was. If she *did* leave, she intended to slip away quietly, so he wouldn't know where she was, and she would probably have to leave everything behind.

In early March, Michael and Monika had another row, and she said she was going back to California unless he agreed to see his psychiatrist. Because of her ultimatum, he made an appointment at St. Andrew's Hospital for the next week, then quietly made other plans: he called his solicitor and said he wanted to divorce Monika.

On Friday morning March 11, 1983, he drove her to an office building near High Wycombe and left her at her temporary job. He promised to pick her up at four-thirty and take her to a nightclub near Windsor Castle. At five o'clock, Monika was still waiting for Michael outdoors in the cold. She hailed a taxi and went to Lambourn House. It was a shambles; he had turned it upside down, and even the television set was gone. He had left a note for Monika, composed for him the day before by his lawyer. It said he no longer wanted to live with her, he had left permanently, and she should contact Mr. Dimmick, who would "tell you what arrangements I am making for your financial support."

Monika ran over to Ettie Turner's house and asked to use her telephone.

"Mom," she said into the phone, "I just came home from work and Michael has smashed up the house again. Half the furniture is gone, and he ripped the telephone off the wall and left me without any money."

Elsa asked what had set him off this time.

It was probably because she had put her foot down and made him promise to see his psychiatrist, Monika said.

"Monika, you gave it your best shot. Why don't you come home now? I'll send you the money for a ticket."

Lou picked up the telephone, and Monika described to him what had happened. He agreed with Elsa: "At Christmas, Michael gave me his word he was going to change, and he hasn't. I think it's time to just get the hell out of there and come home, throw in the towel. If you don't have the money, we'll send you a ticket. Right now, I think continuing your own recovery is more important than Michael's problems."

Monika drove to Lane End and told Cheryl and Richard what had happened, then used their telephone to call home again.

During the second call, Lou urged her to hire a lawyer to institute divorce proceedings.

"The only lawyer I know in England is Michael's cousin," she said.

Lou suggested she ask her sponsor in A.A. to recommend a lawyer. Because of the prenuptial agreement, Monika didn't have a claim on Lambourn House or Michael's inheritance, but she was entitled to a share of their joint assets and anything she had brought with her from America. A lawyer could arrange it.

Monika explained that Michael's note had said his solicitor would be contacting her about financial support.

"You're going to need something to get started on when you come back," Elsa said, "something to live on for a few months."

"Do you think it would be too much if I said I wanted $25,000 or $30,000?"

"No, Monika," Elsa said. "That's not too much. You gave up your job to marry Michael. You were making that much a year. You've been gone for over two years. I don't think you know how bad the inflation is here. No, I don't think that's too much. You gave up your career to marry him."

Michael's family, Lou interjected, should also pay for shipping her furniture and other belongings home. Then he said he wanted to tell Monika about something that had happened in Santa Rosa when they were home for Christmas—something he and Elsa hadn't told her about before. It was something that happened New Year's Eve. Knowing about it might help her when she saw the lawyer, but she should not mention it to Michael.

Monika listened to what Lou had to say, then promised not to repeat it to Michael.

32.

After her second call to Santa Rosa, Monika invited Cheryl to Lambourn House to inspect the mess left by Michael. As they toured the nearly empty country house, she spotted something he had left untouched: a wine rack containing his most expensive vintages. She picked up a bottle of French claret and said Michael had paid £200 for it.

"Let's drink it."

"It's red wine," Cheryl said. "Red wine always gives me a migraine." She knew Monika had fought hard to stop drinking and didn't want to encourage her.

"To hell with your migraine—it's Michael's wine and I want to drink it."

They finished the bottle, then a second, and opened a third, and only a few days after Lou had sent Monika a token from Alcoholics Anonymous commemorating her first year of sobriety, she leaped off the wagon. And, with her tongue loosened by alcohol, she told Cheryl a secret: since moving to England, she had had sexual experiences with women. It had begun in Tunbridge Wells, she said, with a neighbor— the wife of a solicitor—when Michael was often away and she was looking for new friends and starting to drink too much. She was fond

of her, she said, but it was brief, experimental, and never fully satis-
fying. Years later, when Cheryl recalled the evening, she said: "I think
it happened because Monika was so lonely. I think all she ever wanted
was to be loved, and she wasn't getting what she needed from Michael.
I think she thought it might make him pay more attention to her."

After more wine, Monika asked Cheryl to go with her to The Boot,
to cash a check.

As always, there was a palpable increase in the energy level in the
pub when Monika arrived. The men twisted around on their seats to
admire her, expecting her familiar smile but no other encouragement.
But several noticed something was different tonight: Monika was tipsy,
and they knew she hadn't had a real drink at the pub in months.

Outside, a thick fog was descending over the Chilterns and turning
the steep road between Bledlow Ridge and West Wycombe slick and
treacherous. At closing time, the two women agreed that neither of
them was sober enough to drive Monika's Pontiac back to West Wycombe, and Cheryl asked for a volunteer.

Joe Stennings was first to volunteer. Slender and wiry, with long
brown hair, he had the boyish, vulnerable look Monika had always
liked in men. At thirty-one, he earned his living as a painter, roofer,
and general handyman in Buckinghamshire. He was among the regulars at The Boot who had lusted after Monika since the first day she
walked in the door.

After Stennings drove them to Lambourn House, he made his move
quickly: to Cheryl's surprise, he tried to kiss Monika, who was now
very drunk, but she pushed him away and he left.

The next morning, Monika awoke with a hangover that reminded
her she had betrayed her Higher Power the night before. But she awoke
with a sense of liberation, a freedom she hadn't known in months:
Michael was gone, she was no longer responsible for him, she could
go home.

At the kitchen table, where Michael had left his note, she composed
a goodbye letter:

Dear Michael:
    Thank you.
    I'm finally free.
    I sincerely hope you find the cure to your illness as I found mine.
    I will always keep the memories of Bermuda and the way I felt when
I opened the door in L.A. and you were standing there, suitcase in
hand.

Those were the happy times. Maybe we should have stayed in L.A. England has never been good to either of us. Leave it as I intend to and don't look back. Watch out for the sunny weather friends. Stand up for yourself. A.A. says: 'We are not better but no worse than the next person.' I am leaving you the dishes and things in the cabinets. Your mail is also there.

If you can't find happiness, please go back to Al-Anon. You found help and friendship there.

Remember the cheese soup, Bermuda and then we both can continue life with good memories of each other.

Goodbye and love always.

Monika

33.

She was going home.

After finishing the letter, Monika called Oceanair International Removals Ltd. in London, the company that seventeen months before shipped her Victorian antiques and other belongings to England, and said she wanted to send a Pontiac Firebird, a cockatoo, several of the same items of furniture, and her personal effects from West Wycombe to Santa Rosa, California. The agent, David Stewart, offered to send a representative to prepare an itemized estimate. But she said no one was to visit and she didn't want any telephone calls or mail at Lambourn House, because she intended to leave England quietly. As if acknowledging it was an unusual request, she told Stewart she was an American who had married an Englishman and the marriage hadn't worked out: she was disappointed in him and England and was going to leave quietly. She didn't want her husband to know she was leaving yet, because he might try to stop her. Stewart said that, without inspecting her property, they could not give her a firm quotation but, based on what she said, it would cost approximately £2,300 to transport her household goods and the bird to the United States, and £700 for the car. Monika replied that she was not concerned about the expense: her husband's solicitor would pay the bill, and Stewart should not pinch pennies. Then she repeated her first instruction: everything had to be done in secrecy. Stewart promised to be discreet.

While Monika was arranging to return her belongings to California, Michael was getting ready to leave England for Australia. After dropping Monika off at her job the morning of March 11, he had returned to Lambourn House, stripped it, loaded his car, stacked several boxes of motorcycle spare parts in the unfinished summer house annex, where the sauna was being installed, then drove to Devon and left some of the things with Alison. The following morning, he arrived unannounced at the home of a half-sister, the daughter of his mother's second husband, in Tunbridge Wells and asked her to store his television set and several boxes of other belongings. He said he was going to Australia until his solicitors had sorted out problems with Monika. Three days later, his half-sister drove him to metropolitan London's secondary airport, Gatwick, to catch a helicopter shuttle flight to Heathrow, where he was booked for Sydney.

At Gatwick, she noticed he was edgy and apprehensive—even fearful—and asked what was bothering him. Without further explanation, Michael said he was afraid Monika would be waiting for him at Heathrow with policemen.

But there were no policemen looking for Michael at Heathrow, and he left for Sydney.

Monika's current sponsor in Alcoholics Anonymous was a titled member of a noble family who had recently gone through a difficult divorce. When Monika asked her to suggest a lawyer, she arranged a meeting in London with one of Britain's best-known divorce specialists.

Afterward, Monika told her parents the meeting had not gone well.

"As soon as he learned who I was, he said he didn't want to take my case. He realized that I didn't have any money and so the Vesteys would be paying his fee, and he didn't want to tangle with them." A second lawyer turned her down for the same reason, she said.

She told her parents that Michael's solicitors had informed her he was in Australia and he had asked them to institute divorce proceedings. They said the family would deposit a few hundred pounds in her account for temporary living expenses, ship her property home, and buy her a return ticket to California. She could also expect a small financial settlement, but she was reminded that in signing the pre-nuptial agreement she had forfeited any claims on Lambourn House or Michael's other assets.

"Just come home and don't worry about the money," Elsa said.

Monika said she couldn't leave yet, because she was scheduled for dental surgery in two weeks: her periodontist said she had a serious gum infection. "I might as well get it done before I come home. The family will pay for it."

Since the periodontist intended to put her under general anesthesia, she would have to spend a day or two in the hospital, she said. After the surgery, it would take several weeks to tidy up her affairs, and instead of coming straight home to California, she might go to France or Italy for several weeks: it would probably be her last chance for a long time.

During the next week, Monika's initial sense of relief at Michael's departure began to fade. Her feelings of exhilaration were crowded out by sadness, then depression, as her headaches got worse and she had trouble sleeping. Despite everything, she still loved Michael. Besides Michael, she knew she would miss other things about England: her friends in West Wycombe and Tunbridge Wells, friends from Alcoholics Anonymous and the antique business, and the pubs where she was as welcome as any of the regulars from West Wycombe; she'd miss the village life, the beautiful Chilterns, and the Thames Valley.

Barbara Lloyd, a nurse who lived near West Wycombe, was having a late lunch at The Boot with her husband, an accountant on his day off, when she whispered to him that she thought she recognized the woman who was sitting alone at a table across from theirs, with a glass of orange juice in front of her, sobbing.

"She looks like she's having a nervous breakdown," her husband said.

Then the nurse remembered where she had seen Monika: a few weeks before, she had bought a glass bowl from her at an antique sale. After hesitating, she walked to her table and said: "Dear, is there anything I can do?"

Monika looked up and broke into heavier sobs. The nurse put an arm around her. "What is it, dear?"

Monika told the nurse that her husband had left her, and the circumstances. They *did* have a troubled marriage, she said, but they loved each other and he needed her: everybody else tried to take advantage of him.

"Would you like a drink?" the woman asked.

No, Monika answered: she didn't drink.

Monika was still crying when Barbara Lloyd and her husband finished lunch thirty minutes later and left The Boot.

A week after Michael's departure, Monika invited Christine Percy and David Wallis, their friends from Tunbridge Wells, to Lambourn House for a weekend—probably their last together, she said, before she returned to California. They arrived Saturday afternoon, forewarned by Monika that, except for an uncomfortable cot, there was only a single bed intact in Lambourn House and they would all have to share it.

Over supper, she told them the details of the most recent problems in her marriage. She said she was tempted to remain in England, but had decided to go home and resume her career. Shortly before midnight, they fell asleep in the bed. At 4:00 A.M., the telephone rang and David answered it.

It was Michael calling from Australia. "He wants to speak to you," David said.

Barely awake, Monika said: "Ask him what he wants."

David said Michael was thinking about coming home.

"Tell him he can come home if he keeps his promise and sees his doctor."

David conveyed the message to Michael, who replied angrily that this was a matter between himself and his wife and demanded to speak to her.

After first sleepily refusing, Monika took the phone and repeated what David had said: that she missed him and wanted him home, but only if he promised to resume his treatment and this time kept his promise.

Michael said he would book a seat on the next flight to England.

Monika, still adrift on the sea between wakefulness and sleep, hung up and slipped back into unconsciousness, uncertain what Michael would do next.

Because their rest had been interrupted, Monika and her guests slept late Sunday morning, then drove to The Boot for lunch. As they ordered fish and chips, Joe Stennings approached the table; it was a rare day when he didn't walk the few steps from his parents' home in Bledlow Ridge to the village's only pub. He asked about Michael, and Monika replied that he was in Australia and she didn't know if she would ever see him again. Stennings joined the group, and after lunch she invited him to Lambourn House for coffee.

When they had finished their coffee, Christine and David took off for Tunbridge Wells, leaving Stennings with Monika. Sipping Coke after Coke, she spent the rest of the afternoon describing the chaos of her marriage. She told Stennings how difficult Michael was and how depressed she was that he was gone—she felt like a failure.

Alluding to Michael's telephone call from Australia, he assured her: "Don't worry; he'll be back."

"You never know what to expect from Michael," Monika said.

She grew more despondent as the shadows of a long afternoon lengthened into a chilly evening, and her mood didn't improve during a pub dinner with Stennings and a friend from A.A. whose husband had also left her. Afterward, Monika and Stennings returned to Lambourn House, where she continued to talk obsessively about Michael.

"He had a horrible childhood," she said. His money had ruined him; his family considered him a black sheep. Yet, despite his problems, he was basically kind and likable and had so much *potential* if he could only free it: "I wish he'd sort himself out. I can't believe the things he does."

It was nearly midnight when Stennings made his move again. "All of a sudden," he said, "we were kissing and cuddling."

This time, Monika, lonely and melancholy, did not resist him. They went to her bedroom and made love.

34.

Stennings and Monika were asleep when the telephone rang in Lambourn House the following morning. It was Michael: he was in Singapore and halfway home. The next morning, he called again: he was at Heathrow and anxious to come home.

Monika telephoned Elsa. "Michael just called; he's back in England and says he wants to see me. I told him he couldn't come here, but I'd meet him in London and we'd talk things over."

"Be careful," Elsa warned. "Don't do or say anything you'll regret later."

The next day, Monika called Santa Rosa from the Hyde Park Hotel. She said she and Michael had reconciled: "He promised he'll go to St. Andrew's if I stay with him and I've promised to help him work things out."

After a pause, she added that Michael had just bought her a diamond necklace at Cartier. It cost £3,000, she said.

"*Big, deal,*" Elsa said. "So what?"

She knew Monika's vulnerabilities: one of the biggest was jewelry.

Now Michael's money, she thought, was as much a curse on Monika as it was on him.

"Are you sure you know what you're doing?"

"Mom, it's different this time. I'm calling the shots."

Lou picked up an extension phone and said he was happy about the reconciliation. It didn't surprise him, because he knew they both had a lot of love to give each other. But he said he and Elsa were emotionally drained by their problems: their marriage was on one day, off the next; if Monika wasn't calling Elsa to complain about Michael, Michael was calling him to complain about her. In the future, he asked, could they please try harder to deal with the problems themselves before calling?

They promised to do so. Michael called St. Andrew's and made an appointment to see his doctor in two days—on Friday, March 25, the day before Monika's dental surgery. Monika called Mr. Dimmick and told him to forget about a divorce settlement; then she called Oceanair International Removals Ltd. and canceled the order to ship her belongings to America. But the following morning—a Thursday—after they awoke at the Hyde Park Hotel, Michael said he had changed his mind and didn't want to go to St. Andrew's after all.

After they argued for a while, Monika called Alex and asked him to drive her to West Wycombe. By the time she arrived at Lambourn House late that afternoon, she was very drunk. During the trip, she accused Michael, sometimes hysterically, of deceiving her once more; he had made her life miserable, driven her to drink again. Now, she was finally giving up on him: "From now on, I don't care what he does."

But within the hour she had reversed herself, after Michael called from the hotel and said he *was* willing to keep his appointment at the hospital. The next morning, they drove to St. Andrew's, and Monika told his psychiatrist Michael was determined once and for all to deal with his emotional problems. Because outpatient therapy hadn't worked, the doctor said he should re-enter the hospital for three months of intensive treatment. Michael objected, but the doctor persisted. It was agreed Michael would return in four days, after Monika's dental surgery, at two o'clock Tuesday afternoon.

After they returned to West Wycombe, Joe Stennings, who had promised Monika to look after her birds while she was in London, came to Lambourn House, unaware she was no longer in the city. Michael told him he wanted to install a new seat in his Mini Cooper and asked if Stennings would come over in the morning to help, after Michael took Monika to the Chiltern Hospital for her dental surgery.

When Stennings arrived Saturday morning, he found Michael in the courtyard of Lambourn House frantically emptying his trash cans on the grass.

"What the hell are you doing?" he asked.

"I'm looking for a piece of paper," Michael said without further explanation. Then, indicating he hadn't found it, he refilled the dust-bins, and they installed the new seat in the Mini.

On Monday morning, Michael brought Monika home from the hospital; her gums were still painful and swollen, but she said she felt like celebrating, because the difficult surgery was behind her and she was happy they were reconciling. When Stennings came by later to inquire how the surgery had gone, Michael asked him to join them for a night out.

Monika was always arresting, but more so than usual when she entered Needham's Snooker Club in High Wycombe that evening: she was wearing a T-shirt emblazoned with the caricature of a camel, and a glittering £3,000 diamond necklace.

While Michael dropped coins in a slot machine, she and Stennings played pool. Stennings remarked that he thought Michael was unusually quiet and remote, to which Monika replied that it was probably because he was anxious about going to the hospital the next day. From time to time, she put down her cue and went over to kiss Michael, comforting him, Stennings thought, in the tender way a mother spoke to a distressed child.

They were an odd couple, he thought—constantly bickering, but very much in love.

When they returned to Lambourn House, Michael began packing for the hospital while Monika made coffee and toasted cheese sand-wiches stuffed with olives and green peppers. Michael suggested that, while he was in the hospital, Monika should take a trip abroad; she said she might go to Europe.

Meanwhile, he packed fitfully: he folded a shirt into his suitcase, removed it and replaced it with another, then repeated the cycle. Every few minutes, he stopped packing and chatted with Stennings, then resumed his packing after Monika reminded him it was getting late.

The hospital he was going to, he told Stennings, was an attractive place: "It's not a nuthouse—it's more like a holiday camp, with lots of trees and lawns. Lots of lovely women, too."

Stennings left Lambourn House at midnight and promised to return in the morning to say goodbye to Michael. When he arrived, shortly before noon, Michael answered the door in his bathrobe and said he wasn't going to the hospital after all—he'd changed his mind—and Monika had decided to take a brief holiday in Europe.

As Stennings drove up the grade back to Bledlow Ridge, he speculated about what might have happened: when Michael changed his mind about the hospital, Monika must have gotten mad and left.

The following weekend—Easter Monday—Michael drove to Devon to collect the things he had left with Alison before going to Australia. He told her he had returned from Sydney to make a last-ditch effort to save his marriage but it hadn't worked: they had had an argument and Monika had left him—for where, he didn't know and didn't care, although she was so anxious to get a big payoff from the family that it wouldn't surprise him if she returned. Michael handed Alison a diamond necklace in a velvet box with a Cartier label and said he felt guilty he hadn't spent more on her before. He wanted to make up for it now; with Monika gone, he appreciated Alison more.

The next week, when Stennings returned to collect a fishing rod Michael had borrowed, Michael introduced him to two new pets: German shepherds, a big female and a puppy. As he petted the dogs, Stennings spotted Monika's Pontiac in the garage and asked if Michael had heard from her.

Yes, he said: "She's left me for good and says she's not coming back." Even if she did, Michael added, he wouldn't take her back: "I'll tell her she can pack her bags and leave."

Michael's dogs growled from behind the brick walls guarding Lambourn House when Ettie Turner took her regular stroll on Radnage Lane, frightening her. She suspected that, if it were given any encouragement, the bigger of the two would hurdle the wall and sink its teeth into her.

The same week the dogs arrived, gardeners planted a thick wall of conifer trees along the road, further shielding Lambourn House from villagers.

Michael reassured Ettie the animals wouldn't harm her. During a brief visit to the Turner home, he thanked her for letting Monika use her telephone while he was in Australia and gave her a £5 note to cover the cost of the calls. When she asked about his dogs, he said they were only pets—not real watchdogs—and wouldn't harm her.

Ettie wasn't surprised when he said Monika had left him: she had spent enough time sipping coffee with Monika as she hovered over the living room heater to know there were problems in her marriage. After he left, it occurred to Ettie that Michael would be lonely by himself in the big house and told herself it wouldn't surprise her if he and Monika tried to make another go of it.

35.

Simon Bonner had been inside some of the grandest houses in the Chilterns and the Thames Valley. Though still an apprentice locksmith, he was already fully experienced in catering to the insecurities and whims of the wealthy country squires who, fearful for their lives and property, asked him to turn their homes into fortresses capable of resisting the most resourceful burglar. But he had never filled a request like the one made by the squire of Lambourn House on April 12, 1983. Michael asked him to fit new locks not only on the outside doors but on every door inside the house as well. Before Bonner had finished this assignment, Michael asked him to install a *second* lock on each of the interior doors—a mortise bolt that could be unlatched only with a one-of-a-kind hexagonal key. Bonner had not yet completed this request when Michael said he had decided he wanted *four* locks on the two outside doors and the door between the lounge and the kitchen, and *three* on the master-bedroom door. He also asked Bonner to replace the door and lock on his floor safe, underneath the carpet in the lounge, and the locks on the garage doors and courtyard gate, and he wanted an electrically powered burglar-alarm system to protect the entire estate.

There must have been a look of curiosity in Bonner's eyes that persuaded Michael to volunteer why he was doing so much to enhance the security at Lambourn House: it was isolated, far from the village, and he expected to be involved in a contentious divorce. He implied he expected a stormy tug of war with his wife over their property, and he didn't want her in the house without his authorization.

Amused by the paranoia that sometimes seized the wealthy, Bonner completed the work and departed, leaving behind a long string of keys for the new locks.

Six days before the locksmith's visit to Lambourn House, Linda Black-stock, a thirty-two-year-old single mother of two who lived in Lane End, twirled the dials of her CB radio seeking respite from the loneliness that still haunted her four months after her husband had deserted her. She heard a vaguely familiar voice, a man using the handle Snake Radio 99.

She had first heard his voice almost a year before; midway through a conversation with him she had angrily turned off her radio: he had been arrogant and full of himself. But now she sensed a vulnerability and sadness in Snake Radio 99 which she found appealing. He sounded lonely. When he came on the air the following night, she accepted an invitation to have a meal with him at a Chinese restaurant in High Wycombe. Over dinner, she confirmed her intuition: Michael was hurt and sad. His wife had walked out on him, just as her husband had walked out on her.

After dinner, Michael invited her to see his house, and she accepted. En route, she asked about his job. Michael said that, because of an illness, he was on a leave of absence from a job that he couldn't discuss because it was covered by the Official Secrets Act. Once they were at Lambourn House, however, he told her he had lied when he said illness had forced him to take the leave of absence. In fact, he said, he was in the SAS and he had gotten himself into trouble during the Falklands war and was under temporary suspension because, unintentionally, he had caused the death of a comrade.

They talked until six the next morning, mostly about Monika. She was all he wanted to talk about: how much he loved her—how much he had spent on her—how well he had treated her—how poorly she had treated him. An alcoholic and a drug addict, she attacked him with fingernails as sharp as talons when she was angry. He was sad and lonely, Linda thought, suffering the same kind of pain she did—the pain of abandonment. Like a lot of men going through a divorce, he was obsessed with his wife. But she understood it and was attracted to him, even after he called her Monika several times and failed, after trying just before dawn, to make love to her. The next day, when he called and suggested another date, she was glad.

—————

Several days later, Michael invited the Richardsons to Lambourn House and asked Cheryl to cook supper for them. When she saw the house, she realized it badly needed Monika's touch. It was a mess: the bed was unmade, dishes were stacked in the sink, and the kitchen needed scrubbing. She offered to come by two or three times a week to clean up until Monika returned, and Michael accepted the offer. Richard, meanwhile, complained that Michael doted too much on his new dogs. After the puppy dirtied the carpet, he waited for Michael to discipline it. When he didn't, Richard grabbed the dog and rubbed its nose into the mess, spanked it, and took it out to the courtyard. "You *have* to rub its nose into it," Richard said when Michael protested, "or it won't stop crapping on the rug."

Michael ignored him and rescued the exiled puppy, caressing it and apologizing for Richard's behavior as he returned to the living room, the grateful puppy licking his face. Richard noticed a spot on the carpet and warned Michael that the whole carpet would become spotted like that if he didn't discipline the dogs. Defensively, Michael said the puppy wasn't responsible for that stain, he was. He had knocked over one of Monika's plants and scattered dirt and gravel on the rug; when he tried to clean it up, he made the mess worse. Cheryl examined the spot and recognized the odor of a disinfectant. "Michael, I sometimes wonder about you," she said. "Only a moron would use a chemical cleaner to clean up dirt."

As they usually did during visits to Lambourn House, Cheryl and Richard asked for news of Monika. Michael said he still hadn't heard from her but suspected she was with her parents in America. Until he did hear from her, he said, he didn't know what to do with her clothes; if she didn't call soon, he was going to put them in storage. He asked Cheryl to help him box up her things: "If you give me a hand, she can shout at you instead of me if she doesn't like the way I packed her flimsies."

Cheryl filled fifteen cardboard boxes with Monika's clothes and cosmetics. Richard, Michael, and one of the Richardsons' two sons carried them to the summer house, the building Monika called "the outhouse." When Cheryl removed Monika's fur jacket from the closet and started to fold it, Michael told her to leave it—he would take care of that.

Each time Monika's friends called, Michael asked if they had heard from her, but no one had any news about her. Christine Percy telephoned at the end of April and inquired if Monika's surgery had been successful. Michael said they had had an argument, she'd left, and he didn't know where she was, although one of his neighbors said he'd seen her drive away with a man in a Mercedes limousine. Christine said she and David might drive up to West Wycombe to visit Michael. He warned her he had installed a burglar-alarm system and bought a pair of guard dogs, so she should call before they came.

For a month after Michael's first date with Linda Blackstock, they saw each other almost every day. Monika was often the central topic of conversation. Although Michael continued to call her by Monika's name, Linda enjoyed his company and the affection he showered on her and her children. He sent her roses and jewelry and bought her a new CB radio, perfume, and other gifts from Harrods. When she admired a $50,000 Porsche, he offered to buy it for her, and one afternoon he arrived at her doorstep with a fur jacket and gave it to her. It was Monika's, he said. She had abandoned it along with him.

After the first week, Linda decided she didn't believe Michael's story about the SAS. His evasiveness and obsession with secrecy, his money and expensive country house, his preoccupation with security (he even locked the bedroom door at night), and the sweet, cloying odor she sometimes smelled in Lambourn House convinced her he was a drug dealer. When she told him about her suspicions, he howled with laughter, but seemed flattered.

Throughout their affair, which lasted into May, Linda often spent the night at Lambourn House. Michael continued to try but was unable to consummate intercourse. He was tender in his attempts at lovemaking, but, Linda told a friend, she felt "he just wanted me to be another Monika." She finally decided there was little future in their relationship; after a month, they began to drift apart.

During one of her visits, Cheryl noticed Monika's fox jacket was missing from the closet. When she asked about it, Michael said he had loaned it to a friend.

"Oh, Michael! Monika will go mad. . . . That was *her* coat. You shouldn't have done that."

"I haven't *given* it away; it's on permanent loan."

"Yes—and your permanent loan means you've given it away!"

"Do you think I should get it back?"

"What you do is entirely up to you, but all I can say is that Monika is going to fly through the roof if she finds out her fur coat is not here."

Michael said he would get it back and added that he now suspected Monika was still in England.

Her bank statement that arrived that morning showed she had used her Cashpoint card to withdraw money from the automatic-teller machine at the Lloyd's Bank branch in High Wycombe repeatedly since leaving him March 29. To track her down, he said he had hired a private detective, who was coming from London the next day.

"Michael, the detective is probably going to ask you for a photograph of Monika," Cheryl said. "If I were you, I'd pick out a recent one."

She saw Monika's face looking down on them from every wall of the living room. Most of the pictures were from her wedding day, before she began to lose weight and let herself go. They wouldn't help the detective, Cheryl said, and offered to help Michael find more recent photographs of Monika.

The photos she selected were waiting on the lacquered redwood table in the living room in Lambourn House—Lou and Elsa's wedding gift—the next afternoon, Friday, the thirteenth of May, when Colin Alastair Finlay arrived. The director of Finlay's Bureau of Investigation in London was a large, husky detective with thick eyeglasses who had been hunting down missing spouses and performing other assignments for solicitors retained by some of England's best families for more than thirty years.

He took notes while Michael recounted how he met Monika's parents in California and his subsequent courtship of their daughter. He said he had realized soon after his marriage that she was interested in him only for his money and the marriage was a mistake. Although there was little chance they would ever reconcile, he wanted Finlay to find her; he wanted to get on with the rest of his life.

Finlay asked him for a list of friends she might have visited or stayed with after leaving, or other places she might be now. Michael said Monika had many friends in the antique trade, but he didn't know them. She liked to visit The Boot in Bledlow Ridge, and someone there might have seen her. But the last time he was there he had asked, and no one had had any news. Before Monika left, he said, she had talked about taking a holiday in Europe, so she might be abroad.

From a drawer, Michael pulled out Monika's address book, which listed the telephone numbers of several friends in the antique business and her family in California, and gave it to Finlay. He also gave him her bank statement, which showed she had withdrawn £100 from a teller machine in High Wycombe the day she left him and more money several times since. At least she had money to live on, he said. Michael handed Finlay seven photographs of Monika, mostly wedding pictures, but also those selected by Cheryl that showed a more haggard-looking woman who only vaguely resembled the bride on her wedding day. He took Finlay outside, opened the double doors to the unfinished summer house, and showed him the stack of boxes containing her clothing, which the Richardsons had packed. He opened one, pulled out a dress, and offered it to Finlay, as if the detective were a bloodhound and it contained a scent that would help him find her. But Finlay said the clothing wouldn't be of any help.

After three hours, the interview ended.

Closing his notebook, Finlay said he didn't have much to work with but would do his best to find Michael's wife.

36.

Four days after Colin Finlay's visit, a parcel shaped like a cannon barrel was delivered to Lambourn House. It was a mailing tube containing Lou's birthday gift for Michael, a large autographed poster of Harley-Davidson's championship motorcycle-racing team, Team Harley. The same day—May 17—Michael called Susan Bright, one of Monika's closest friends, and asked if she had heard from her.

"No, Michael, I'm sorry," Sue said, "I haven't."

"I haven't, either."

Sue heard a sigh. He sounded lonely—and hurt.

Michael said it was his thirty-third birthday and he was alone. He asked her to help him celebrate his birthday at Frederick's, a restaurant on the Thames in Maidenhead, and she accepted.

Sue, like Linda Blackstock, was a single mother in her early thirties. She and Monika had been friends for several months, after they met at an office in High Wycombe where she was a secretary and Monika a temp. When they arrived at Frederick's, Michael seemed very nervous. She suspected it was because he felt guilty about asking one of Monika's best friends out to dinner. But Michael said that, as far as both he and Monika were concerned, their marriage was over. It had been her decision to leave him—and good riddance to her.

Michael ate his meal enthusiastically while they enjoyed a view of the river. With Monika gone, he had taken himself off the diet she had put him on. A paunch was asserting itself around his waist, and his face was becoming more fleshy and rounder. He was beginning to lose his hair.

The birthday dinner began an affair that lasted through the summer.

As always, Michael hinted during its first days that he worked for a clandestine government agency that was covered by the Official Secrets Act, and he showered the new woman in his life with expensive gifts. As he had with Linda, he sometimes called Sue "Monika." Most, although not all, of his attempts at sexual intimacy were successful.

In early June, Betsy Ligon, the wife of a pharmacist who operated a stall at the Chinnor antique fair, drove to Lambourn House after trying unsuccessfully to contact Monika by telephone. She wanted to ask her if she intended to rent a stall at the next fair; when she telephoned, she was told the number had been changed and the new one was unpublished. As she knocked at the door, Michael's German shepherds, Mandy and Midge, ran out from the garden and surrounded her. Perhaps assuming she was one of the tourists who occasionally strayed onto Radnage Lane while searching for Sir Francis Dashwood's erotic caves, Michael cracked open the top half of the Dutch door and asked if she was lost.

Betsy Ligon was twenty-nine, blonde, and as petite as Monika. In a crowd she might be mistaken for her.

Michael smiled and looked firmly into her eyes—a look of carnal interest, she thought.

She realized he didn't remember her.

"I've been trying to reach Monika," she said. "About next month's fair."

When he understood she wasn't a lost tourist, Michael explained that Monika didn't live there any more. She had gone back to the States.

It didn't surprise Betsy. She'd once seen Michael and Monika have a loud, public argument at one of the antique fairs. They'd been introduced on that occasion, but he didn't remember. As she started to reply, Michael's dogs bounded across the courtyard, made a few orbits around the grass, then sat down on their haunches in front of the summer house.

"Oh, I didn't know that," she said. "She didn't tell us."

Not expecting Michael to tell a stranger more about his marital problems, she left; when Monika failed to reserve a stall for the next antique fair, it didn't surprise her. Still, she thought it odd that Monika hadn't taken the time to say goodbye to her friends.

Betsy Ligon wasn't the only resident of Buckinghamshire puzzled because she had not heard from Monika. Cheryl Richardson didn't understand it, either. In mid-June, she persuaded Richard to call Monika's family in California to ask where she was. Although they didn't have a telephone number for the family, they knew her parents lived near San Francisco and called directory assistance in that city. The operator said there were no listings for Zumsteg in San Francisco, but she found one in a suburb of Oakland—the listing for Monika's grandparents.

Richard's call brought Isabella Zumsteg out of a deep sleep.

He introduced himself and said he was trying to contact Monika.

"Do you know what time it is here?" Monika's grandmother asked.

Richard, whose voice still had touches of the brogue he had acquired as a child at a camp for displaced persons in Scotland, apologized and said it hadn't occurred to him it was the middle of the night in California.

"No, Monika's not here," she said. "I haven't heard from her for some time. She's in England."

He apologized again for the lateness of the hour and hung up. "That's strange," Cheryl said. "Monika was always on the line to her folks."

When Cheryl told Michael about the call, he said he wasn't surprised. He had always suspected she was still in England. According to her bank statement, she had used her Cashpoint card repeatedly since walking out on him, and she'd almost emptied one of their accounts.

After Richard's call, there were others at unusual hours to the house near Oakland where Monika's grandparents lived—from Finlay and investigators he recruited to help find her.

"Could I speak to Monika?" they usually asked, or they said: "May I speak to Mrs. Telling?"

"*Monika's in England,*" Isabella Zumsteg always said. "She's not here."

"I was told she might be staying with you," the voices said.

"No, if she was in America, she'd probably be with her parents in Santa Rosa; I haven't seen her."

When she told Elsa about the calls, Elsa said she and Lou hadn't spoken to Monika or Michael in several months, and they were growing concerned. It had been a tough few months for Lou and Elsa: he'd lost his job with a labor-relations consulting firm, and the import-export business was doing poorly.

Elsa said she had mailed several letters to Monika but hadn't had a reply. She was never a good letter writer. The last time she had called, Lou had asked her and Michael not to bother them as often with their problems; that might explain why she hadn't called. The last time they had spoken, Elsa said, Monika had told them Michael was entering the hospital and, after having dental surgery, she might take a trip to Europe with a friend. Elsa and Lou had tried several times to call her, she added, but they were told the telephone number had been changed.

"I'm getting worried," Elsa said.

"I am, too," her mother-in-law said.

In early July, Lou sent a registered letter to Monika:

July 5, 1983

Dear Monika:

It has now been about four months since we last heard from you or Michael and, needless to say, we are at least curious about this lapse. Even more so, since your grandparents are receiving various calls from men and women who purport to be friends of yours. Whether or not that is true, they do have the folks' phone number. The last of these calls was from some guy at One A.M. in the morning last Saturday.

These calls are upsetting to your grandparents and I want you to do everything you can to put an end to them . . . *immediately*. They would, of course, be delighted to hear from you personally . . . as we would. Since you have an unlisted number, it is not possible for us to call you except by going through the British Police. I can assure you that unless the calls are stopped to the folks and I do not hear from you, I will resort to that measure. I do wish you would let us have the phone number, for emergency purposes, if none other.

Of other news, I visited with your Uncle Eddie and family in Chicago and then rode a bike back to here. . . . Your mother and I are busy with the boot business and managing to pay the bills.

I hope that you and Michael are resolving your individual and collective problems. You both have a lot of good when you let it surface.

All our love to you both,
Dad

The letter arrived at the High Wycombe Post Office a week later, and a notice of its arrival was delivered to Lambourn House. But Michael wasn't there. He was vacationing in Monte Carlo.

The letter remained uncollected at the post office while England endured a summer of scorching heat. The month of July was the hottest since 1659, and the blistering heat wave continued into August while a drought turned much of the Bucks countryside brown and gray.

Before leaving for Monte Carlo, Michael had asked Richard and Cheryl to keep an eye on the house, feed the dogs and birds, and open his bills; he promised to call every other day to learn if anything important demanded his attention. He also asked Richard to make some minor repairs at the house, which his family would pay for. Richard was glad to have the work: Britain was still in the grip of a punishing recession. The task of keeping the old house livable never ended. He went from room to room, making repairs as needed. He fixed the roof, patched the ceiling, and tried without success to fix the broken hot tub. One morning, he decided to air out the summer house, but couldn't find a key. The next time Michael called, he asked about it. Michael said he had taken it with him by mistake.

When he asked if anything important had come up, Richard said: "Do you want the good news or the bad news first?"

Michael was silent for a moment. "The bad news."

"You got a letter from the tax man."

"Is that all?" Michael said. "What's the good news?"

"There's a bloody refund check in it for £1,700."

"Everything else all right?"

"Everything's fine. Enjoy yourself."

He also mentioned there was a notice of a registered letter waiting for him at the High Wycombe post office.

———————

After Michael came back from Monte Carlo, Colin Finlay called to say he and his staff had been unable to find Monika.

They had confirmed that she had used her Cashpoint card at least eight times since leaving him, but there was no other trace of her. Until something else turned up, there was nothing more they could do. Michael thanked him and promised to call him if he heard from her.

After waiting several weeks for a reply, Lou drove to the post office in Santa Rosa and filed a notice requesting a trace on the registered letter that he had sent to Monika July 5.

On August 15, a second notice advising the occupants of Lambourn House that a registered letter was waiting for them at the post office in High Wycombe was delivered.

Like the first, it met with no response.

But a few days later, Michael opened another letter—a letter from Mr. Brown—and it mobilized him to take action.

37.

In the southwest of England, near the forbidding wilderness called Dartmoor, the site of the terror and murder Sir Arthur Conan Doyle wrote of in *The Hound of the Baskervilles*, there is an important highway junction. Five miles south of the city of Exeter, the main route from London divides at the base of a steep vertical escarpment, the eastern flank of the Haldon Hills.

The southern fork becomes the A380 and takes travelers across the top of the Haldon Hills, a densely forested plateau overlooking the Exe River, toward Torquay and a necklace of other resort towns that look toward the sea from a coast Britons call the English Riviera. The northern route, the A38, skirts Dartmoor's primeval moonscape of moors and peat bogs to the city of Plymouth, before continuing on to the westernmost point of mainland England, Land's End.

The two roads climb the slopes of the Haldon Hills less than a mile apart. At the summit, they are linked by a narrow country lane. Near it is a two-foot-deep depression in the forest, evidence that, since at least the Iron Age, man has walked the Haldon Hills.

On the afternoon of September 3, 1983, most of the world was preoccupied with a tragedy—the murder two days before of 269 people aboard a Korean airliner by a Soviet fighter pilot. But Colin Marshall, a plumber employed by the Exeter Building Society, was more concerned that afternoon with his bladder.

It was Saturday, and, as he often did on weekends, he was moonlighting to earn extra cash. The week before, he had installed a central heating system at a home in one of the villages tucked among the Haldon Hills, and he'd returned to fire up the boiler for the first time. By the time he finished, it was almost one. He packed up his tools and left the house to pick up his wife and two children, whom he had dropped off several hours before at her parents' home. On his way to collect them, he turned off the A380 onto the country lane between the two highways, using it, as he often did, as a shortcut to reach the Plymouth road. He knew that about two hundred yards past the turnoff there was a clearing in the woods where motorists had once been invited to enjoy a panoramic vista of Exeter and the estuary of the Exe River as it reached toward the English Channel. Two years before, the Forestry Commission had closed and fenced the little-used lookout, and the forest had begun to reclaim it, creating a secluded trysting spot for courting couples.

Marshall parked his Ford Escort station wagon, climbed the fence, and entered the abandoned viewing site. It was about twenty yards wide and fifty yards long and shrouded by shrubbery, ferns, and towering trees.

He circled the edge of the forest, looking for an opening where he could relieve himself, and spotted a gap in the woods shielded on three sides by ferns. The natural fern grotto was perfect for his mission. As he entered, he noticed that the grass underneath his feet was bent, as if it had been walked on recently. A few feet in front of him, he saw what looked like a soggy mattress on the ground. After another halfpace, he saw a human foot. The toes were pointed straight up, the sole pointed away from him. The skin looked chalky and yellow; it was the color of a rotting apple. A horrible smell engulfed him. It was at this moment that Colin Marshall realized that what he had thought was a mattress was a human being.

———

Jeff Henthorne was the first man from CID at the scene.

The body was on its side in a semifetal position. He wanted to roll it over and look at it, but knew not to touch it until the doctor arrived. Unfortunately, the local man was out of town for the weekend, and it was almost four hours before he heard the hard chopping sound of the police helicopter overhead. The pilot hovered a few moments to test the wind, then descended slowly and made a soft landing in the clearing.

Dr. Kellett ran from the aircraft directly to the fern grotto. From the air, he had seen the floodlights illuminating the forest and knew where to go.

He touched the body: it was cold and damp.

As his gloved hands groped beneath the bright glare of the lights, he turned over the body. It was a woman or a girl, he said.

A puzzled look—then an icy expression—appeared on Kellett's face. He looked up at Henthorne and said:

"The head's missing."

V

The body is the chief witness in every murder. . . .

G. K. CHESTERTON

38.

The autopsy at the Royal Devon and Exeter Hospital began at 9:40 P.M. and was not finished until just before dawn. The most important tasks facing Dr. Robert Kellett of the Home Office Forensic Science Laboratory at Chepston, Wales, were to determine the cause of the victim's death, to estimate the time of death, and, most important, to search for clues that could help the police identify the heap of flesh abandoned in Exeter Forest. As Detective Inspector Jeffrey Henthorne of the Devon and Cornwall Constabulary told a reporter: "Before you can start on the whodunit, you've got to identify who it was done to."

Like detectives the world over, Henthorne believed it was important to attend the postmortem examinations in murder cases, to observe and listen for anything that might lead him to the person whose conduct had put the cadaver on a mortuary slab. His boss, Detective Superintendent Brian Rundle, deputy head of CID, felt the same way. For this reason, neither slept the night after the headless corpse was found in the Haldon Hills.

For a century, homicide detectives from London's Metropolitan Police Department were routinely dispatched to the provinces to solve murder cases. But in the 1960s, increases in the population and the murder rate began to make it impossible for detectives from Scotland

Yard to investigate every murder. Provincial police forces started developing their own homicide specialists; this was pleasing to local policemen, who believed local knowledge and rapport with local people were often needed to catch murderers.

The Devon and Cornwall Constabulary was one of fifty-two police departments in England. From its headquarters in Exeter, it enforced the law in a region larger than almost all the others: a jurisdiction encompassing two counties, 1.4 million permanent residents and as many summer vacationers, a breadth of 180 miles, a 500-mile coastline, and almost 4,000 square miles, from Devon's border with Dorset and Somerset across the desolation of Dartmoor to the rocky tip of Land's End and, beyond it, the Isles of Scilly.

The head of its 250-member detective branch—the Criminal Investigation Department—was Detective Chief Superintendent John Bissett, a silver-haired manager in his fifties who was nearing retirement. In a few days, he was scheduled to leave on a holiday. From the moment Brian Rundle's wife called him out of the vegetable garden in the backyard of their home near Exeter on a Saturday afternoon to tell him his office was calling about a murder, he knew he would be in charge of the investigation.

Bissett's deputy was a large, well-built man who stood six feet five inches tall. Although steel-framed eyeglasses and his constant companion—a crooked pipe usually afire with sweet-burning tobacco from Sweden—suggested an academic vocation, his bulk bestowed on him a sense of authority that had served him well in police work. He had been born in 1937 in a home with neither central heating nor inside plumbing, a home that was also the police station in a remote North Devon village where his father, a country bobby, enforced the law from a bicycle. At eighteen, after high school and army service, he decided to follow the path of his father and older brother and become a policeman. He first joined a provincial force in Wiltshire, then, in 1958, became a police constable in Plymouth. After nine years in uniform, he was assigned to the CID. His salary was unchanged, but as a detective he got an additional 10 shillings a week "beer money"— for making telephone calls and buying drinks for informants—and £10 a year for civilian clothes.

To members of the Devon-Cornwall force, he was an unrelenting, introverted investigator with a high degree of insight into human nature and an ability to ingratiate himself with suspects and troublemakers. Friends said he suffered fools poorly.

Jeff Henthorne was four inches shorter and two years younger than his boss—more voluble, more excitable, less introverted, a trench-coated bloodhound who hated paperwork, bridled at bureaucracy and was unhappy when he wasn't on a difficult case. As it was for Rundle, police work was his life. Son of a bus driver, he had joined the Devon constabulary as a cadet at sixteen, and became a police constable at nineteen and a detective at twenty-six. After his wedding two years later, he told his bride: "Anybody who marries a CID man knows she won't see him at home much; as the saying goes: 'You work from nine to one and from two to six and from seven until whenever you finish.' "

Despite the large population in England's two southwestern counties, relatively few murders were committed in Devon and Cornwall—about a dozen a year. Henthorne usually was assigned to solve them.

Although their personalities were different, Henthorne and Rundle had something in common: for both, the murder investigation that began on a Saturday afternoon in the Haldon Hills was the biggest case of their careers.

The mortuary room at the Royal Devon and Exeter Hospital was white and sterile, with stainless-steel trays all around, an examining table, and a long bank of refrigerator doors that concealed trays of human bodies and organs under cold storage.

As he began the autopsy, Dr. Kellett said the missing head appeared to have been deliberately severed—hacked off the body with a cleaver, a knife, or an ax. It was a sharp cut—not the kind you'd expect if it were the work of animals.

X-rays revealed seven fragments of lead in the victim's body—in her chest and bowels and beneath the right diaphragm. Any one of several of them could have caused her death, in the pathologist's judgment.

The bullets, he said, had inflicted a great deal of internal damage. The pattern of wounds was different from any he had ever seen: in some ways, they were like wounds inflicted by a shotgun, but the fragments of lead were too large. They reminded him of wounds made by shrapnel during a war. It appeared, Kellett said, that two or possibly three bullets had entered her chest, then disintegrated. He removed the victim's T-shirt and showed it to the detectives. Holes in her clothing lined up perfectly with wounds in her chest and back. The victim also appeared to have been hit in the neck by one or two bullets.

Otherwise, the Home Office pathologist continued, the body was in too poor a condition to be a very helpful witness as to the circumstances of its death. The body was putrefied. It was impossible to type the blood or determine if drugs or alcohol was in her system when she died, or to determine with any degree of confidence whether she was a victim of a sexual assault. And, of course, the absence of her head made it difficult to establish other facts about her, including her size and age. She was slender and petite, with a twenty-one-inch waist, Kellett said, and though she appeared to be of child-bearing age, there was no evidence she had ever had children. His best estimate was that she had been five feet one inch tall when she was alive and between fifteen and thirty years old.

A staple of detective fiction is the arrival of a doctor at a murder scene, or after an autopsy, to proclaim how long the victim has been dead. In reality, calculating the time of death of a murdered man or woman is not so exact a science: too many variables defy exactitude. According to the British text *An Outline of Scientific Criminology*, "Almost nowhere in forensic medicine is there greater potential for error than in estimating time of death."

After expressing this caveat, Dr. Kellett said that, based on the condition of the body, his best estimate was that she had been dead between three and sixteen days.

There was not much to go on, Rundle and Henthorne agreed as they left the hospital. It was a Code One—departmental parlance meaning they didn't have any leads.

39.

The Haldon Hills were blanketed with forests of pine and fir trees during the nineteenth century by aristocratic landowners who wanted to create woodland plantations not only for scenic beauty but as profitable sources of timber. By the mid-twentieth century, most of the wealthy families had long since given up trying to operate the plantations and had leased them to the government Forestry Commission, which managed Exeter Forest as a nature preserve while allowing the selective cutting of lumber. It was wild country abounding in badgers, deer, foxes, and other wildlife, including poisonous adders, all of which were on the minds of the men and women, almost a hundred of them, who began sweeping through Exeter Forest at dawn Sunday morning, the day after the headless body was found.

They were looking for the victim's head, which, it was suspected, might have been carried away by a badger or some other animal. Pausing only for tea and sandwiches served by a mobile canteen, they advanced with dogs in an ever-widening circle through chest-high bracken, scouring the soil on hands and knees and using chain saws and axes to penetrate deeper into the forest. Meanwhile, other searchers—first with rubber-gloved fingertips, then with gardener's trowels—explored the soil underneath and immediately around the site where the body had been found. Within a few hours, they had excavated a gravelike hollow in the earth that was twelve feet square and two feet deep. The soil was shoveled into garbage cans hastily commandeered from the Exeter corporation yard, carted to a police station, and screened through metal sieves.

By nightfall on Sunday, the searchers had not found the head, although Jeff Henthorne reported one discovery to Detective Chief Superintendent Bissett.

"What did you find?" Bissett asked.

"A tooth—a whole tooth and nothing but a tooth," he joked.

In fact, the searchers had found *four* teeth in the damp soil of the fern grotto. Dr. Kellett said they might be human teeth, but until they could be examined by dental surgeons, he wasn't sure. It was a critical issue: teeth are among the most durable elements of the human body, and some criminologists considered them nearly as distinctive as fingerprints. If they *were* the victim's teeth, Kellett said, it might indicate she was killed and decapitated where she was found. Although no spent cartridges were found, she might have been executed on the spot by a barrage of bullets that cut off her head and knocked out her teeth.

The fingertip search of Exeter Forest grew wider, extending half a mile from the fern grotto. As they pushed farther into the wild, detectives found several scraps of bone—human or animal, it was too early to tell; a human fingernail, broken and painted with a reddish-purple polish; a condom unopened in its wrapper; an empty condom wrapper; a rusty pocket knife; a rotting bedspread; a woman's leather handbag; half a dozen beer cans; three pairs of women's panties, each a different color; and seven other assorted items of female apparel.

Brian Rundle and Jeff Henthorne shared the view held by many policemen that behind almost all serious crimes there was usually one of two motives: money or sex.

The killing they were investigating had the appearance of a sex crime. The circumstances suggested that Miss X might have been the victim of a *serial* murderer: a man who sexually assaulted and exterminated one woman after another and disposed of their bodies in remote areas as if they were yesterday's newspaper. But the detectives also knew that *most* murders were committed by people who know their victims, very often by family members.

The severing of the victim's head suggested an attempt to conceal her identity. But the brutality with which it had been hacked off and the callous way she had been dumped in the damp forest glade weighed against a family murder. Hatred, it was true, often festered deepest within families, but it was not usual for people to inflict such mayhem on the physical being of someone who, once in their lives, they had loved.

Until Miss X was identified or someone reported her missing, all they had to work with was her clothing—a pair of shorts and a T-shirt. They were dried, photographed, and sent to the Home Office laboratory in Wales. Meanwhile, the detectives began their investigation with a working theory that she was a hitchhiker who had been given a ride by a stranger, then was raped, murdered, and abandoned.

There was, of course, one obvious suspect: Colin Marshall.

Most murder investigations began with the person who had found the body, and this one was no different. Two years before, Henthorne had been called to another murder site near the Haldon Hills after a man and his girlfriend stumbled across the body of a young woman. The detectives were suspicious; the man was questioned and eventually convicted of killing the woman. He had brought his new girl to the woods to establish an alibi when he uncovered the body.

For this reason alone, Colin Marshall was a suspect. But there was something peculiar about his story, Rundle told Henthorne: "He leaves a place where he's doing a job, where he could have gone to the toilet, and within five minutes of leaving there he says he has to stop, even though he could have been home in ten minutes. It doesn't make sense."

But after almost a day of questioning, Marshall convinced the detectives that his decision to answer the call of nature in Exeter Forest was simply that.

———

The first priority remained identifying the victim.

At a police station in Exeter, Bissett and Rundle established an Incident Room. The command post for the investigation was an oversized conference room jammed with desks, typewriters, telephones, computer terminals, and radio apparatus, along with dozens of detectives and uniformed policemen; large diagrams of Exeter Forest and aerial photographs of the death scene papered the walls.

Computer records were checked, first in Devon and Cornwall, then throughout England, for reports of missing women between the ages of fifteen and thirty. Unsolved serial-murder cases reaching back a decade were reviewed without success in a search for parallels. When the missing-persons files failed to suggest an identity for Miss X, Bissett and Rundle decided to seek help from the national press.

They did not have to try hard. Once news reached London that a headless body had been found near Exeter, the highways and trains to Devon were crowded with reporters. On Monday morning, every major daily in England carried a story about the Headless Corpse.

40.

The British press has long had a macabre fascination with headless corpses. The gruesome and final act of decapitation arouses curiosity and horror in all people, but nowhere more than in England, a venue for some of the most celebrated examples of the grisly genre of murder. There was Dr. Hawley Harven Crippen, a patent-medicine salesman whose innocence or guilt is still debated in England. He was executed for poisoning his shrewish wife in 1910 and burying her headless torso beneath the floor of their London home. There was Patrick Mahon, a vain, married philanderer who in 1923 bludgeoned his mistress, Emily Kaye, after she said she was pregnant and insisted he leave his wife, then dismembered her body and kept it in a trunk in his bedroom, to which he invited another young woman. Mahon brought the woman home, he explained, "because the damn place was *haunted*. I wanted human companionship. . . . I should have gone stark staring mad if I had not had her with me." After she departed, Mahon built a fire in his sitting-room fireplace and placed the head of Emily Kaye on the grate. As he watched, he said, he heard a mountainous clap of thunder and Emily's eyes suddenly opened very wide and fixed a steely gaze upon him; he fled the room in terror.

There was Buck Ruxton, a London physician who in 1935 discarded *two* headless corpses—one his wife, of whom he was insanely if unduly jealous, the other his children's nursemaid, who had the misfortune of walking in on him while he was killing his wife. After they vanished, Ruxton told some of his friends that his wife had left him and moved out of England and others that she had deserted him for another man. When two heads—one wrapped in his children's rompers—were found in a country ravine, Ruxton was arrested. At his trial, he admitted quarreling with his wife, but said, "We were the kind of people who could not live without each other," and quoted a French proverb, "Who loves most, chastises most." Like Crippen and Mahon, he died on the gallows.

These were but three of the headless-corpse cases that had fascinated the British tabloids and their readers during the twentieth century. When the police in Devon convened a press conference to discuss the discovery of another headless corpse—as almost all the others had been, it was a headless young woman—it was like inviting children to a circus.

Through the assembled journalists, Detective Chief Superintendent Bissett appealed to Britons to call the Incident Room to report if any girl or young woman they knew had recently failed to return home, or to a job or holiday lodging. "This was a brutal murder which appears to be premeditated," he said. "This young woman was shot at close range and then decapitated. We ask the public's help in identifying her." He outlined what little the detectives had surmised about Miss X and said they did not know yet whether she had been killed on the spot or shot elsewhere and dumped. "The head was severed at the shoulders and we have not found any trace of it. There is still a great deal for the forensic people and the pathologist to do. We are at the start of what could be a very difficult enquiry. We are in the hands of the scientists. . . ."

After the news conference, more than seventy mothers, fathers, and husbands in England called the Incident Room to report missing daughters and wives. Detectives were assigned to investigate all of the reports.

On Monday morning, four more teeth were found in the soil excavated from Exeter Forrest. The detectives sifting the earth also found two more fingernails painted with the same reddish-purple polish as the one discovered on the first day of the search.

Sitting at his desk, Brian Rundle dropped a plastic envelope containing the fingernails onto his palm and tried to imagine the hands they had once adorned. The nails were so shiny they might have been part of a lacquered Chinese vase. Whoever she was, Miss X must have cared about her looks.

At a Home Office laboratory in Cambridge, forensic experts concluded that the victim was shot four times at close range with a high-powered rifle. The violence inflicted inside her body was too massive to have been produced by a pistol: the killer appeared to have used soft-pointed bullets that explode on impact, like those some deer hunters use to increase their killing power. Because the slugs had shattered into so many pieces, determining the caliber was difficult, but a microscopic analysis of the fragments indicated the murder gun may have been a .30.30-caliber Marlin repeater—a hunting rifle.

As the shards of lead were being weighed, measured, and studied in Cambridge, criminologists at the Home Office laboratory in Wales carefully washed the clothing worn by Miss X. Initially, they thought her muddied, blackened shorts had been beige, but after laundering them and opening a seam, they discovered the fabric had been pink. Inside the waistband there was a label:

```
           TOGETHER
           With L A I
        100% spun polyester

     AN14924 MADE IN THAILAND
```

A few hours after the police released a sketch of the label, a woman in Exeter telephoned the Incident Room and said her daughter owned shorts and a sweatshirt with an identical marking.

"Where were they purchased, madam?" a detective asked.

She said her daughter had bought the shorts and sweatshirt for about £4 during a holiday in San Francisco four years before. She still had the receipt with the shop's telephone number.

The detective called the shopkeeper in California and he confirmed that he stocked shorts like those worn by Miss X and identified the New York wholesaler who distributed the product. Hoping to get a list of stores in England that carried the same garment, the detective contacted the wholesaler. But he said that, as far as he knew, products with an LAI label were sold only in America, largely in California.

The detectives pursued other leads. An Exeter hotel clerk reported that four dark-skinned men, apparently Middle Easterners, had checked out abruptly only three days before the body was found and left behind a bloodstained sweatshirt. His report raised suspicions that the murdered Miss X had been part of a terrorist organization. A nationwide hunt found no trace of the men. More than two dozen other men who had records as sex offenders and frequented a race-course in the Haldon Hills were tracked down and interviewed. The chef at a restaurant not far from the racetrack reported seeing a stranger drop something in the restaurant's outdoor incinerator shortly before the body had been found. The ashes yielded a piece of charred bone and part of a woman's wristwatch strap. They were sent to Wales for analysis.

After re-examining the victim, Dr. Kellett narrowed his previous estimate of her age to between twenty and thirty. Dental surgeons, meanwhile, concluded that several if not all of the teeth found near her body were human. But until her dental records were available for comparison, the teeth were of little use in the investigation.

When the victim's discolored T-shirt was washed, the dim outline of a camel appeared on the chest, along with several words in Arabic and French. A police artist sketched the design, and Rundle released it to the press.

By late Thursday, five days after the body was found, the names of 103 missing women and girls had found their way to the Incident Room. Detectives had located seventy of them and still did not know the identity of Miss X, nor had they found her head. At their press briefings, they said they were beginning to develop a clearer picture of what had occurred in Exeter Forest: "I am now beginning to believe that it is more than likely the woman was killed where she was found," Bissett said. The position of her body suggested she had been forced to kneel before being executed, he added.

Bored with a lack of significant new developments, the reporters began stepping up their pressure on the detectives to solve the mystery and developed their own theories on the case. On Friday morning, the *Times* of London reported: "Despite nationwide inquiries, police are still baffled about her identity." The *Daily Mail* suggested an under-world connection: "The killing has every sign of a gangland murder and the theory being considered by the police is that the woman was involved in drug smuggling. A senior police officer said: 'She may have been a courier of some sort. Her Moroccan and Thai clothing could indicate she has been abroad recently. . . .' "

But, unknown to the reporters who wrote these words, a telephone call to the Incident Room two days earlier had changed everything.

VI

*No man likes to live under the eye of
perpetual disapprobation.*

SAMUEL JOHNSON

41.

It was the T-shirt that finally persuaded Cheryl to make the call: when the news announcer reported that the headless corpse found in Devon was clad in a T-shirt possibly purchased in Morocco, she dialed the special number at which, the TV announcer said, policemen were standing by to receive "any information that might help them in their inquiries."

Cheryl was connected to a detective seated before a glowing computer monitor in the Incident Room. Mechanically, he logged her statement in the computer: a friend of hers—an American—had bought a T-shirt during a holiday in Morocco the previous winter. Although she may have returned to America, Cheryl hadn't heard from her since March, and she was puzzled by it.

The next day, a uniformed bobby from the Thames Valley Constabulary drove from High Wycombe to Lane End and interviewed Cheryl. She repeated her remarks of the previous day, adding that it wouldn't surprise her if her friend *had* returned to America: she had threatened to do so many times. But it *did* surprise her that her friend hadn't sent a card or a letter, because they were good friends.

The policeman asked for a photograph, and Cheryl gave him a

197

framed picture of Monika on her wedding day. She didn't look exactly like that now, Cheryl said—she looked more tired and run-down.

The policeman relayed Cheryl's report to Exeter, where it fell atop a stack of similar accounts of women and girls who had mysteriously dropped out of the lives of people who cared for them. But something elevated it in the eyes of Brian Rundle: Cheryl Richardson's friend was an American, a Californian—and the forensic team said the pink shorts worn by Miss X might have been bought in California.

The next day, Cheryl was called to the telephone at the hostel in High Wycombe where she worked. The bobby from the previous day said two detectives had driven up from Exeter to interview her. Could they pick her up for a chat?

In her living room, Cheryl told the detectives more about Monika. She had moved to West Wycombe two years before, after marrying a wealthy Englishman, but they had had problems and she had talked about returning to California after dental surgery the previous spring. That's what her husband, Michael, thought she had done. Since then, Cheryl hadn't heard from her.

Because five months had elapsed without someone's reporting Monika missing, the policemen were initially skeptical: if someone had disappeared *that* long ago, a friend or relative would surely have reported it by now.

"As you can understand, Mrs. Richardson," one of the detectives said, "our first task is to identify the victim, and it is especially difficult in this case."

For obvious reasons, the picture of Monika that Cheryl had given the police the previous day was of limited help to the investigation. "Is there anything you can remember about your friend that would help us identify a *headless* body?"

Cheryl thought a moment, trying to imagine Monika without her head.

"Not really," she said.

The detectives showed her the sketch of the T-shirt prepared by a police artist. It depicted a camel, *Souvenir du Maroc*, "Souvenir of Morocco" in French, and the same words in Arabic.

Cheryl said it looked very much like the T-shirt her friend had purchased in Morocco.

"Is there anything else you can think of that might be of help in identifying a headless body?"

"The only thing I can think of is that Monika had very beautiful fingernails," Cheryl said. "She always kept her nails absolutely beautiful."

"What color polish did she use?"

"Red with a purplish tint—more like a *mauve* red, I would say."

When Richard Richardson arrived home, the detectives asked him if he knew of any unusual behavior by Monika's husband recently.

The only thing he could remember, Richard said, was that, the previous weekend, he had hired a van and hauled some rubbish to the local tip.

As the interview extended into a third hour, Cheryl was haunted by words Michael had blurted out to her four days before, during a ride home from the Tesco supermarket in High Wycombe. But she could not bring herself to repeat them. She didn't want to condemn Michael for the rest of his life, especially when she wasn't *sure*. Maybe he had been joking.

———

After the detectives from Exeter relayed their report to Brian Rundle, he moved swiftly. At dawn on Friday, he sent four more detectives to West Wycombe, led by Jeff Henthorne. Officers of the Thames Valley Constabulary, which had jurisdiction over the village, joined the investigation and told them Monika Telling's husband was a member of one of England's richest and most powerful families. They also said he had been arrested the previous year for keeping a large cache of illegal firearms at his estate and had to be considered dangerous.

Alerted by Cheryl Richardson's comment that her friend had been scheduled for oral surgery shortly before she dropped out of sight, Henthorne tracked down Monika's dentist. This dentist produced not only her dental X-rays but the name of a friend—another dentist—who was regarded as one of Britain's leading experts on identifying victims of airline crashes from their dental charts. The X-rays and the teeth found in Exeter Forest were rushed to him in a police car.

At eight that evening, a policeman drove Cheryl Richardson to High Wycombe to be interviewed by Henthorne. As they were leaving the house in an unmarked police car, Michael arrived in one of the several cars he owned, a Volkswagen Golf. Cheryl spotted him and ducked.

After Richard offered him a cup of coffee, Michael asked: "Where's Cheryl?"

"She's out."

"Where?"

"At the police station," Richard said.

"What for?"

"I don't bloody know. There's some silly business going on."

Michael looked at him suspiciously, then asked if he had anything to eat.

"John," Richard told his son, "fix Michael a burger."

For an hour or so, they discussed new CB equipment; then Michael left.

Cheryl was still at the police station. Shortly before midnight, she told Henthorne what Michael had told her during the drive from Tesco's.

"I didn't say anything before, she said, "because I thought he was joking."

42.

Henthorne left the room, called Brian Rundle, and repeated what Cheryl had told him. At midnight, the dentist telephoned: he had examined the X-rays and was 90-percent sure the teeth found in Exeter Forest were those of Monika Telling.

Shortly after dawn the next morning, a group of deliverymen and workmen dressed in overalls appeared on Radnage Lane. Several brought ladders and went to work on the roof of Alf and Ettie Turner's house. They were detectives armed with .38-caliber Smith and Wesson revolvers. Of the twenty-eight hundred members of the Devon and Cornwall Constabulary, only 150 or so carried guns. Rundle sent more than a dozen to West Wycombe. If Michael Telling had indeed killed his wife with a hunting rifle, he might still have it with him. Rundle told the detectives to wait outside until their suspect had left the house: "The last thing we want is a siege situation in which we have to go in after an armed man."

Shortly after 10:00 A.M., the phone rang in the Richardson home. Michael told Richard he was driving over to watch him pull the engine out of his car for overhaul. A policeman posted in the home alerted the detectives staked out near Lambourn House.

A few moments later, Michael backed his Volkswagen out of the garage. His dogs were perched behind him on the back seat. As the car pulled out of the garage, two policemen wearing civilian clothes approached.

"Do you know where Beacons Bottom is, please?" Detective Constable Bruce Pearce asked, referring to a road.

"No—sorry. You would do better to ask next door," Michael said.

"Are you talking about those roofers next door?" the second man, Detective Constable Brian Stocker, asked, referring to the policemen in mufti standing on ladders several hundred yards away.

When Michael turned his head to look at them, Stocker opened the car door and Pearce leaned in, pulled out the ignition key, and grasped Michael's arm.

"We're police officers," he said. "Release your seat-belt catch and get out of the car slowly."

Michael, wearing his usual blue jeans, T-shirt, and leather jacket, climbed out of the car and put his hands on the roof. He was searched, handcuffed, and seated in the rear of a police car while his dogs were led away by a bobby. One of the detectives said: "You have been arrested in relation to a murder inquiry at Exeter. You are not obliged to say anything unless you wish to do so. But what you say may be put in writing and put in evidence."

Michael asked for a cigarette but said nothing else during the fifteen-minute ride to the High Wycombe police station. When Henthorne saw him arrive, he telephoned Rundle and said he thought they had their man.

A few moments later, Rundle began his daily briefing for the increasingly restless corps of reporters camped in Exeter.

"Would it be fair, Mr. Rundle," one local reporter asked, to say that, in the time you've been running this inquiry, you haven't made *any* progress?"

"That would appear to be the case," Rundle said. To himself he thought: "That's not *really* a lie."

When the briefing was over, Rundle left the station through a rear door and entered a black Ford Grenada that was waiting for him. He said he wanted to get to High Wycombe as fast as he could. The driver took him at his word and covered the 120 miles in less than ninety minutes.

———

As Rundle was departing for High Wycombe, two visitors entered Michael's cell in High Wycombe.

"I'm Detective Inspector Henthorne from Exeter," he said, "and this is Detective Sergeant Rudd. You know you have been arrested in connection with a body found in Exeter, and I just want to tell you now that you will be detained here to await the arrival of Detective Superintendent Rundle, who is in charge of the inquiry and who is traveling up to interview you later today. Is there anything you want to say?"

"No, I don't think I want to say anything until my solicitor gets here."

Considering his circumstances, Henthorne thought Michael was a subdued, even calm man.

"Is there anything you want?" he asked.

"Can I have bail?"

His question surprised Henthorne.

"You know why you have been arrested. There is no question of bail. Is there anything you want to say about what you have done?"

"I think you know what I've done."

"Is there anything you want to say about that now?"

"Can I see you on your own?"

After Detective Sergeant Rudd left the cell, Michael burst into tears. "I want to see my dogs," he said. "They're inside the house. . . . I suppose I'll be in prison for thirty, forty, fifty years, won't I?"

"You are not obliged to say anything," Henthorne said, "but anything you do say may be taken down and given in evidence."

"I did it," Michael said.

"Did what, Michael?"

"Murdered my wife?"

"When was that?"

"In March, I think."

43.

West Wycombe,
March 29, 1983

There were only two of them in Lambourn House when it happened, and one of them would never speak again; Michael made sure of that. And so it was left to him alone to tell the story.

He shot her *three* times, not four, as the Home Office ballistics experts had speculated.

She was standing in a corner of the living room shouting at him.

He said he didn't want to return to the hospital. She said he *had* to go back.

He chased her though the lounge, and when she turned to face him, he raised the rifle and fired.

The first bullet hit her in the throat and pushed her back with a jerk.

As her knees began to fold, Monika didn't say a word, made no sound.

The only sound in Lambourn House was the echo of the blast from his rifle.

If you're going to shoot someone, shoot to kill, someone had once told Michael. Without lowering the rifle from his shoulder, he cocked it again and, as Monika tumbled toward the floor, fired. This time, the bullet smashed into her chest.

While she continued to fall, Michael pressed again on the steel lever of the hunting rifle and with a metallic clap pushed another soft-pointed bullet into the chamber.

He pulled the trigger and fired. Before Monika hit the floor and her blond curls spilled across the carpet, inches from the Victorian settee that she had lovingly brought from California, the third slug burst inside her, sending a cascade of shrapnel through her chest like an exploding skyrocket.

As Monika's blood streamed onto the carpet, Michael put down the rifle, bent over her, and raised one of her arms. It was limp. He looked into her eyes. They were blank.

For once, she was silent.

———

He went to the kitchen and vomited.

Trembling, he realized his blood sugar must be near zero. For half an hour, he sat at the kitchen table drinking coffee laced with sugar. Then he returned to the living room and looked down at Monika again.

An hour later, he was in the shower when Joe Stennings knocked at the kitchen door.

After sending him on his way, he covered Monika with a sheet, slid the rifle he had smuggled into England a few days before into a vinyl sheath, and threw the empty shell casings into a dustbin. He had bought 240 bullets in Australia, but he had needed only three.

Shortly before two o'clock—the hour when he was supposed to register at St. Andrew's—Michael called the hospital and said he wouldn't be coming after all.

He didn't have to go back now.

She couldn't make him go back now.

———

As the day passed, Michael expected the police to knock at his door: someone must know what had happened. But once Joe Stennings left, no one else came.

The house was silent except for the occasional sound of gunshots fired by distant marksmen in the Chiltern Hills. That evening, he withdrew £100 from a cash machine in High Wycombe, using Monika's credit card.

For two or three days, he left her on the floor where she had fallen. Then he wrapped her in a plastic blanket—a motorcycle cover—and dragged her to the bedroom at the end of the hall. He laid her down on a camp cot, covered her with the glossy motorcycle shroud, leaned over, looked into her face, and kissed her.

During the next two weeks, Michael said, he often paused at the bedroom doorway and spoke to Monika, then walked over and kissed her. Then he bought a wheelbarrow and, after dark one evening, lifted her off the cot and rolled her to the summer house.

He opened the double doors, then the door to the unfinished sauna, lifted her from the wheelbarrow, and laid her on the tiled floor.

There she remained for nearly five months, through one of the hottest summers in England in centuries.

After two or three weeks, he began to think he would get away with it. He burned her passport and all her personal papers. He went out, invited friends over, made new friends via the CB circuit, brought women to Monika's bed. Like Patrick Mahon, the philandering killer who made love to a tart inches from a trunk containing the pieces of his dismembered wife, Michael sought out human companionship. When people asked about Monika, he said she had gone back to America or had left him for another man, or he made up a different story. When he handed detective Colin Finlay one of her dresses and said it might help him find her, she was on the floor of the sauna a few feet from them. Again and again, he used her Cashpoint card, emptying her account save for a few pounds, to prove she was alive. The detective believed him. Everybody believed him. But as the summer passed, he began to grow apprehensive once more: people wouldn't stop asking about her—they wouldn't stop *talking* about her—everyone wanted to know where she was—everyone said how *wonderful* Monika was—everyone said how *strange* it was that no one had heard from her. Most of all, he worried about Lou and Elsa. He worried they would arrive at his doorstep and ask about Monika. He changed his telephone number, bought the dogs, installed the new locks and burglar alarm, and planted a forest of trees beside the house to help guard his secret. When letters arrived from California, he burned them. He began to suspect that strangers were following him, photographing his house, and tapping his telephone. He paid a parking ticket the day it was issued, afraid that if he didn't he would be arrested. And if he ever needed reminding that Monika was rotting in the sauna, he had only to watch his dogs: for hours at a time, they sat on their haunches outside the summer house, guarding it like loyal sentries, tails wagging.

It was the letter from Mr. Brown that arrived in late August that finally convinced him to remove Monika from the sauna: the letter said painters would be arriving in early September to redecorate Lambourn House.

On Thursday, September 1, he rented a van at a car agency in High Wycombe and asked Richard to drive him there to pick it up. He said he had accumulated a large amount of rubbish and needed the van to haul it to the local tip—the municipal dump.

After dark, several hours later—shortly before nine o'clock—he loaded a tent, sleeping bag, fishing tackle, bait, a spade, an ax, and a pitchfork into the black-and-yellow van and headed to the southwest of England.

With his dog Mandy seated beside him, he drove toward Devon, his favorite county in England. A few minutes past midnight, he turned off the A38 to a narrow country lane a few miles south of Exeter and stopped beside a gate near a clearing in the woods.

It was a windy night, a prelude to a fierce storm that during the next twenty-four hours would rip scores of boats from their moorings on the Devon coast, uproot trees, and smash the Haldon Hills with gales of fifty miles an hour.

He tried the gate. It was unlocked.

About nine o'clock the next morning, Richard Richardson drove to Lambourn House. The night before, Michael had telephoned and asked him to let his puppy out of the house in the morning because he expected to be gone. But when he and Cheryl arrived at Lambourn House, both of Michael's dogs and Michael himself were outside to greet them. The rented van was parked near the garage, its back door open. A hose was coiled on the lawn nearby, and water was dripping from the rear bumper.

Cheryl asked for a cup of coffee before Richard drove her to work, and they chatted a few minutes. Afterward, Michael knocked at the door of Alf and Ettie Turner and said: "Anything I can take for you to the tip? I've got some rubbish to go."

Alf said he wanted to get rid of two paraffin heaters and helped load them on the van; he offered to accompany Michael to the tip, but Michael said he was going to wait for another day, until the weather improved. Buckinghamshire was being pummeled by the same storm as Devon. It had already ruined the annual Wycombe Show, where Bucks each year exhibited their best flowers, fruits, and vegetables.

That evening, Michael called Alison and invited her to bring Matthew to West Wycombe for a few days, so they could see his house for the first time. She promised to come on Monday, in three days.

"What's the weather like in Devon?" he asked.

"It's stormy," Alison said.

"It's the same here."

———

The next morning, Saturday, September 3, the winds were still blowing angrily when Michael arrived at the Richardson home. Richard offered to show him how to find the tip, and the two of them unloaded the Turners' paraffin heaters and half a dozen heavy plastic bags Michael had filled with garbage. They went back to Lambourn House, and Richard helped him clean out the van.

After Michael returned the vehicle to the Wycombe Car Hire agency, he asked Cheryl to go with him to Tesco's to help him stock up on groceries for the next week. As she pushed her shopping cart down the aisle, Michael became impatient with her, annoyed that she had decided to do some shopping of her own while they were there. She would make him get another parking ticket, he said, and he didn't want to get arrested. "For God's sake, Michael, you don't get arrested for a parking ticket,"she said. But the worry in his face didn't fade until they were in the parking lot and saw that the windshield of his car was clear.

As they drove toward West Wycombe, Cheryl said again she was worried about Monika: it had been five months since anyone had heard from her, and that wasn't like her.

"I killed her," Michael said. Then he mumbled several syllables Cheryl only dimly discerned: she thought she heard "sauna" and "stinking."

"What are you talking about? Have you flipped your lid?"

Michael fixed his eyes on the road and didn't say anything more. Cheryl decided he must have been joking, and that evening she didn't think it was important enough to mention to Richard.

The next day was Sunday. About 9:00 A.M., Michael drove to the

Richardson home to pick up their son Scott, who had offered to help with some chores. When Cheryl arrived at Lambourn House several hours later with their second son, John, to collect Scott, Michael urged her to call Richard and ask him to join all of them for dinner. It was agreed, and she and John, an aspiring chef, volunteered to cook.

As they were preparing dinner, the evening news came on the television set. A BBC announcer said: ". . . A headless corpse, the body of a woman believed to be between the ages of fifteen and thirty, was found abandoned Saturday afternoon at a beauty spot near Exeter. . . ."

Michael looked quickly at Cheryl, turned his back, and went to the bathroom. A moment later, she heard him vomiting. She followed and saw him standing over the toilet. It wasn't the first time she had seen him become ill suddenly, because of his diabetes. Michael said he was all right and asked her to go with him to the rose garden Monika had planted in the courtyard.

"Why was John staring at me during the news broadcast?" he asked.

"Michael, he wasn't staring at you. Why should he? He had no reason to. . . ."

At that moment, Richard arrived for dinner, saw them standing in the twilight among Monika's roses, and asked: "What's up?"

"I've got some problems with my roses, and Cheryl's giving me some advice," Michael said.

When she arrived with Matthew the next day, Alison quickly realized Michael was in one of his quiet, depressed moods. He handed her an envelope containing a woman's wristwatch and two rings, one crowned by a large emerald, which she recognized as Monika's engagement and wedding rings from her visit in Devon. Michael said he planned to sell the jewelry later, but wanted Alison to have it for now.

An hour later, the Richardsons brought Scott over to play with Matthew. Michael told them one of his Harleys had dripped a lot of oil on the floor of the summer house and he needed advice on how to clean it up.

Cheryl and Richard hadn't been inside the summer house for months. The humidifier Monika had given Michael the previous Valentine's Day to filter air in the "Radio Shack" was whirring noisily, scattering a powerful lemon scent.

Richard, who got headaches around air-purifying machinery, said: "Michael, would you switch that thing off?"

Michael refused: the place needed an airing out, he said. Richard turned around and left, leaving Cheryl alone with Michael. When she saw the spots on the floor, she recommended the name of a liquid cleaner that she said would remove them. Looking up, she was surprised to see the boxes she and Richard had packed several months before with Monika's clothing.

"Michael, how come these are still here?"

He said Monika still hadn't come round to pick them up, and he'd been too busy to ship them to America.

Then he looked at her and asked: "Do you think it smells in here?"

44.

As if he were the driver of a bulldozer clearing a path for a new highway, or a surgeon performing the same operation he had done many times, Jeff Henthorne now went about his job methodically and unemotionally. His detachment, he knew, often surprised people with vocations other than his own. "People tend to believe we are incensed by what has occurred and react accordingly, as if it were happening to one of our own family," he once said, "but I don't necessarily look down on murderers, and I don't moralize about them—sometimes I even feel compassion for the murderer. It's the chase I enjoy."

As a young bobby, he had learned that the pace of questioning was often crucial in interrogating a suspect: asking questions too slowly invited deception; questions that came too rapidly might unnerve the suspect and undermine whatever willingness he had to tell the truth. With Michael Telling, he decided to ask his questions slowly, even sympathetically.

"What did you use to kill her, Michael?" he asked, drawing out his words slowly, encouraging him to tell the rest of the story at his own pace.

"Rifle."

"What sort of rifle?"

"Marlin .30-.30."

"Where did you get that?"

"Australia."

"Where is the rifle now?"

"Gone," Michael said.

He said he had broken it apart; some of the parts he had discarded in the rubbish, and "some I threw away on motorways into the banks. I stripped it. There you are, I've confessed. I knew you'd want a confession. Will you promise to look after my dogs, please?"

Henthorne departed, leaving a detective constable outside the cell with a notebook in case Michael volunteered anything more.

After ten minutes, Michael asked the detective to pass a message to Henthorne: "Can you tell the detective inspector—the head, it's at home. It's in the garage. The keys are here. It's the whole head. I didn't do anything to the head. I couldn't."

Henthorne returned and said: "I understand you want to tell me something about the head."

"It's in the garage," Michael said. "Have you contacted my solicitor?"

"Who's your solicitor?" Henthorne asked.

"Kenneth Dimmick. Monika's head is in the garage."

"Whereabouts?"

"In the boot of the Mini."

"Why is it still there?"

"I just couldn't, you know. . . . The same with the body, the same with the body, I had it for five months. I didn't want to dump it. I didn't want to do anything with it. I couldn't stop. You would have identified it anyhow. I didn't want to take the clothing off, either. She didn't have much on."

Michael explained that after he killed Monika he had kept her on a bed in the house for two or three weeks, then put her in the sauna, and, five months after killing her, took her to Devon, to a spot he had once visited to enjoy the view of Exeter.

"What can you say to me now about the way you managed to keep the head?" Henthorne asked.

"I just left it there. I chopped it off with an ax."

"In the outhouse?"

"No, down in Devon. Can I have a cigarette?"

"In Devon, you say—when you dumped the body?" Henthorne asked, after handing Michael a cigarette.

"Yes."

"Why did you do it?"

"There were a hundred and one reasons. I can't really explain. I walked out and was back home in Australia. I wish I'd stayed there. She kept pushing me. I don't mean she pushed me over—I just snapped in the end. I don't just mean nagging—she was horrible in most ways—but it doesn't justify killing. What can justify killing?"

At that, Michael said he didn't want to say anything more until his solicitor arrived.

At Lambourn House, Rundle and Henthorne watched as a scene-of-crime officer from the Devon and Cornwall CID used one of Michael's keys to open the luggage compartment of his orange Mini Cooper. In the center of it, they saw a round package, melon-sized, and wrapped in a black plastic bag. He opened the bag and discovered an identical polyethylene bag; when he opened that one, he found another, then another and another.

Like the multiple boxes of a Chinese puzzle, the scene-of-crime man opened each bag in sequence. When he opened the seventh bag, the senses of the detectives were assaulted by a corrosive, ghastly odor and a grotesque sight: the rotted face of Monika Elizabeth Zumsteg-Telling staring up at them sightlessly. Her skin was putrefied and falling from her skull like rotted bark from a diseased tree. Her teeth—the few that remained—were askew and falling out of the sockets. Her eyes were dark and gruesome holes, her blond hair matted and rotting.

"We've got ourselves a problem," Rundle said. "We've got a torso that's the responsibility of the coroner in Exeter and a head that's the responsibility of the coroner in High Wycombe."

In the irreverent fashion of policemen everywhere, a detective from the Thames Valley force said: "Let's flip a coin—heads or tails?"

After several minutes of more serious consultation, the coroner in High Wycombe agreed to allow the members of the Devon and Cornwall Constabulary to take the head to Exeter. Now the out-of-town detectives faced another problem: they needed a container to preserve the evidence until they got to Exeter. Checking his watch, Rundle realized it was twenty minutes past five. The shops in High Wycombe would be closing in ten minutes.

"Go over to the High Street and see what you can find: get any kind of container with a lid," he told a detective, "and hurry."

When the detective returned fifteen minutes later, his face brimmed with the triumphant expression of a man who thought he had accomplished a difficult mission with aplomb: at Woolworth's, he had purchased a beer-making kit that included, along with ingredients for making home brew, a large plastic container for fermenting it.

———

Given the flashing lights and police cars all round, it had been impossible for the few residents of Radnage Lane to miss the commotion at Lambourn House. Soon rumors were flying. No one was more shocked by the rumor that her neighbor had beheaded his wife than Ettie Turner. She loved Monika like a daughter. Monika was the kindest, sweetest, most compassionate young woman she had ever known.

For several hours, all she could see in her mind was a vision of Monika sitting across from her, next to the oil heater, a cup of coffee in one hand—without her head.

After Michael's arrest the year before, Monika had told Ettie he had boasted that a member of his family could get away with anything in England.

She looked over at Alf. "I wonder if the Vesteys will find a way to get him off this time."

VII

There is nothing so powerful as truth, and often nothing so strange. . . .

DANIEL WEBSTER

45.

After meeting alone with his lawyer, Michael signed a confession in which he not only admitted killing Monika but established what was to become the foundation of his defense for doing it: she had it coming to her.

In the statement, prepared with his solicitor's help, he said that, shortly after the marriage, he had learned Monika was an alcoholic and a drug addict who was interested in him only for his money. She used cocaine, heroin, and marijuana; she hadn't slept with him in months; she was a bisexual who belittled him and assaulted him physically and took others to her bed, "because I was only good for money."

Michael said that, on the morning of her death, "Monika was in a bad mood and kept following me around, going on at me as before. She kept telling me to hurry and go in to hospital so that she could lead her own life and she kept taunting me as before. She would not stop so I went in to another room and picked up the rifle and returned to the living room. I put the rifle against the wall and she then came charging towards me, shouting. I thought she was going to attack me so I picked up the rifle and shot her."

He kept Monika at Lambourn House because "I did not want her to leave the house. When I realized that eventually I had to move the

217

body away, I wanted to do so as decently as possible. I decided to put her in a forest which I knew. I cut off her head and brought it home with me. I am not clear why I did this but I thought that later on, if the body was not discovered, I could collect and bury it with the head in our house. Also I did not want her identified because of my family. They had been good to me and stuck by me when I was in trouble and I did not want to get them involved. At all times, I really loved Monika and never wanted to kill her. If only she had stopped going on at me this would not have happened."

After signing the statement, Michael was transported to Exeter in the rear of Rundle's Ford Grenada. In the front seat, the detective superintendent had reason to feel happy: in less than a week, he'd gone from a Code One to a confession.

But before Michael was charged, another postmortem exam was required, to confirm that the head found in the boot of his car had once been attached to the torso abandoned in Exeter Forest.

Moments before it began, Rundle was called to a telephone at the Royal Devon and Exeter Hospital a few steps from the mortuary room. As he spoke to the caller, he suddenly heard loud, stampeding feet. He looked up and saw the two detectives he had left behind sprinting down the hallway as fast as they could run. A second later, he knew why: an odor unlike anything he had ever experienced engulfed him. It was the odor of hell—the odor of putrefied brain tissue, tapped by a pathologist's battery-powered saw.

It smothered him, almost knocked him down. And it was still with him long hours later, after he went home to bed.

As expected, the head and vertebrae fit perfectly. Monika's mouth provided the final connection: the dental surgeon said the teeth in the forest were from the head found in Michael's Mini. Michael's ax, he speculated, had probably knocked out the teeth when he decapitated her. If he hadn't hit her so violently, Rundle said, they wouldn't have the final link proving she was Michael's twenty-six-year-old wife.

After the second postmortem exam, Michael was arraigned in Exeter's Wonford Magistrates Court. Standing handcuffed to a policeman, he heard the charge against him: "That at West Wycombe, Buckinghamshire, or elsewhere, between March 27 and September 4, 1983, Michael Henry Maxwell Telling, age thirty-three, did murder Monika Elizabeth Zumsteg-Telling contrary to law."

After the ninety-second hearing, Michael was booked into Exeter Prison, a dank, overcrowded fortress that had housed the miscreants of Devonshire for almost a century. On his booking form, prison officials listed his occupation: "Non-employed." "That's different than *unemployed*," a policeman told a reporter. "When you've got as much money as he does, you don't have to work. That's 'non-employed.' "

46.

The telephone rang in Santa Rosa at seven-thirty Sunday morning, September 11. When Lou answered, the caller identified himself as the Los Angeles correspondent for London's *Daily Mirror* and said he wanted a comment from Lou about his daughter's murder.

Sleepily, Lou tried to get his thoughts together.

"What?"

The reporter said the police had identified his daughter, Monika Zumsteg-Telling, as the headless corpse found the week before at a beauty spot in Devon.

More words followed from the reporter, in a torrent. Lou deciphered only a few.

"It's a reporter," he whispered to Elsa. "He says Monika is dead and that Michael has been arrested for murdering her."

He didn't tell Elsa—yet—that the reporter said Monika had been decapitated.

Elsa stared at him in shock, then became hysterical.

Lou asked the reporter to repeat what he had said.

When he had finished, Lou asked for the telephone number of the police in Exeter, so he could confirm the report.

He hung up slowly, then burst into sobs, and he and Elsa hugged each other without finding solace.

After that, the telephone didn't stop ringing. Within hours, their leafy, quiet neighborhood was crowded with taxis, vans, and rented cars containing reporters and camera crews, more arriving each hour.

After repeatedly trying, Lou got through to the police in Exeter. A detective in the Incident Room confirmed what the reporter had told him and said he was sorry that Lou had had to learn it in such a way. With Elsa continuing to cry hysterically, Lou fought to gain control of himself, while journalists telephoned and knocked at his door.

If the London tabloids had been titillated by the discovery of a headless corpse in Devon, they were rapacious now that it belonged to a member of a noble family.

Although Britain imposed some of the world's strictest restrictions on pretrial publicity in criminal cases, the rules did not apply to the dead, not did they prevent a journalistic feeding frenzy.

In a stampede Monday morning, Fleet Street competed to produce the most ghoulish portrayals of life at Lambourn House and the "rich, American party girl" who lived there. The relatively sedate *Daily Express* trumpeted: "NEW SCANDAL ROCKS THE VESTEY EMPIRE." The *Daily Mirror* headlined its story: "SOCIETY WIFE'S BODY 'KEPT IN FREEZER,' " apparently based on speculation that Monika's body could not have survived five months in the state it had without cold storage. And, less than twenty-four hours after Monika was identified as the headless corpse, the *Daily Star* managed to buy a complete set of her wedding photographs and splashed them across several pages. The next day, it scooped its rivals again with a three-page layout of photographs taken of Monika when she had modeled designer clothes at a charity luncheon for African-famine relief. Many of the articles focused on the Cinderella elements of her life: an American beauty falls in love with a handsome British tourist, then discovers he is a scion of one of the world's richest families; they move to a splendid country house, but instead of living happily ever after, she dies grotesquely—a Barbara Cartland romance novel transmuted by an ax into a Gothic horror story. In the United States, there was also morbid interest in this aspect of the story. *Time* began its report: "A gruesome murder and a lucky tip, a pretty American victim and a jet-setting suspect from a dazzlingly

wealthy British family. The case could have been a thriller co-written
by Agatha Christie and Evelyn Waugh." After describing Michael's
arrest, *Time* noted: "Some of the Vesteys were quick to point out, as a
spokesman put it, that he 'was not a close member of the family.' "

———————

As ordinary people often do when they are suddenly caught up in a
sensational event, Lou and Elsa, despite their grief, tried initially as
best they could to respond to the reporters' questions.

"Yes, they made a positive identification, she's our daughter," he
said on his front steps while, a reporter noted, he tried unsuccessfully
to fight back tears. Lou tried to weave for the reporters a coherent fabric
from the events that had occurred and perhaps, in so doing, understand it himself. He described their meeting with Michael in
Sausalito and Michael's whirlwind courtship of Monika. After the
marriage, he said, they had had problems, but so did many newlyweds:
"My daughter was a career-oriented gal. Michael was among the idle
rich. He lived in a social and career vacuum; he didn't have any
purpose at all. That's normal for people from that background, but
Monika needed purpose. She applied to Oxford. She wanted to go
back to school in order to work. She tried antiques as a hobby and
trading and also took some odd jobs that were not too successful. But
finding a place to work and being a member of England's second-
richest family is a hard thing to do."

He said he and Elsa had tried repeatedly to contact Monika by
phone during the previous five months. He had also sent her a registered letter in July, but to no avail. Asked what he thought now of the
man to whom he had introduced his daughter, he answered:

"When they called me Sunday and told me what had happened, it
wasn't like I lost just one member of my family. He was like a son to
me. I loved him like a son. Now I've got mixed emotions, from anger
to recriminations. I wonder: God, how could I have introduced him to
my daughter—my joy?

"As for Michael," he added, "I can't afford to spit venom at him for
the sake of my own sanity. I feel terribly sorry for him. I know the kind
of help he needs is beyond my ability to give."

As much as Monika's grieving parents tried to help the invading
troupe of British newsmen, they learned it was impossible to satisfy
them: the reporters always wanted more. From their windows, they
saw telephoto lenses stalking them from neighbors' yards and balco-

nies; reporters pounced on them when they left the house, tried to follow Lou to his A.A. meetings. Their faith in Fleet Street began to fade even more when reports of what the British papers were printing about Monika were played back to them: she was "a society jet-set girl from a wealthy American family," a "playgirl" and "high-society hostess" who socialized with royalty and film and rock stars and entertained the super-rich at wild parties in her country house.

But this, they learned soon enough, was only the beginning of the violence the British press and the British legal system would perpetrate on their daughter.

47.

Aunty Liz sent a note of condolence, but from other members of the Vestey family, the response was silence: no words of sympathy, no expressions of sorrow, no apologies to Lou and Elsa.

It was as if Michael's second wife, despite her presence on the roster of Britain's aristocratic families, had never existed. In life, the family had tried to use her to help Michael. In death, they abandoned her.

Lou didn't know whom to turn to. After learning Jeff Henthorne's name from a reporter, he telephoned him and offered to fly to Exeter to help with the investigation. But Henthorne said there was nothing he could do and encouraged him to stay home.

Not knowing what else to do, he wrote to Michael's cousin Christopher, whom he had met at the wedding. He said he and Elsa were in shock but would fly to England if it would help: he wanted to collect Monika's body, assure that her affairs were taken care of, and join the family in holding a memorial service for her. Remembering that Christopher was a trustee of the family trust, he asked if the family would help pay their expenses. Lou did not tell him that he and Elsa had lost much of their savings to the export-import business he had started with Michael and he was still unemployed.

Christopher did not reply to Lou's letter. Instead, Kenneth Dimmick, Michael's solicitor, responded indirectly through a British lawyer the Vesteys paid to represent Monika's interests. Dimmick said trustees of the Vestey Settlement did not want to communicate directly with members of Monika's family—only through lawyers—and quickly put to rest any notion Michael's family felt obliged to make a financial settlement to his wife's family simply because he had killed her. Indeed, he made clear they could expect nothing. Monika appeared to have died intestate, he said, and thus Michael was legally entitled to her entire estate unless he was subsequently determined to have killed her by murder or manslaughter. In the strictest sense, therefore, her family appeared to have no legal rights to any of her property. However, he said this was probably a moot point since Michael currently didn't expect to press his claim. In any case, he said, Monika appeared to have few assets. Although she maintained an account at Lloyd's Bank, it was virtually empty and, of course, she had no claim on their home. Alluding to an offer by Lou to visit Lambourn House and collect her things, the lawyer said it was sealed and its contents in storage. "It is owned by the Trustees of the Vestey Settlement and there would appear to be no reason why Mr. Zumsteg should want to inspect the property."

Monika's clothing and personal effects, he continued, were in storage, and Mr. Zumsteg could have them if he came to England. Her Pontiac was also in storage; he proposed it be sold as quickly as possible: storage costs were running up, and they would have to be deducted from any proceeds realized by the Zumstegs from the sale of the car.

As to Lou's question about whether Michael's family would help pay his and Elsa's expenses to England, Dimmick said the trustees agreed to reimburse reasonable expenses—against appropriate vouchers—for *his* expenses while he arranged to ship Monika's body to America, but would pay none of Elsa's expenses. He concluded by saying his clients strongly opposed holding a memorial service for Monika in High Wycombe, as Mr. Zumsteg suggested. Under no circumstances, he emphasized, would the trustees help underwrite any expense for such a service or any additional hotel or living expenses for Mr. Zumsteg in conjunction with one. "It is of questionable taste, is bound to attract publicity (which Mr. Zumsteg says he is anxious to minimize) and I doubt whether Monika's limited circle of friends in that area are of the type to attend."

Lou was stunned and furious over the icy, insensitive tone of the letter. Replying to the lawyer who had forwarded it to him, he said: "I cannot fathom Dimmick's remark about a memorial service being of 'questionable taste,' nor do I believe he had more than a scant knowledge of Monika's 'limited circle of friends.' "

When Chief Inspector Brian Rundle drove up the long driveway toward the sixty-five-room country estate of Lord Samuel Vestey, he didn't know what to expect. It was not unknown in his country for the rich and powerful to attempt to manipulate the machinery of justice. The Vestey family's enormous wealth made it a foregone conclusion that Michael Telling would be defended by a barrister from the front ranks of the British bar. But Rundle was anxious to learn what else, if anything, his family was likely to do in his behalf, and he drove to Stowell Park, a sweeping woodland preserve crowned by the castlelike home of Lord Vestey, in search of clues to a possible campaign of obstruction.

After Lord Vestey offered him coffee, they got down to business. Rundle outlined the prosecution's case against Michael while the man the tabloids called "Lord Spam" listened quietly, as if, Rundle thought, he were weighing the pros and cons of a pending business deal. When Rundle finished, the head of Michael's branch of the family appeared to be convinced that the case against Michael was strong. He said the family would stand fully behind Michael but would let justice run its course.

Rundle left convinced that Lord Vestey wanted to get things over with as quickly and painlessly as possible.

For the Vesteys, there was really only one choice to defend Michael: George Alfred Carman, Q.C. Every generation in England produced a defense lawyer whose style and courtroom success, insight into the minds of jurors, and ability to bewitch and persuade them, to make speeches as finely woven as the silk gowns they wore, inspired awe among their peers.

George Carman was a 1952 graduate of Oxford's Balliol College with a first-class honors degree. After rising to minor prominence at the bar during the 1960s, he was designated a Queen's Counsel in 1971, a title granted Britain's most distinguished barristers. Along with other Q.C.s, he wore a silken gown instead of the cotton or polyester robes of less distinguished opponents—and could charge the swollen fees considered appropriate for the best lawyers in the land. Beginning in the late 1970s, a string of prominent defendants placed their fate in his hands, and he delivered for them at a series of sensational trials that gained him enormous publicity. Journalists called him a "legal genius" and "invincible" as his reputation grew. He won acquittals for Jeremy Thorpe, leader of the British Liberal Party, on charges of conspiring to murder a male model; for a doctor accused of murdering a child with Down's syndrome; for one of Britain's most beloved television actors, who was accused of molesting a child. He was unable to prevent the conviction of a celebrated Soviet spy, Geoffrey Prime, but performed so skillfully he earned further plaudits anyway. Following another of his victories, shortly before Michael's arrest, the *Daily Express* wrote: "George Carman, QC, has become one of the highest paid and most fashionable courtroom defenders of our time." The *Daily Mail* said: "He has achieved a reputation as a brilliant defense lawyer who pays great attention to detail and has a turn of phrase that makes complex legal points comprehensible to jurors and public alike."

Now the fate of Michael Telling was in his hands.

48.

Lou landed in England during a rainstorm. The bleak and stormy November sky reflected the sorrow of his mission. Before Lou left California, Kenneth Dimmick had appealed to him to reconsider his decision to fly to England: it would only add to the publicity. But Lou persisted and eluded the reporters who were waiting to interview him at Heathrow.

His first task was to make arrangements to ship Monika's body home. The lawyer suggested cremating Monika and sending her ashes to California instead, to simplify things. Lou telephoned Elsa and asked what she thought about this proposal.

"No, Lou. *I want her back*. I'm not going to make it easy on them."

None of the Vesteys would see Lou—not even Michael's cousin Christopher, whose dark, cryptic glance on Monika's wedding day had a meaning Lou only now comprehended.

If was as if Lou, like Monika, didn't exist any more in the eyes of Michael's family. Even Alex, the chauffeur, who had been friendly to him before, said apologetically that he had been asked by the family's lawyers not to speak to Lou.

Lou brought with him a list prepared by Elsa of the things Monika had taken with her to England: the antique furniture she had bought in the Gold Country, an expensive set of French china, silver dinnerware, the burled-redwood coffee table she and Lou had given Monika and Michael for their wedding. She asked Lou to have Monika's things packed up and shipped to Santa Rosa, along with any clocks or jewelry that might be left over from her antique business: "I know they're not going to bring her back, but they're all we're ever going to have of Monika."

But everything—or almost everything—was gone.

In the warehouse where Lou was escorted to examine the material taken from Lambourn House, he found virtually nothing on Elsa's list—only smelly, mildewed cardboard boxes containing Monika's clothing and cosmetics and the burled-redwood coffee table Monika had wanted to remind her of California.

Everything else was gone. After he killed her, Michael had given away her jewelry and her fur coat and several of her most prized antiques, and later—before Lou arrived in England—one of his relatives had picked over what was left and taken what she wanted from Lambourn House.

As Michael's solicitor had indicated, Monika's bank account—the account she had opened with dreams of saving enough money to use as a down payment for an investment property and reduce their dependence on Michael's family—was empty: starting the day he killed her, Michael had plundered it.

Lou was incapable of complaining. Disoriented, oppressed by grief and guilt, he wanted to leave England as quickly as he could.

With help from the consular officials at the U.S. Embassy in London who specialized in such things, he completed the paperwork necessary to ship Monika's body to California. And on Thanksgiving Day—his fifty-third birthday and what would have been her twenty-seventh—he dined in High Wycombe with several of her friends from Alcoholics Anonymous. They joined Lou in toasting Monika's courage, which had enabled her to look at a bottle of alcohol for more than a year without succumbing to temptation. This was as much of a memorial service as Lou could arrange for Monika without help from the Vestey family.

While he and Monika's friends were toasting her with orange juice and soft drinks at an A.A. meeting in High Wycombe, Michael was dining on steak and red wine at Exeter Prison.

Under British law, remand prisoners—those arraigned and awaiting trial without bail—could order meals from restaurants if they had the means. Michael, who had often found solace in food, did so enthusiastically: "I am looking forward to a *decent* breakfast—a glass of O.J., shredded wheat, a kipper and some kidneys and scrambled eggs," he wrote to Cheryl and Richard Richardson, who had been informed they would be called as witnesses at Michael's trial. "I guess lunch will be simple—steak, spinach and *real* mashed potatoes. . . . I will have a half bottle of something decent. I have to stick to red as I don't see how they could keep white cool. . . ."

———

Before returning to California, Lou met with Jeff Henthorne and offered to return to England for Michael's trial, but the detective urged him not to come: he had seen too many parents sitting in the backs of courtrooms unnecessarily reliving their grief at the loss of a child, Henthorne said.

Elsa had asked Lou to bring home Monika's cockatoo if he could arrange it. "It will probably outlive us," she said, "and, in a way, always remind us of her." Although one of the family's lawyers promised to send the bird after an appropriate period of quarantine, it never arrived in Santa Rosa. The bird had died, the Zumstegs were told. "Baloney," Elsa said. "That bird was the only witness to what Michael did, and they didn't want it to live."

———

When Lou arrived back in Santa Rosa, British reporters continued to hound him. Only an outraged Catholic priest kept them away from Monika's funeral, a requiem mass at St. Eugene's Cathedral, the church where Monika had once dreamed of marrying Michael in a long white brocade gown with six attendants dressed in simple Victorian sack dresses.

Afterward, she was buried on the side of a grassy hill at Calvary Cemetery. A few days before the funeral, Lou had composed a eulogy for Monika, but he was unable to deliver it. As he sobbed quietly, the words he had written were spoken by his brother, Edward:

"At last you are home, Monika. Your final journey from England to your native California has ended. . . . Monika, you were a woman of beauty and bright promise who touched many lives here and in England. Those closest to you knew of your deep sensitivities, although you frequently tried to conceal them. Your earlier work with sick and elderly folk and your special compassion for the aged revealed a richness of desire to be of help to others. Your studies in humanities and plans to further your education were more steps in finding social and personal purpose in helping others. . . .

"You had many talents and were particularly good with the written word. You once wrote:

> If reason sat upon a throne
> And actions sat below
> Understanding would be their child
> And humanity their soul. . . .

"This, and the many other poems and letters you have left us, showed a rare perception of life and humanity, which many would call love. In the final year of your life, you became active in a fellowship where you found deep spiritual meaning and purpose in helping others. You discovered that not only is love giving something without expecting anything in return, but that God is love. You carried this message to your family and to your friends. You did your best to improve the lives of your husband and others by helping them find purpose and meaning.

"The shock of your tragic death has receded; now we mourn your passing and remember you with love in a communion of spirit and fellowship. We have sought understanding for your untimely passing, but in following your own example, we must believe in faith, in a Higher Power. That it is: 'Thy will not ours be done." And that: 'Nothing, absolutely nothing, happens in God's world by mistake.' In this belief, we can find the same consolation that you once found yourself. Rest in peace, Monika, our beloved daughter, sister, and friend. . . . At last you are home."

Unbeknownst to those at the funeral, a few miles away, in San Francisco, a private detective hired by Michael's family had begun to make inquiries about Monika.

49.

Brian Rundle believed Monika Zumsteg-Telling was murdered in cold blood. He reached the conclusion during the ride back to Exeter, with Michael in the back seat of his car, after he interviewed him in jail. His conviction grew stronger after Jeff Henthorne stayed behind and discovered more about Michael's life and marriage. Henthorne told him the marriage had been very stormy: "They weren't a very compatible couple."

"Yes," Rundle said. "But the usual solution to that is divorce, not murder."

If nothing else convinced him that the murder of Monika Zumsteg-Telling was premeditated—an act of planning and malice afore-thought—Michael's trip to Australia did: "I'm satisfied," he told Henthorne, "that when he went to Australia, he went there for the express purpose of getting the gun he used to kill her."

Rundle was equally convinced Michael's lawyers would argue he had killed his wife during a moment of irrationality in which he was not legally accountable for the crime—was guilty, at most, of man-slaughter. The stakes in such a distinction were substantial. Convicted of murder—the killing of someone with malice aforethought—

Michael Telling faced a mandatory life sentence; convicted of man-slaughter—the taking of another's life without malice or intent to do harm—he could be free in a few years or released immediately.

Rundle's first mission was to convince prosecutors that the murder was cold and premeditated. It was his responsibility to gather evidence and submit it to the Director of Public Prosecutions. If he satisfied the Crown's prosecutor, the evidence was referred to the Attorney-General, who retained a senior barrister and an assistant to present the evidence at trial. Although policemen could press cases on their own, Rundle knew that in practice he needed to convince the Crown prosecutor that Michael Telling was guilty of and should be tried for premeditated murder.

In late February 1984, five months after his arrest and four months before Michael's trial was scheduled to start, John Hamilton, the medical director of Broadmoor Special Hospital, drove to Exeter to interview Michael at the request of the Director of Public Prosecutions. He was one of the United Kingdom's most experienced specialists on the criminal mind. The institution he helped oversee, a Victorian madhouse known for more than a century as the Broad-moor Criminal Lunatic Asylum, was a sprawling cage of stone and concrete—part psychiatric hospital, part maximum-security prison—spread over acres of heavily guarded countryside near a picturesque village in the county of Berkshire. The forty-year-old psychiatrist had grown up in the shadow of Broadmoor. Now in his custody were hundreds of psychotic murderers and other insane criminals, the worst and most dangerous in England. The Department of Public Prosecutions wanted his opinion of Michael Telling before deciding on a strategy for his trial.

In a small, white-walled prison interview room, Michael's words spilled out in a torrent. Hamilton couldn't get him to stop. He complained about overcrowding at the prison, his guards, and the policemen who had put him there; he complained about the prison food and not being able to take more showers. But most of all, he complained about Monika. After almost two hours, the psychiatrist closed his notebook and said he would return in a week to complete the interview. Before leaving Exeter, he met with prison administrators. They called Michael a manipulative, demanding prisoner

who had not expressed a word of remorse for murdering his wife and
repeatedly offered to bankroll expensive parties for fellow inmates to
gain their favor. After Hamilton's interview, Michael complained to
Cheryl Richardson about having to have his mind probed by yet another psychiatrist. "I don't think that the public realizes how I am
treated in prison," he said. The only thing that lifted his morale
were visits from friends and his restaurant lunches. He said he had
given up hope of a fair trial "because of who I am and what I represent. . . ."

In another letter, he told Cheryl: "I hate the waiting, not knowing
what is happening, or what the final result will be . . . why don't they
bring back hanging? At least it would all be over and maybe I could see
Monika, even if it was only for a little while. . . ."

After Hamilton's second interview with Michael, one week later, the
psychiatrist told Brian Rundle that he not only agreed with him that
Michael was a cunning and cold-blooded murderer, but that Michael
had *admitted* that he had begun plotting his wife's murder two or three
days before he did it—clearly evidence of premeditation. Now, Hamilton said, he was trying desperately to avoid a prison sentence by
claiming his wife *deserved* it.

"He spent a great deal of time trying to persuade me that his victim
had provoked him into killing her and he was not in any way responsible for his actions," Hamilton said.

The psychiatrist described his interview more fully in a report filed
with the Department of Public Prosecutions:

> Telling admitted to me that he did not kill his wife in the heat of the
> moment. He said that the seeds were sown two or three days previously
> when the two were staying together in a London hotel. He said resent-
> ment had been building up inside him at the way she had been treating
> him and throughout these days he had been harbouring a wish to obtain
> his revenge. He told me he made the decision to kill her by shooting her
> the night before the killing. A considerable period therefore elapsed
> between the time he made the decision and the time he deliberately
> shot her.

After the second interview, Brian Rundle had no difficulty convincing
the Department of Public Prosecutions that Michael Telling had killed

with malice aforethought. It was murder, not manslaughter. But he knew George Carman would present other psychiatrists, who would argue differently. That's how the system worked, in England as in America. Almost certainly, the upcoming trial in Exeter Crown Court—*Regina* v. *Michael Henry Maxwell Telling*—would be a trial within a trial over the defendant's sanity.

50.

The legal systems of the world have grappled for centuries with the challenge of trying to define when a person accused of a crime is so mentally impaired that he or she should not be held accountable for it. In thirteenth-century England, advocates for the damned argued that imbeciles and lunatics should not be executed for crimes if they were clearly incapable of understanding right from wrong. In 1618, a manual for British jurists advised: "If one that is 'non compos mentis,' or an ideot, kills a man, this is no felony, for they have not knowledge of Good and Evil, nor can have a felonious intent, nor a will or mind to do harm." British courts later applied the "wild beast test": insofar as men or women "act like wild beasts," they are not accountable for a crime.

But the courts' efforts to protect the demented have often collided with another responsibility—their responsibility to mete out appropriate punishment for the ultimate crime, murder—not least because society's efforts to protect the demented have often provided the only potential escape route to sane, guilty men who are clever enough to convince a court that they are neither. If he can blame an illness for his crime, a guilty man can claim he wasn't responsible for it—a devil inside him made him do it.

In the seventeenth century, Sir Edward Coke, one of the fathers of British common law, writing what was to become the foundation of homicide statutes in much of the world, composed the following definition of murder: "When a person of sound memory and discretion unlawfully killeth any reasonable creature in being, and under the king's peace, with malice aforethought, either express or implied."

Two centuries later, a Scottish woodworker named Daniel M'Naghten was charged with murdering the private secretary of British Prime Minister Sir Robert Peel, whom he mistook for Peel. A court judged him insane and committed him to an asylum. Because of an uproar over the decision, the House of Lords opened an inquiry that in 1843 forced British jurists to promulgate new principles defining the insanity of criminal defendants. Called the M'Naghten Rule, it is still relied on, a century and a half later, by many courts in the United States and elsewhere in the English-speaking world: "We submit our opinion to be that the jury ought to be told in all cases that every man is to be presumed to be sane and to possess a sufficient degree of reason to be responsible for his crimes, until the contrary be proved to their satisfaction; and that to establish a defense on the ground of insanity it must be clearly proved that, at the time of committing the act, the accused was laboring under such defect of reason, from disease of the mind, as not to know the nature and quality of the act he was doing, or, if he did know it, that he did now know he was doing what was wrong."

Accused murderers who pleaded "guilty but insane" and could persuade jurors they were mad under the new standard were spared and committed to a mental hospital; those who could not were usually sentenced to death. Some defense lawyers, judges, and the practitioners of a new medical specialty—psychiatry—began arguing, after the turn of the century for an even broader definition of insanity, claiming that the M'Naghten Rule's right-and-wrong test was too narrow: some people, they said, killed when they were overtaken by an urge over which they had no control. At a 1919 trial, Sir Edward Marshall Hall, a renowned British defense lawyer, while representing a former British infantry officer accused of killing his girlfriend, postulated a new legal excuse for murder: the irresistible-impulse defense. He claimed his client had killed during an irrational moment triggered by syphilis and the after effects of shell shock. "Will is different from reason," he argued. "A man may know the difference between right and wrong and appreciate the nature and quality of his acts and the consequences therefor, and yet be deprived of that instinctive choice between right and wrong which is characteristic of a sane person." The court rejected the defense and his client was hanged, but three years later, Hall was instrumental in shaping the recommendations of a panel of lawyers and medical people appointed to review the M'Naghten standard: "It should be recognized that a person charged criminally with an offence is irresponsible for his act when the act is committed under an impulse which the prisoner may be, by mental disease, deprived of any power to resist." The panel's recommendation was unpopular, however, with ordinary Britons and many judges, who claimed it was impossible to distinguish between an impulse that was irresistible because of a mental illness and one irresistible because of jealousy, rage, lust, hatred, revenge, or any other motive in the palette of human emotions. The proposal was voted down, and the irresistible-impulse defense was expressly prohibited in British courts. In America, however, the concept gained a foothold. By the late 1920s, courts in more than twenty states allowed it.

For decades, defense lawyers on both sides of the Atlantic continued trying to broaden the M'Naghten Rule. In the 1950s, they gained an ally: psychiatrists began to assert that advances in their field gave them the skill to see inside a defendant's mind, reconstruct his state of mind when he had killed, and determine whether a mental aberration over which he had no control made him do it. Relying in part on these claims, the British Parliament opened a door to the prohibited irresistible-impulse defense when it passed the Homicide Act of 1957, the first in a series of laws that would limit, then abolish capital punishment. The new law embraced the concept of "diminished responsibility," which had been applied in Scotland for more than a century. According to the new law:

1. Where a person kills or is a party to the killing of another, he shall not be convicted of murder if he was suffering from such abnormality of mind (whether arising from a condition of arrested or retarded development of mind or any inherent causes or induced by disease or injury) as substantially impaired his mental responsibility for his acts and omissions in doing or being a party to the killing.

2. On a charge of murder, it shall be for the defense to prove that the person charged is by virtue of this section not liable to be convicted of murder.

3. A person who but for this section would be liable as principal or accessory, to be convicted of murder should be liable instead to be convicted of manslaughter.

Influenced, as they had often been in the past, by British legal precedents, U.S. courts adopted an American version of the diminished-responsibility concept—"diminished capacity"—that further legitimized the irresistible-impulse defense. Courts in more than half the states endorsed it, and psychiatrists claiming the ability to determine the state of mind of accused killers—often months or years after they had killed—became nearly as common at murder trials as lawyers. Trials were often battlegrounds between rival psychiatrists hired by the defense and prosecution lawyers. They frequently offered diametrically opposite opinions, depending who hired them. In California, Sirhan Sirhan blamed his decision to assassinate Robert F. Kennedy in 1968 on an irresistible impulse set off in part by bright lights. Ten years later, a San Francisco supervisor who killed the city's mayor and a fellow supervisor was acquitted of murder after a psychiatrist blamed his state of mind partly on eating too much junk food. The verdict of voluntary manslaughter touched off a riot in San Francisco. Three years later, there was an even louder uproar when John Hinckley, Jr., was found not guilty by reason of insanity for trying to assassinate President Ronald Reagan.

––––––––

There is a saying common among American criminal lawyers: "If you look long enough and pay enough, you can find a psychiatrist who will say anything you want about your client. Just keep asking psychiatrists until you find one who gives you the right answer."

This is not to say that psychiatrists, any more than other men and women, are necessarily venal or corrupt, although, for the ethically deficient, it is a calling where easy money awaits the hired gun, and hired guns are not hard to find. The problem is that psychiatry, like long-range weather forecasting and betting on the horses, is an inexact science, based largely on insight, experience, and informed guesses—not objective, scientific measurements. It is a field in which the opinions of "experts" can easily be shaded by vanity, ignorance, obstinacy, simple prejudices. It is a subbranch of medicine that the cunning malingerer has often found easy to manipulate. But, unfortunately, until something better comes along, psychiatrists are all the courts have to help them see into the minds of murderers.

––––––––

While policemen, lawyers, and psychiatrists prepared for his trial, Michael continued his once-a-week correspondence with Cheryl and Richard. His letters were filled with complaints about the police and prison life and plaintive expressions of fear about his future. In one, he wrote: "I look forward to the day when I can once again hear and feel the rumble of a Harley Davidson and lay back and go where and when and as far as I please. Have been caged like an animal or worse for 263 days. I wonder how much longer? I hope not much. . . ."

The letters grieved Cheryl.

He was in jail because of *her*. On the streets of London where she grew up, friends didn't "shop" their friends—didn't inform on them. Monika, her friend, was dead. There was nothing she could do to help her. But she could help Michael. During the months leading up to his trial, she wrote him often and, with Richard, visited him at Exeter Prison. It was the least she could do. "I felt partly to blame because he was in prison," she said years later. "I felt guilty for the part I played. It was like I had an obligation . . . he trusted me enough to tell me what he had done and yet I betrayed his trust in me when I handed him over to the police."

A few days before the trial, Michael wrote again to Cheryl and Richard. "I guess after my trial," he said, "I will know 101% who are my enemies and who are pretending to be friends and who really are my true friends."

"How do you plead?"

"My Lord, not guilty to murder, but guilty to manslaughter by reason of diminished responsibility."

The Crown rejected Michael's plea, and the trial began June 19, 1984.

VIII

Murder
When a person of sound memory and discretion
unlawfully killeth any reasonable creature in being,
and under the king's peace, with malice aforethought,
either express or implied.

SIR EDWARD COKE, *The Law of Life*

Justice, though due to the accused, is due to the
accuser also.

ASSOCIATE JUSTICE BENJAMIN N. CARDOZO

51.

After a bloody siege that lasted eighteen days, the people of Exeter capitulated to the invading army of William the Conqueror in 1068. To crown his conquest, the Norman duke built a huge stone castle on a hill overlooking the Exe River. By the spring of 1984, all that remained of Rougemont Castle was a mighty stone arch guarding the entrance to several colonnaded eighteenth-century buildings known collectively as "The Castle." There, since 1774, the judges of Great Britain had decided the fate of the accused in Devon.

Courtroom Number Two was a large room with a high ceiling that easily attracted the reluctant rays of the Devon sun. It soared more than twenty-five feet high, and at the top, above walls veneered with slabs of hardwood so neatly fitted they all seemed to have been cut from the same tree, were huge rounded windows. Presiding over the room from its highest point, wearing scarlet and black and a gray wig that curled down his neck like the pelt of an aging ram, was Sir John Gervase Sheldon of Kensington. As presiding judge of the Western Circuit of the High Court of Britain, he was called Mr. Justice Sheldon. Like most of Britain's high-court judges, he was male and elderly— a former barrister, public-school boy, Cambridge man, part of the establishment.

The opposing counsel introduced themselves:

George Carman, Q.C., was short, rounded, and fifty-four years old. He had a simple face largely hidden by tinted pink glasses with dark rims that at times gave him an owlish appearance. Without his silk gown and gray wig, it would have been easy to imagine him in an apron hovering behind the counter of a Dewhurst butcher shop, solicitously responding to a customer's request for a lean pork chop.

The handsome dark-haired man opposing him also wore a silk gown. He was Alan David Rawley, Q.C.—forty-nine, an Oxford graduate, once the commander of a British tank regiment. A Queen's Counsel since 1977, he was much less renowned than George Carman.

Under the British trial system, it was the obligation of the prosecutor to present the evidence in a neutral manner. In the broadest sense, it was not Rawley's duty to *win*, but simply to present the evidence collected by the police in an unbiased way and leave it to jurors to decide the truth.

In his opening statement, he read Michael's confession to the jury, then said it would be for them to decide, first, whether he was suffering from a mental abnormality when he murdered his wife, and, second, whether the abnormality was severe enough to absolve him of responsibility for it.

"The jury might think that anyone who kept a body rotting in a summer house must be out of their mind; anyone who cuts off a head must be out of their mind." But, he said, the facts of the case were more complex.

"It seems," Rawley continued, "that his wife was a rather difficult young woman." It also appeared that he had experienced emotional problems as a child and may even have been suffering a degree of mental impairment at the time he killed his wife. But when everything was put before them, Rawley said, the jurors may determine that Michael Telling had murdered his wife in cold blood in an act of intelligence and cunning and, in equally cunning fashion, took careful and elaborate steps to cover up his actions.

The first witness was Joe Stennings, the last person, other than Michael, to have seen Monika alive. He said he knew both of the Tellings, whom he had met at the public house called The Boot.

On the night before Monika entered a Buckinghamshire hospital for dental surgery, Rawley asked, "Do you remember whether anything was said by the deceased, Mrs. Telling, to her husband in your presence?"

"She mentioned about a gun that he may have bought."

"Can you remember what she said?" Rawley asked.

"She said, 'You bought a fucking gun.' "

Stennings had a thin, reedy voice, and his words echoed, as did most sounds in the cavernous courtroom, a few milliseconds after he spoke them, as if he were speaking inside a giant cave.

"Did he make any reply?"

"No, he just said, 'Don't be silly,' or words to that effect."

"How often did she mention this gun?"

"Over a period, two or three times."

"Did you ever hear him say whether he had got one or not?"

"No, he never said he had bought one."

As Rawley turned his attention to other matters, the judge and the jury, the reporters, and other spectators in the airy courtroom were left with the impression that Monika was referring to the .30.30-caliber Marlin rifle that was to take her life.

———

Stennings described for Rawley his recollections of Michael packing his suitcase for St. Andrew's: "We would be sitting there drinking tea or coffee, and there was a suitcase open in the other room, and he would go in to the bedroom, put one item into the bag, and chat, and then minutes later, he might go back and put in another item, and that is how it went on. Or he would change his mind and take something out."

"What was his attitude toward this packing, so far as you could tell?"

"That he did not want to do it."

"Did Mrs. Telling say anything to you, in Mr. Telling's presence, about what he was doing, or why?"

"She said, 'You have to go away and get sorted out,' or words to that effect."

Stennings next described his visit to Lambourn House the following morning, when Michael, still wearing a bathrobe, peered out at him from the top half of the Dutch door of the kitchen.

"What impression did you get about your presence there?" he was asked.

"That it was not wanted."

Rawley asked Stennings to summarize his opinion of the marriage of Michael and Monika Telling.

"They were always arguing or bickering about something. They were close, but they were always at loggerheads with one another, bickering . . . not really bad arguing, bickering."

"Was one more quarrelsome than the other in this bickering?"

"Yes."

"From your observations?"

"Monika did sometimes seem to pick on him more than she needed to, and saying the odd thing that was really not necessary. That is my opinion."

Rawley asked Stennings to describe Michael.

He was a "nice chap," but "seemed to wander off, thinking about other things or talking about other things. He did not take in what you said to him. If I explained about something, he would be interested for the first few seconds, and then wandered off mentally."

Stennings was not asked about his brief affair with Monika, and he did not volunteer anything about it.

———

George Carman rose to speak.

In Great Britain, it is the obligation of a barrister to raise every issue, advance every argument, ask every question that might help his client without purposely misleading the court. Nothing in the canons of his profession makes it unlawful or unethical to put the victim of a murder on trial.

George Carman now began his assault—on Michael's wife:

"Would it be right to say that he was a young man who clearly wanted to show affection to his wife?"

A few feet from him, Michael sat in a sleek pinstripe suit, sandwiched between two uniformed prison wardens.

"Yes," Stennings said.

"And, equally clearly, she began not to favor that or react to it."

"I would say equally as clearly."

"Is this fair, that he appeared to dote on her and she did not respond?"

"She mentioned things to him in my presence, how nice he was, and that sometimes he was too soft. She said he was kind and things like that."

Stennings' answer was more equivocal than Carman desired.

"You know that Monika was an *alcoholic*?"

"Yes."

"How long had you known that before March 1983?"

"I would say about a year previous."

"It was clearly something which caused Mr. Telling considerable concern, because he tried to stop her drinking?"

"Yes."

"And although he tried to stop her, she did not always agree, because she went her own way and drank when she should not?"

Another equivocal answer: "As far as I know, she knew the problem she had, and I do not think she would go out of her way to go to a pub, to take drink."

Carman changed the subject. He asked questions in a soft voice, placing an extra atom of emphasis on the words he most wanted the witness and jurors to hear.

"Did you know that she took *drugs?*"

"Yes."

"Did you ever hear her boast of her ability to get *cocaine?*"

"No."

"What drugs did you understand her to be taking?"

"Pills of different sorts. There were always a few bottles lying around."

"What about *cannabis?*"

"No."

A disappointing answer. Once again, Carman shifted gears: "Did you know that Monika was a *lesbian?*"

In an American court, the prosecutor in a murder case might have risen now to object to such an interrogation, with its implied assumptions about the victim of a crime. But Rawley was silent.

"No."

"Had you any *suspicions?*"

"No, none whatsoever."

Carman changed the subject again.

Was it true Monika Telling insisted that Michael admit himself to a psychiatric hospital?

"Yes."

"She mentioned this and said it in front of you?"

"Yes."

"It was not her habit to mince words with her husband on occasions?"

"No, not at all."

"Of the two, she was clearly the more dominant person."

"Yes, I would say so."

"More intelligent?"

"I do not know that."

Carman raised the temperature of his campaign to depict Monika as a shrew: "She really picked on him sometimes, more than was necessary in your presence?"

"I would not say 'picked on him,' but *bickering* with him. I would not say 'picked on him.' "

"*Critical* of him on occasions, would you say?"

"Yes."

"Did you know that Monika Telling refused to allow her husband to keep a dog?"

"No."

"He acquired the two dogs after what you now know was after her death in March 1983?"

"Yes."

"Clearly, he was very fond of the dogs."

"Yes."

Excused, Stennings left the witness box.

He had not given all the answers Carmen wanted, but the lawyer had had a victory of sorts: he had left the impression with the jury that Monika did not like dogs.

The next witness was Cheryl Richardson.

Interrogated at a casual pace by the prosecutor, she traced the evolution of her friendship with Monika and Michael, starting with her husband's meeting with him via the CB, through the drive home from Tesco's a year and a half later when he murmured that he had murdered Monika.

"Did you say anything?"

"I thought the guy had flipped his lid and I asked if he was kidding or words to that effect."

"What did he say?"

"He then told me no, it was true, and the body was stinking."

"Did he say where the body was?"

"Yes, in the sauna."

"Had you accepted it as serious?"

"No, I thought it was a sort of joke."

In the newspapers the next morning, it was not Cheryl's account of the trip from Tesco's, or Michael's admission that he had killed his wife, that most preoccupied the journalists at the trial. It was Cheryl's description of life in Lambourn House before Monika's death.

"Did Mrs. Telling smoke cigarettes?" Rawley inquired.

"Yes," Cheryl said.

"Did she smoke anything else?"

"Yes, what I would term as 'weed' but she said that it was cannabis."

"Did she take in other drugs, to your knowledge?"

"Cocaine."

"Did you ever see her doing it?"

"No." But Michael had told her about it after Monika's death, she said.

"What sort of temper did she have?"

"A very quick temper. She did not like a peaceful life. She liked especially with Michael to down him all the time."

"It was as though she enjoyed it, was it?"

"Sort of humiliating Michael in front of other people," Cheryl agreed. Sometimes she had taunted Michael about his sexual prowess.

Perhaps Americans in the courtroom would have found it odd to hear a prosecutor press ahead with questions maligning the victim of a brutal murder. But under British practice, the prosecutor was obligated to be neutral and pursue any evidence that helped the jury reach its verdict. Besides, as events would show, in this case, the prosecution and the defense had a common interest. He continued:

"Tell us about her sexual inclinations," Rawley asked. "Did you know anything about that?"

"Only that Monika confirmed to me that she was a lesbian. To quote her exact words, she said if she screwed me I would never want another man."

"Let us make it quite clear," Carman said during his cross-examination. "She, to your knowledge, took back girlfriends of a lesbian character in her husband's home while her husband was there?"

"Yes."

"And that is something of which she made no secret whatsoever."

"Not to him, she didn't."

"And you have personally witnessed her really enjoying *humiliating* Michael?"

"Yes," Cheryl said.

At the prosecution table, Rawley was silent.

Who spoke for the victim?

No one.

Cheryl, her testimony over, left the witness box. The following morning, the assault on Monika's character continued.

Like Cheryl, Richard Richardson portrayed Monika as a drunken, money-grubbing drug abuser and sexual deviant and Michael as a gentle man trapped in the snare of a shrew.

"Monika always wanted money. That was all she wanted," he said.

"So far as Michael Telling was concerned, did he appear to be affected from the dominance of his wife, frightened of his wife?"

"Oh, yes, very much so."

Carman asked him to elaborate.

"If she got a bruise on her leg, for instance, 'I will call the police' and 'I have been beaten' is what Monika would say. She went on about 'If he ever gets a gun, I will call the police, or 'If he does that, I will call the police.' She said, if Michael ever hurt her and put her in hospital, her father and mother would come from the States and sort him out. . . ."

Did anyone rise to challenge Richard or suggest that Monika had been motivated by a fear for her life? No, but Mr. Justice Sheldon looked down at him from the bench and asked: "You say, if she had a bruise, she threatened to call the police?"

"Yes."

"Was that a bruise that was inflicted by Michael?"

"All the bruise I saw on her was by her goose, because she did not give it water and it attacked her."

The answer drew laughter in the courtroom. Not only did the murder victim not like dogs, she hadn't treated her goose kindly, either.

"You have given My Lord and the jury quite a picture," Carman said as he approached the end of his cross-examination. "Does this summarize it fairly: that he is an emotional man, seeking affection, as you say?"

"Yes."

"And a rather lonely and insecure man?"

"Yes, very lonely and insecure."

Rawley posed only one question during his re-examination of Richard: "Can you tell us, did you ever see Mrs. Telling behave pleasantly towards her husband?"

"No, very seldom. I cannot remember any special occasion—oh, yes, when she wanted money."

———

The prosecutor called his fourth witness.

"You are Joyce Strong?" he said.

"Yes."

Michael's mother looked so frail as she entered the witness box that Mr. Justice Sheldon encouraged her to sit rather than stand while giving evidence.

"In February 1949, did you marry Henry Maxwell Telling?" Rawley asked.

"Yes."

"Your first husband?"

"Yes."

"On the seventeenth May 1950, did you have a son, Michael Henry Maxwell Telling, the defendant in this case?"

"Yes."

As the prosecutor led the witness through a chronology of her life and that of her only son, tears began to roll down Michael's cheeks and he poked one of his lawyers and handed him a note.

"When he was thirteen years of age . . . I think you married again, to Mr. Strong, in 1966?" Rawley continued.

"Yes," his mother answered.

"At the end of 1969, you and your husband moved to Sydney, Australia, where you live now?"

"Yes."

George Carman stared at the note that had been handed to him: "You get mum away from this awful trial or I will get up, let the bloody prossquter here [sic] what I think off."

Carman rose to speak:

"My Lord, I have a message from the defendant. Would Your Lordship indulge me for ten minutes?"

"Certainly," the judge said, and he adjourned the trial for a recess.

Michael was still crying.

52.

Joyce Vestey did not marry until several months after her twenty-eighth birthday. Sadly, when at last she had her chance, she did not make a wise choice.

The eldest daughter of Captain Leonard Vestey, late of the Royal Field Artillery, third son of the first Baron Vestey, grew up in what she called a sheltered world of nannies and governesses, of enormous wealth and vast family estates. She was born in 1920, a year and two weeks after her father returned from World War I and married her mother, Hilda Thompson, of Grays, Essex. He was a rogue and wild in his life, and when Joyce was six, he ran off with his mistress, abandoning her mother, a nervous and insecure woman who never remarried and died of lung cancer at fifty-four.

Although Joyce Vestey was not extraordinarily pretty, fate had made her a woman of great wealth. Still, there does not appear to have been a long line of suitors pressing their case on her. Her sister, Elizabeth, who was three years younger than Joyce, married at twenty-three.

When she did marry, on February 16, 1949, it was to an executive who worked for the Vestey family. Although Henry Willis Maxwell Telling married well, it was not a happy union. Shortly after the wedding, Joyce discovered he was the prisoner of a prodigious drinking problem. If she complained about his drinking, she said, he became a violent and mean man.

On May 17, 1950, their only child, Michael Henry Maxwell Telling, was born after a difficult pregnancy. He weighed only five and a half pounds, and as an infant was unusually vulnerable to illnesses. She nursed him briefly, then turned him over to the first of what would be a long succession of nursemaids and governesses. He lived with his nannies in a separate suite of the family's London mansion, far from his parents' rooms, but he could still hear their relentless, sometimes violent combat. Among his first memories, he told a psychiatrist, was that of trying to intervene in one of their battles—an undersized toddler rising to protect his mother from his father's assault.

Michael saw little of his mother and received neither solace nor attention from his alcoholic father. He was reared in a household impoverished of affection except for the small amount he could coax from the nannies who entered and left his life with the regularity of express trains.

Early on, his mother said, Michael was a good baby, but later he became very difficult. He didn't like being cuddled and was a fidgety, nervous child—especially after he overheard still another quarrel between his parents, his nursemaid took a day off, or, worse, a new girl arrived to replace one to whom he had grown attached.

Shortly after Michael was born, Joyce Telling abandoned him emotionally, distancing herself from him and giving him neither love nor attention. Why? Perhaps it had something to do with the role models she herself had observed during her privileged but difficult childhood; perhaps she was reacting to a painful pregnancy. Perhaps the innate instincts of motherhood were overwhelmed by the challenges of trying to endure a horrible marriage; or perhaps a shy and coddled woman from a rarefied world, in confronting the downside of life for the first time, simply turned her back on a child she found hard to love.

Michael had just turned two when Joyce Telling divorced her husband. Although she was awarded custody of Michael, she conveyed it to the lengthening procession of nursemaids, nannies, and au-pair girls from Germany who became the women in his life, however briefly. Between the ages of two and four, Michael did not eat a single meal with his mother; at most, she saw him an hour a day. He spent virtually the entirety of his life with his young nannies, who trundled him in a perambulator back and forth on London sidewalks, under orders from his mother to keep him away from home as long as they could.

The rare moments he spent with his mother often ended in tantrums. If he suspected she was going to abandon him again, he ran to his room and threw furniture and toys out the window to persuade her to stay. She learned to leave the house quietly and lie to him about her plans.

When he was five, shortly after his diabetes was diagnosed, Michael's mother sent him to a nursery school, and he saw even less of her. He attended North Bridge House in St. John's Wood until he was six and a half, when he was forced to leave because teachers were unable to break him of his habit of chasing classmates with lighted matches. A psychologist told his mother he threw the matches at his playmates because he was seeking her love and attention.

In June 1957, Michael's mother moved to Dulwich, a village favored by the well-to-do at the rim of metropolitan London; three months later, she sent Michael to Pinehurst, a boarding school in rural Kent. He was seven years old. Within a week, doctors were summoned to the school by an emergency: Michael had broken into the tuck-shop, raided its stock of candy and cakes, and induced a diabetic coma. When he was conscious, he demanded to be sent home, but his mother said he had to remain at school. He induced a second diabetic coma, but this also failed to persuade her.

A cunning mind, born of a desperation perhaps found only among the forsaken, was in the making; Michael began trying other stratagems designed to get his mother to let him come home. The next time he broke into the tuck-shop, instead of sweets he stole cash for bus fare home, where he told his mother the school had been destroyed by a fire. After confirming that Pinehurst was still very much intact, she said he had to go back. Michael ran out the door, took off his clothes, and threw himself down on the road in the path of oncoming cars, only to run out of the way seconds before they hit him.

That didn't work, either, and his mother sent him back to Pinehurst. During the next two years, he repeatedly ran away from the school, but each time she returned him. He also escaped to the homes of his grandmother and Aunty Liz; they, too, said he had to go back to school.

Pinehurst School, whose campus was a large Victorian house in the Kentish countryside, had a dozen or so boarders and half again as many day-boys. Its specialty was helping troubled boys from well-off families turn their lives around.

In their youthful slang, British schoolboys have a nickname for thin, weak-looking classmates—"weed." The boys at Pinehurst used this term to describe Michael. Slightly built, undersized for his age, needing twice-a-day insulin injections, he was not clever at sports, and was more vulnerable than most of his classmates to minor illnesses. From the first day, he hated the place. Miss Feek, the headmistress, quickly became convinced he was a malingerer who feigned illness in order to gain her pity; therefore, she offered little of it, even when it may have been deserved. She told Michael's mother that he was an artful and manipulative liar willing to say or do anything to get his way.

Michael made few friends at Pinehurst, and most of them, one classmate observed later, "tended to be friends in name only." The classmate said his diminutive size and status as the wealthiest boy at the school made him vulnerable to predatory older boys. Frail and weak, he was bullied relentlessly. Once several boys ordered him to roll around in a bed of thorns before they would let him play a game. He was bloodied from head to toe, but still they wouldn't let him play. To raise cash to pay the tribute demanded by the bigger boys, he pilfered his mother's purse, and stole to buy cigarettes; by nine, he was a heavy smoker. There was one bright passage for him during his years at Pinehurst: unexpectedly, his father visited and took him out for a meal—his first attempt to establish a relationship with his son. But after another visit or two, Michael again lost contact with his father.

When Michael went home on term holidays, he didn't find love, either. He and his mother quarreled more than ever. Every time she said he had to go back to school, he exploded in a violent temper tantrum, kicking and swearing at her, hurling toys and furniture out the window. So often did he do this, she said later, that she stripped his room bare except for a simple bed and a chair.

After he had tried without success for two years to persuade his mother to let him come home, Michael took the matter into his own hands. One night, while his classmates were asleep, he crept out of bed and set fire to a stack of mattresses stored beneath the staircase. The headmistress awoke as flames raced up the staircase, and the blaze was extinguished before reaching the other boys' bedrooms, but, the next day, Michael got his wish: he was expelled from Pinehurst, and his mother had to let him come home. At home, however, his troubles continued. During an argument with the local vicar's daughter, he broke a milk bottle over her head—after one spat with his mother, he drank half a bottle of sherry—after another, he took four carving knives from the kitchen to his room and, when she asked for them, threatened to kill her with one.

A few weeks later—on June 7, 1960—Michael's mother, on the advice of a psychologist, admitted him to Maudsley Hospital in South London, perhaps England's foremost psychiatric clinic. He passed into adolescence in the ward of this hospital, having virtually no contact with the world beyond it. Psychologists who tested him said he was of above-average intelligence but possessed few fundamental reading, writing, or mathematical skills—nor, they said, did he have much self-esteem, although on the surface he was self-centered and egocentric. His doctors said Michael had a "low tolerance of frustration," got along poorly with fellow patients, and was suspicious and mistrustful of them, because he believed other children were interested in him only for his money.

Twenty-seven months after he entered Maudsley Hospital, Michael's doctors decided he had improved sufficiently to leave and attend a special boarding school for maladjusted boys. But less than five months later, he returned to Maudsley after a stormy schoolterm and a disastrous Christmas visit home. The registrar who readmitted him wrote.

Transferred from his boarding school from which he had been expelled on day before admission.

Present complaint: Continual thieving, will not submit to any form of authority. Violent behaviour—smashes things if he cannot get his own way.

Present status: Eating habits, faddy. Tendency to disregard diabetic diet. Recently difficult about going to bed . . . unhappy, aggressive, recently threatened mother with a knife. One friend, Alistair, with whom he gets on, except if a third person present. Has taken a great dislike to present au pair girl and calls her names. Jealous of mother. Anti-social behaviour. In holidays broke things up at home until threatened with police by mother. Disobedient. Steals money from home. Swears. Smokes 'like a chimney.' Having great difficulty in concentrating.

Progress at school: poor until finally expelled for stealing, tantrums and truanting.

Family and social history: little change since last admission. Father on even worse terms with his family.

Mental examination: cheeky, petulant manner. Initially friendly but soon loses interest. Anxious about possibility his mother does not want him.

During Michael's second residency at Maudsley, a male nurse took an interest in him and for a few months introduced a father figure into his life. His doctors decided he had improved enough to send him to the William Penn Comprehensive School in London as a day-boy while he continued to sleep at the hospital. The experiment was more successful than several of the psychiatrists expected, probably, they concluded, because his visits home were kept to a minimum. According to the hospital's records, his mother said she was "completely unable to tolerate his behaviour" and didn't want him at home, even on summer holidays, when he was dispatched to a London County Council boarding school.

When Michael was released a second time from Maudsley Hospital, September 7, 1963, the psychiatrist who had supervised his care was cautiously optimistic:

Condition on Discharge: Very much improved. Looking forward to Boarding School and a continuation at the William Penn School.

Prognosis: Very uncertain but may mature over the years given the opportunity of a stable environment. Long term treatment by psycho-analysis was discussed but a final decision not taken.

Diabetes controlled.

Further action: Out-patient appointments for Michael. This is particularly important if he is taken on for analysis as he may act out during this course and require readmission to Hospital.

At thirteen, instead of returning to the William Penn School, Michael entered Bredinghurst, like Pinehurst a boarding school for troubled boys. He remained almost five years, despite a record of poor adjustment to the school. His doctor has said, "He found it difficult to trust other people and always thought they were trying to exploit him," and he also had "a chip on his shoulder about his diabetes because it meant that he would be unable to join the army or the navy."

At thirteen, he already understood the special status of his family in England and was aware of the expectations imposed on its young members. Male Vesteys were part of Britain's ruling class; they were expected to attend Oxford or Cambridge, enter the Scots Guards, have a life of accomplishment. He had watched some of his relatives fulfill these expectations. Christopher, the cousin to whom he was closest, attended a respected public school before going on to Oxford. But for Michael there was no chance of that. At sixteen, he scored disastrously on examinations that might have assured him a place at a university and experienced still another disappointment when his mother married Thomas Hugh Strong, a diplomat and a specialist on agricultural development, and the couple moved to Africa, where he was posted.

Michael left Bedinghurst School at eighteen but would not become a full-fledged beneficiary of the Vestey Settlement for another three years. His mother sent him money while he lived in a London hostel and bought him expensive cars and other toys. Perhaps he hoped for a job at one of the Vestey companies, but, aside from his medical history, the family discouraged nepotism. William and Edmund Vestey had established that policy, as they had planned virtually everything about the global enterprise they left behind. Inviting all future sons and grandsons into the business, they concluded, would produce recurrent power struggles and family feuds that would undermine the company. They had seen other great British family businesses disabled by warfare between rival factions of the founders' descendants. Their solution was to establish a narrow line of succession in the business while providing generously for all future members of the family.

Poorly educated, without a trade, unable to carry on a family tradition of military service or follow the route to Oxford or Cambridge expected of him, Michael drifted. His first job, selling menswear in a department store, ended after six months when he was dismissed for theft. Subsequent jobs were even briefer. When he was nineteen, his mother and stepfather moved to Australia, where the Vesteys owned cattle stations almost as large as some British counties, and Michael followed, arriving in Sydney a few days before his twentieth birthday.

For a time, his life was tranquil and marked by a level of success that had eluded him before. He found work on a transformer-factory assembly line, then at an automobile-parts plant. He became an Australian citizen, attended a technical college, and was promoted to foreman. Then things started to go wrong again. In 1973, he met a Roman Catholic girl who was pregnant because of a rape. He fell in love with her and doted on her during her pregnancy, expecting to marry her. But after her baby was born, she turned him down, and

Michael took an overdose of sleeping pills that put him in a Sydney psychiatric hospital.

A year later, he was rejected by another young woman, induced another diabetic coma, and was unconscious for two days. In each case, he told his doctors that he hadn't intended to kill himself but had hoped to gain the sympathy of the women who spurned him.

At twenty-six, Michael lost the foreman's job during an economic retrenchment and moved four thousand miles across Australia to Perth. Still without a skill or a trade, he worked at odd jobs, none lasting more than a few weeks, and after a while gave up looking for work altogether and began devoting all his time to his toys—guns, motorcycles, CB radio, and reading about soldiers of fortune. He didn't need a job. His bills were paid faithfully each month by trustees of the Vestey Settlement. In Perth, Michael met Alison Ruth Webber, a plain—some would say homely—eighteen-year-old immigrant from England who worked as a waitress. He told her he was a veteran of the Vietnam War and showed her his uniform. He also confided he was a member of a secret, elite British commando unit, the SAS. In April 1977, after five months of dating, they moved in together; a year later, they were married. Soon after that, with Alison pregnant, they moved to England, where the trustees of the Vestey Settlement bought them a home in Devon, near Alison's hometown of Torquay, and their son, Matthew, was born.

In October 1980, Michael flew to California to buy a Harley-Davidson.

53.

"I hope you understand that I have to try to return back in some detail to Michael's early life and his first marriage," George Carman inquired deferentially of the woman whose family would pay his bill.

"I hope you understand it is necessary to do that?" he repeated as he began his cross-examination of Michael's mother.

"Yes," she said.

During the recess, Michael had regained his composure. He sat between his guards looking impassively at his mother.

"Your maiden name is Vestey?"

"Yes."

"And you are the granddaughter of the first Lord Vestey?"

"Yes . . ."

Outdoors, the temperature was climbing into the seventies. Indoors, beneath the vaulted ceiling and huge Georgian windows that flooded the courtroom with sunlight, it was becoming very warm. Many reporters and spectators were in shirtsleeves as the dark-robed, bewigged defense lawyer continued the interrogation begun by the prosecutor, which had taken Joyce Vestey Telling Strong chronologically through her financially secure and pampered childhood, her marriages, and the early life of her son.

"I do not want to say this in any way critically," Carman said, "but, so far as that young child was concerned, you really found it very hard to cope as his mother when he was very young?"

"Yes," she said.

"And without in any way attributing blame, because of your marriage problems and because of Michael's own character, it seems there was no real affection possible between you and him when he was a young child?"

"No," she said.

"Is that right?"

"That is right."

"His own father did not show him affection."

"No."

Was it a true statement, Carman asked, that as a young mother she had been "too distressed by those problems—and I do not use this unkindly—but either unable to cope or thought it best to leave it to the nanny or nursemaid?"

"Yes."

Carman had a voice that rose and fell with subtle nuances that could express surprise, sympathy, contempt, and other emotions with the seamless ease of an actor. Under his gentle prodding, Michael's mother continued to affirm that she had given her child no love and abandoned him emotionally. Sometimes he repeated questions in different words, to reinforce the impact of an answer he wanted to inscribe in the minds of jurors.

"I suppose, looking back on those early years of his life, you would accept that he was clearly a boy, a young boy, deprived of affection and love?"

"Yes."

"Do you think he resented the fact that he was not achieving success in life compared with the other, very distinguished members of his family? Was something of a failure?"

"Yes," she said, continuing her half of the colloquy with monosyllables.

Looking occasionally at the jury to alert them that they were listening to something pathetic and affecting, but seldom at the defendant, Carman elicited still more descriptions of Michael's lonely childhood from his mother, then indicated he was coming to the end of the cross-examination:

"I think you, of your own voluntary accord, flew from Australia before this trial in order to be here."

"Yes."

"And you have seen Michael Telling in prison on a number of occasions in recent days and weeks?"

"Yes."

"Have you seen more of him now than you have for virtually the whole of his life, while he has been in prison?"

"I have seen a lot of him."

"Can I put it this way: have you got to know him better in the last twelve months than ever you knew him before?"

"Yes."

"When you visited him in prison, has he shown you affection?"

"Yes."

"Have you felt yourself able readily to respond or not?"

"Yes, I have felt able."

"Is that mutual affection something which was lacking and absent when he was a young child?"

"Yes."

After Michael's mother walked slowly from the witness box, the prosecution resumed the presentation of its case. The proprietor of a High Wycombe carpet-cleaning firm testified that Michael had summoned him to Lambourn House in April to remove a large stain from the living-room carpet. Police forensic experts said they had found bloodstains at this location beneath the carpet, elsewhere in the house, and in the summer house. A telephone repairman said he had seen a rifle in its case while making a service call at Lambourn House in June. Apprentice locksmith Simon Bonner described Michael's orders to make his house impregnable. Colin Marshall, the plumber who had briefly been a murder suspect, described the discovery of Monika's body. Alison Telling testified about her unsuccessful marriage to Michael and described his gift of Monika's jewelry shortly before her body was found. Jeff Henthorne and other policemen described Michael's arrest and confession and the discovery of Monika's head in his car. Her dental surgeon confirmed that the teeth found in the Haldon Hills were Monika's. Two executives of Lloyd's Bank said her bank account had been emptied after her death. Private eye Colin Finlay described his visit to Lambourn House and Michael's instructions to find his missing wife. Linda Blackstock and Susan Bright described their affairs with Michael and how he had attempted to make love to them at Lambourn House while, unbeknownst to them, his wife's decaying body was in the sauna. A twenty-one-year-old college student, Julie Chamberlain, testified that she had visited Monika at Lambourn House and said they had smoked marijuana, "kissed and fondled," and spent the night in a lovemaking encounter that was unsatisfying to both of them. David Wallis and Christine Percy described the arguments between Michael and Monika when they lived in Tunbridge Wells, including Michael's destruction of the banister; David said Michael had once told him he would kill Monika if she ever left him.

Each time he cross-examined a witness, Carman sought to shift jurors' attention from killer to victim. If a witness resisted his efforts to malign Monika, he repeated his questions until something disparaging was said about her.

A reporter for the *Bucks Free Press* wrote:

> From the start of the trial a week ago, it has been Monika Telling, not Michael, who has been stalked by one of the great legal minds in the world, George Carman QC. One by one the witnesses come forward to tell in their various ways of the brief periods when their lives touched those of the star-crossed Tellings. To begin with they are led through their evidence by the counsel prosecuting for the Crown, Alan Rawley QC, a squirelike figure, gregarious and generously built. Then, quietly, Mr. Carman rises to consider again and again what they have said. He's a small man, owl-like in profile, a tiny white scar on his left cheek, beautifully spoken. . . . He never refers to Michael Telling as the accused, never looks at him sitting behind the serried ranks of lawyers, flanked by two prisoner warders. No, to everyone, Mr. Carman talks of Michael this and Michael that. As the hours pass, you—and probably the jury—begin to think of him as someone close, an acquaintance of some standing. It is a lawyer's trick, one of his many, and you marvel at his skill. . . .

The previous autumn, after a member of one of Britain's most privileged families had been accused of murdering his American wife and chopping her head off, the British press had gone into a frenzy. It was now delirious over the testimony depicting her as a drunken, fortune-hunting bisexual. For more than a week, the trial knocked lesser stories off the front pages. Overnight the unidentified wife of a solicitor from Tunbridge Wells who, it was reported, had had a torrid love affair with Monika, became the most infamous mystery woman in

England. Brian Rundle was offered £20,000 for a photograph she had taken of Monika in a bathtub with a plastic duck. "The photograph revealed nothing," Rundle told his wife. "She was naked, but it wasn't revealing. You couldn't see anything."

If the tabloids couldn't buy salacious information, they offered it up nevertheless: Monika carried a gun; she beat Michael with a whip; she had a strange sexual fetish for plastic ducks; she rode naked into her wild parties at Lambourn House atop one of Michael's thunderous Harley-Davidsons; she trained her cockatoo to spit and swear at him and refused to sleep with him while taking so many other men and women to her bed—noble and commoners alike, none of whom were identified—that if all the stories were true the queue could have encircled Buckingham Palace. One article began: " 'Monika was evil,' says a woman who claims to be an ex-lover. 'She had only one aim in mind with whoever she touched. That was to destroy them—to wreck their lives.' " Another newspaper summarized the journalistic circus:

> It would be an exaggeration to call this the murder trial of the century but certainly few have contained so many ingredients of a blood 'n' lust best seller. There in the dock sits a chubby, rather timid man, Michael Telling, the rejected and stunted sprig of a mighty family tree. Grandson of the incredibly wealthy first Lord Vestey, he was born with a silver albatross about his neck. . . . [He married] a pleasant, everyday woman, unable, as she put it, to shoulder the responsibility of being a husband and a father. Then, from her safe arms, he drops into the talons of a woman who has surely became one of the most celebrated wicked ladies in the history of British jurisprudence—his second wife, Monika.

No one—least of all the prosecutor—spoke up for Monika.

His task was to convict Michael. And in George Carman's relentless and uncompromising campaign to portray her as a slut and a shrew, the prosecution and the defense had a common interest: according to the prosecution, it gave Michael a motive for premeditated murder; according to the defense, it simply gave Michael an excuse to kill her.

54.

"How did he present to you as a psychologist?" Rawley asked Dr. John Hamilton.

"My initial impression was that he was an extremely talkative man and it was difficult to get him to stop talking. The essence of his talking was to portray himself in the best possible light and to portray Monika—his victim—in the worst possible light."

"Was he cooperative?"

"Yes, by and large, and he generally answered all the questions I asked him, although at times he tended to steer the conversation the way he wanted it to go, rather than the way I wanted it to go. I do not feel at all times he was necessarily truthful to the questions I was asking him."

What about the testimony we have heard, Rawley asked, that he was deprived of affection as a child and suffered emotionally because of it?

Although the defendant did have a troubled childhood, Hamilton said, several strengths had been overlooked at the trial. As a child, he had received care at one of England's best psychiatric hospitals, and there was evidence that the treatment there had helped him. In Australia, he had successfully held a job for several years, been promoted

265

to foreman, and had completed work at a technical college. "He was not, in later life, a total failure in many ways."

"Did he tell you anything about the killing itself?"

"Yes, he did. He told me that he had made up his mind to kill his wife quite some time before he actually did it. He told me that it was really in two stages: there was a time when he decided that he would kill her, and he told me there was a time when he decided exactly when and how he would kill her.

"He said the first stage was when the couple were in the hotel in London together, the Hyde Park Hotel, on the day when Monika had returned home but had instructed him to remain in the hotel . . . so he would go direct to the psychiatric hospital the next day for the outpatient appointment. He decided, he said, on the Monday afternoon, the day after Monika had returned from her appointment, that he would kill her the next morning. . . ."

"Monday, being the twenty-eighth?"

"Yes."

"He would kill her the next morning?"

"Yes, and he would do it by shooting her."

Like Carman, Rawley used repetition to engrave in the jurors' minds the images he most wanted to establish: Did you say that the defendant, Michael Telling, *admitted* to you that he decided to kill Monika when they were at the Hyde Park Hotel almost *three days* before he actually did it?

Hamilton nodded affirmatively.

At the hotel, he said, Michael had become increasingly upset with Monika because she continued to insist he re-enter St. Andrew's. He claimed she had belittled him and "made him feel resentment and angry towards her and made him decide to kill her."

"How do you regard the information he gave to you about his decision-making processes?" Rawley asked.

Based on his interviews with the defendant, Hamilton said he believed Michael was fully capable of making rational judgments and controlling his impulses.

"Let us come to the shooting itself," Rawley said. "We know that three shots were fired. We know that the gun is a lever-action rifle and has to be cocked between each shot. The fact that three shots were fired and each time the rifle is cocked before it is fired, does that indicate anything to you?"

"Again, knowing or believing what Mr. Telling told me, that there had been a time between when he decided to kill his wife and when he did it, even if that were not the case, I believe if it had been an impulsive heat-of-the-moment action the firing of the first shot might have brought him to his senses, as it were. But the cocking of the rifle three times underlines to me the cold-blooded, calculated way in which he killed her."

Rawley paused a moment to let the words "cold-blooded, calculated" echo on the courtroom. Then he retraced Michael's actions after he had shot Monika: using her Cashpoint card to create a trail of false evidence—hiding her body in the sauna—installing new locks at Lambourn House—hiring a private detective to find her. . . .

These were the acts of a rational man, Hamilton said, not those of one suddenly overtaken by emotions he was powerless to control. "In general, I formed the opinion that the whole matter of keeping the body, and the final disposal of it, was a cold-blooded, calculated, and clever cover-up," he said. "I think this is evident in many of the different aspects of the case that we have heard over the last few days: this ranges from the careful way in which the small matters, such as the cleaning of the carpets in the house—installing an electric air freshener to get rid of the smell—engaging a private detective to look for his supposed[ly] missing wife—the withdrawal of his wife's cash by means of her cash card, which started on the evening of the day he killed her—the way in which he dismantled and disposed of the rifle and later the ax—the method in which he finally disposed of the corpse with the removal of the head to prevent, I think, detection, and when he did have the head back home, to insert maggots. . . ."

George Carman suddenly interrupted:

"That is not in evidence in this court. The doctor appears to be referring to evidence given in this court, and there is no evidence."

The judge agreed: "There is no evidence in the parts of the forensic evidence that was read to the jury referring to maggots. . . ."

Rawley agreed, too. He produced a file, offered it as evidence, and handed it to the witness.

"Read it," he told Hamilton. "Tell us what the information is. . . ."

It was a report written by one of the two psychiatrists who were waiting to testify for the defense. According to the report, Hamilton said, Michael had told the psychiatrist that when he took Monika's body to Devon in a rented van he also took an assortment of fishing gear for the purpose of establishing an alibi if one was needed to justify the trip.

"Telling had some maggots with him for use as bait on the fishing trip," Hamilton continued. "The maggots, of course, were not used, and when he had returned home with the head in a plastic bag, he tipped the maggots into the bag containing the head, hoping that this would speed up the decomposition of the head to reduce it to a skeleton."

This additional evidence convinced Hamilton that the defendant was a cunning and clever man, and contradicted what he had told a detective after his arrest—that he had kept Monika's head because he couldn't bear to leave all of her in Devon and wanted part of her with him always in West Wycombe. This claim, Hamilton said, was discredited by the fact he took an ax and plastic bags to carry the head in when he left West Buckinghamshire. And if Michael had really felt such a devotion to his dead wife, he wouldn't have taken two women to her bed and or given them some of her belongings.

"Do you take the view that Mr. Telling is insane?" the prosecutor asked.

"No, I believe he is not insane, and I do not believe his mental condition in any way borders on insanity."

He had an "abnormality of mind," Hamilton said, but it was a "personality disorder of moderate degree."

Attempting to close the escape hatch Michael was tying to use to flee a murder conviction—the diminished-responsibility provision of the Homicide Act of 1957—Rawley asked: "Did that personality disorder, as at the time of the killing, substantially impair Mr. Telling's mental responsibility in doing the acts in the killing?"

"No," Hamilton said. "I believe, although he had an abnormality of mind, this was not such an abnormality of mind as substantially to impair his mental responsibility for his acts."

Mr. Justice Sheldon spoke up: "Let me get this, as I understand the position: he did have a personality disorder but it was one of moderate degree?"

"Yes."

"Does that mean, the judge continued, that you believe his personality disorder was not severe enough to substantially impair his actions under the Homicide Act of 1957?

"Yes," Hamilton said.

Following a recess, George Carman began his cross-examination of the psychiatrist.

55.

After two hours of blistering combat, the duel between the witness and his interrogator had been reduced to two words: "substantially impaired." John Hamilton agreed that Michael had an "abnormality of mind," but was adamant that it was not severe enough to impair his reasoning "substantially" or seize control of his will power when he killed his wife. Michael's fate was wrapped in subtle distinctions between words that drifted ambiguously between the precincts of law and psychiatry—"moderate," "substantial," "severe," "profound"—words with meanings as vague as they were crucial to the Homicide Act of 1957.

It was a topic Hamilton knew something about. At Broadmoor, he had researched the role troubled childhoods play in shaping the adult psyche of murderers and was the author of a theory, soon to be published by the British Association for the Advancement of Science, that attributed Adolf Hitler's monstrous crimes partly to a tyrannical and brutish father who had left him with an "insatiable hatred." Hamilton believed that a tortured childhood could reach into the adult mind and make it do horrible things. But he said his interviews with Michael Telling had convinced him that the defendant was a cunning, selfish,

and manipulative man who had killed his wife with malice aforethought and possessed the will to stop himself from pulling the trigger.

His voice echoing so loudly across the upper reaches of the courtroom that it might have been amplified electronically, Carman asked
sarcastically: "Do you regard a man who leaves his wife's body to rot for
five months, then takes it to Devon, cuts off its head, brings it back
home, then confesses, is anything other than *abnormal?*"

"He is an abnormal man, but with a moderate personality disorder."

Given the defendant's background, Carman continued, wasn't it
predictable that "something may go seriously wrong in his adult life?"

"I would not necessarily say that. I think I would have thought he
would have to resolve the situation, perhaps by leaving his wife and
getting a divorce, or finding some way of escaping from the situation."

Carman circled his target with the courtliness of a matador, appearing gracious while searching for vulnerability. He required Hamilton
to retrace the details of Michael's upbringing, once again laying before
jurors the circumstances of his lonely youth, then asked: "In William
Wordsworth's words, 'The child is father to the man,' and in broad
terms, that is an accepted principle of psychology, is it not?"

"I will answer that question with saying 'yes,' without implying
anything else by agreeing to that question," Hamilton said.

"The seeds of how we behave in adult life are sown in our infancy?"

"Yes."

"And the seeds of how we behave in our adult life, if sown in
infancy, depend upon two things in infancy and early childhood—
one, what we inherit from our parents, which is known as the genetic
inheritance?"

"Yes," Hamilton agreed.

"And two, how we are brought up—namely, the environment in
which we live and operate as small children."

"Yes."

Didn't the childhood of Michael Telling "reveal, on close analysis,
a child who was most profoundly disturbed?"

"Yes, he was disturbed."

"That was not the words I put to you. He was most profoundly
disturbed?"

"He was profoundly disturbed," Hamilton said.

As Carman continued his inquisition, Michael sipped from a cup of
water and sifted through a pile of documents. Occasionally, he scrib-

bled a note and handed it to one of the several lawyers queued behind Carman, the famous advocate's supporting cast.

"The red light was there to be seen by anybody who had any knowledge of children?" Carman asked.

"And the red light was seen," Hamilton said.

"I will come to that," Carman said.

"Let me come to this other fact in Michael Telling's life," Carman said. "At twenty-one, he became, as you know, a beneficiary under the Vestey Trust?"

"Yes."

"That family is a byword for distinction, integrity, success, and wealth, and high standing socially in this country. Would you accept that?"

"I am afraid I know very little about the Vestey family."

"Will you accept from me and what you know of the case that it is quite clear that the family were extremely wealthy?"

"I certainly understand that."

"Did it ever cross your mind that this young man, who had suffered from emotional deprivation in the way we have mentioned, might resent his relationship with that family and feel himself to be something of a failure?"

Hamilton said that, though it was true Michael considered himself a failure, "I am not sure how it can be related to the family."

"Would Hamilton agree," Carman pressed, "that money for him was very much of a mixed blessing?"

"It certainly turned out to be."

"Because money and wealth are no substitute for emotional security? And money without emotional security may provide greater insecurity than normal?"

"I am not sure what you mean," Hamilton said.

"If someone has not got emotional security but has to go and earn their living and working in the ordinary world from day to day, then they may be forced to try and mix in socially in a work situation?"

"Yes."

"But if money can enable you to remain isolated and enable you not to work, then in a case such as Michael Telling, this is a handicap?"

"I would agree."

After Michael came into the world burdened with a tarnished silver spoon in his mouth, didn't something worse happen to him when

Monika entered his life? "In retrospect, wasn't it a grave misfortune in his life to fall in love [with] and be attracted by Monika?"

"In retrospect, yes," Hamilton said.

"Because it is very obvious, is it not, that the mix of this fun-seeking, drug-taking, sexually promiscuous Californian was, for Michael Telling, the very worst sort of mix in marriage?"

"That is right."

"And the marriage to Monika and her attitude to him would, of necessity, reactivate the tensions he had endured earlier in his life?"

"At times, yes," Hamilton said, "but at other times I believe she was affectionate and caring and acted very responsibly to him and for him."

Carman did not allow anything to be said charitably about the woman he had put on trial. His response was full of scorn: "Have you heard all the evidence from this witness box that has been given this week?"

"I believe so."

Hadn't several witnesses testified that Monika had *taunted* Michael about his sexual prowess, belittled him, ridiculed him?

"Yes," Hamilton said, "but I heard other witnesses say she was not quite like that all the time." Indeed, he was skeptical about some of the things he'd heard about Monika. Some witnesses sympathetic to Michael might have shaded their testimony, he implied. "I think what I have heard from the witness box is a series of scraps of what happened," Hamilton said.

Skipping not a beat, Carman ignored Hamilton's effort to inject more balance into the dialogue.

"It was a brief marriage—November 1981 until her death in March 1983," he said. "We are talking of some fifteen or sixteen months. The taunts and the humiliation would operate more upon a person with a personality disorder than they would upon the normal healthy man?"

"Yes, I am sure of that," Hamilton conceded.

"Quite apart from the taunting and humiliation," Carman continued, "periodic suggestions that he is 'mental' and requires mental treatment—that, again, would be a matter that would humiliate and distress a person with the personality of Michael Telling?"

"I do not necessarily think so," Hamilton said. There was considerable evidence that indicated Monika had tried to persuade Michael to return to the hospital for his own good, simply because she had cared for him. "It is not that she said, 'You need treatment and go and get it,' but she went with him to help him get treatment."

Again someone had suggested that Monika was not Carman's caricature of evil: once again he refused to let it pass unridiculed. "But insofar as those matters on which the jury have heard in great detail, and we have had quite a lot from people who know them, so far as the picture presents itself, you would agree it was the worst possible remedy or medicine for someone with a personality of Michael Telling" to be married to someone like Monika?

"I think that it did not do him a great deal of good."

"Is that not a little bit of English understatement?" the Q.C. mocked.

"I am sorry . . . but I did not hear from the witnesses describing a great deal of suffering on his part as a result of these things," Hamilton answered, standing his ground.

Carman turned to Hamilton's most damaging statement: that Michael had told him he had decided to kill Monika several days before pulling the trigger that cut her down at Lambourn House. It was the linchpin of the prosecution's case for premeditation and malice aforethought.

Holding Hamilton's report and the handwritten notes he had made during the interviews with Michael, Carman said he couldn't find any references to several points the defendant had made during the interviews—for example, that he sometimes drove his motorcycle at high speeds after an argument with Monika to relieve his tension.

"I have not included in my report every single thing," Hamilton said.

But nowhere, Carman said, "do you record that he made a decision to kill her in the Hyde Park Hotel."

"I'm sorry, I think it does say that," Hamilton said.

"Please show where it is."

Hamilton scanned his notes quickly. "No, you are right, I did not make a note of that. . . . Mr. Telling was speaking rapidly and it was impossible to get everything down, but I started writing some things down."

Carman paused in triumph while Hamilton continued to scan the notes. Then, with a flash of satisfaction, he said he had found his reference to Michael's admission that he had decided to kill Monika when they were in London, and decided subsequently *when* he would kill her. Hamilton pointed to the passages:

London, seeds sown . . . Friday, he back Lambourn House. Saturday morning—she came out of hospital Monday 10 A.M.—eve. de-

cided to kill her. She belittled him—treated him like a dog. . . .1)
know she sleeping with others—taunts sexual prowess. 2) mental insta-
bility. 3) black sheep family—never achieved anything, felt all alone,
rejected—only M. had valued him. "If I can't have you, no one else
will." Decided to kill her. . . .

It was clear from his notes, he said, what Michael had told him: "I
put it down in reference to what he said then. That is the words he
used. He said 'seeds were sown' then, making the decision. . . . My
report says he said the seeds were sown. . . . If I can explain further,
what Telling told me was he decided in the London hotel that he
would do it and he decided exactly when and how he would do it the
evening before."

"Doctor, is it elementary," Carman asked sneeringly, "that, if a
patient told you he decided to kill her when he was in the hotel, you
would record that fact?"

"I have not put it clearly enough."

"You have not put it at all expressly."

"I believe I have," Hamilton said.

"In your contemporaneous notes . . . if Michael Telling told you in
clear terms he decided to kill his wife in the Hyde Park Hotel, would
you not have written that down?"

"I am sorry," the psychiatrist said. "I did not have time to write it
down when I was interviewing him, but I knew when I put 'the seeds
were sown,' I knew it when I came to detail that report, what that
indicated."

"May I suggest that your recollection is a little at fault in terms of
exactly what Michael Telling told you?"

"I believe my recollection is totally accurate."

The craggy voice of seventy-two-year-old Mr. Justice Sheldon suddenly intervened. Breaking the tension that had momentarily brought
silence to the courtroom, he looked down at the witness and inquired:
"Have you any doubt that it was in the Hyde Park Hotel that he
decided to kill his wife—that he *told* you?"

"I have no doubt."

The witness was dismissed.

With John Hamilton's testimony, the prosecution rested its case.

56.

The first defense witness was a gaunt, slender man of fifty-three with a high forehead crowned by thin folds of curly blond hair. Dr. Robert Bluglass was an avid amateur watercolor painter, a professor of forensic psychiatry at the University of Birmingham, a Fellow of the Royal College of Psychiatrists, a leading member of Britain's psychiatric establishment. As an expert witness, he had testified approximately four hundred times, on the state of mind of accused murderers.

George Carman got quickly to the point: "Would you tell My Lord and the jury in terms of Section Two of the Homicide Act of 1957 what your professional opinion is about the absence or presence of abnormality of mind" in the defendant, Michael Telling?

"In my opinion, My Lord," the psychiatrist said, "there is no doubt that he has suffered from an abnormality of mind, clearly since childhood, and suffered from an abnormality of mind at the time of his wife's death."

"Would you give My Lord and the jury more of an indication of the *nature* of that abnormality of mind, Professor?"

"It is my opinion that he suffers and has suffered and suffered at the time from a severe personality disorder."

"Dr. Hamilton thinks that it is not and was not diminished responsibility?"

"Yes."

"You think he is wrong?"

"Yes."

Addressing his witness with the deferential honorific of "Professor"—sending a message to the jurors that *now* a distinguished scientist was in the witness box—Carman took still another opportunity to lay before them the story of Michael's troubled childhood, and to reprise his portrayal of the woman he had decapitated as a shrewish, alcoholic lesbian. Then Carman asked: "What was the attraction of Monika Zumsteg for Michael Telling?"

"I think she was, as I piece it together, a very different sort of girl from Alison," the witness said. "Alison has been seen here, and she is a homely, stable, pleasant girl. Monika, as I understand it, is—or was—a very attractive girl of a very different kind of personality, perhaps rather flamboyant and very active and exciting. She was apparently very dominating, and in many ways, paradoxically, this might have been the attraction for him in a kind of way, that he enjoyed it—initially, at any rate."

Was Monika in love with Michael when she married him?

Although the defense psychiatrist had neither interviewed nor even met Monika, he ventured his professional opinion as to the state of mind of the woman who had been dead for almost fifteen months: "Her attitude towards him, the way she criticized him and behaved towards him, as reported by him, very soon after they met and decided to marry, I think, might suggest her feelings were not simply those of love and affection. . . . She certainly was not obsessively in love. It was plain she presumably must have been by this account, if it is true, a disturbed personality herself, of unusual and abnormal interests and predilections." Paradoxically, he added, the more Monika rejected Michael and treated him badly, "the more he still wanted her and was striving to get her approval and her affection. . . ."

The depth of Michael's devotion to his wife, he continued, was revealed by his actions once he had killed her. Michael had told him that, after he drove her body to Devon, "he could not bear to part with her and on impulse, he said to me, he cut off her head with the ax. He wanted to take some of her back with him. He said he felt very screwed up, more even than when he killed her. He took the head and wrapped it in the bin bag, put it in the van, and came back to his home."

"What did he do with the head?"

"At first he left it in the van, in the center of the garage floor, for several days, but it began to smell and he realized it was deteriorating and was rotten. He said it certainly occurred to him on one occasion, because there were already maggots in it, that it might assist the deteriorating if he tipped the maggots in which he had with him for the supposed fishing trip to Devon. He tipped them into the bag, he said, one week later, in order to complete the decomposition process."

With this image to ponder over lunch, Mr. Justice Sheldon declared the noon recess.

After the break, journalists quickly reoccupied every seat in the press gallery. Elsewhere, a nation followed their reports as a welcome respite from the persistent bad news of a stubborn recession.

"Do you see any echoes or parallels between his experiences in childhood and those in his adult life, in particularly his adult life with Monika?" Carman asked.

Yes, Bluglass said: "From a very early age, he was subjected to the aggressive voice of his father attacking his mother, and the rejection of his mother by her own account which she has given. She found it difficult to love him and she distanced herself from him."

To get her attention, he responded with acts of aggression, stealing, and temper tantrums. "Then he became in turn attached to the other women in his small life, to nannies, and they left, and it seemed to him that they were rejecting him again, and he responded in a violent way which was taking root and developing. Then he was sent away to school, and it seemed again like a rejection. It was his mother who spoke in those terms, to say he demonstrated by constantly wanting to get back. He did want his mother's affection and love, which was never forthcoming. So he wanted to get home, he would steal to get home, but once he got there he still could not achieve the love that he needed. . . . Later, in his relationship with Monika, it seems that he became attached to the same personality, who had many similar features to the mother whose affection he sought when he was a child. He was constantly trying to gain a demonstration of Monika's love and affection, but instead he was humiliated and put down."

What explained Michael's interest in guns?

"They, like motorcycles, must represent power, masculinity, aggression, and provide a sort of boost to his personality, his feelings of inadequacy," Bluglass replied. "It helped him to have guns. They fascinated him."

Now Michael's defense lawyer tackled frontally the most damaging testimony against him.

"Dr. Hamilton thought that the killing was cold-blooded, calculated, and so on. What do you say to that opinion, Professor?"

"I do not consider, in my opinion, that Michael Telling is a cool, cold-blooded, calculating individual or that he is capable of it. He is a man of mixed and considerable emotions who acts on impulses, not on planning, nor calculated work. . . . I find it difficult to reconcile the reported behavior and the position reported by Dr. Hamilton that he decided to kill her in the Hyde Park Hotel."

Alan Rawley opened his cross-examination by saying he found something puzzling: During his testimony, Dr. Bluglass had offered an unqualified opinion that Michael had "severe" mental problems that substantially impaired his responsibility when he killed his wife. Yet, in the written report he had prepared after interviewing him in prison, he had described the problem as "moderate" and said it was impossible to determine in a scientific way whether it had substantially impaired his mental capacity at the time of the murder.

Dr. Bluglass said that, after attending the trial and hearing other witnesses describe Michael's life, he was better able to "place him on some sort of scale in my head. I have now come to the conclusion finally, in giving my evidence, that he has a severe personality disorder."

Rawley reminded him that Dr. Hamilton had testified that the defendant had *admitted* to him that he had decided to kill his wife several days before he did it and had argued that the murder of Monika Zumsteg-Telling was not the act of an impulsive man. "You do not accept it as being true?" Rawley asked.

"I certainly do not think it was true," Dr. Bluglass said. "I cannot account for Dr. Hamilton's interpretation of what was said to him . . . [but] I do not think [the defendant] formulated a clear, cold, calculated plan. . . . He was going to visit her in hospital and it does not seem to me consistent if he had formulated a plan to kill her."

Perhaps, Dr. Bluglass suggested, Michael had not been telling the truth when he spoke to Dr. Hamilton. "I think Mr. Telling is not able to give a clear and truthful account. . . . If pressed, he may say 'yes' to a question. But I do not think he is capable of saying exactly *when* he decided to take his wife's life. I think his behavior indicates he decided that morning."

"Before he picked up the gun or after?"

"When he picked up the gun, probably, I would say. It is difficult to know, but it was probably that morning, when he came down and she was shouting at him, he was shouting back, and he lost his temper and picked up the gun."

"Even if what he said to Dr. Hamilton is true in detail, there is still no doubt in your mind that this was a case of substantially diminished responsibility?"

"No—no doubt."

"No doubt at all."

"No." Even if what Dr. Hamilton said were true, Bluglass said, it would not change his opinion. It was likely, he said, that Monika had provoked the defendant into killing her.

The message implicit in his remark was that Monika was responsible for her own death.

"Do I understand you accept his account—because it is his account—that the reason for keeping the body was that he could not really bear to be parted from her and wanted to keep her with him?" Rawley said.

"Yes."

"You accept he is telling the truth about that?"

"Yes, I think he is. . . ."

"Supposing he had done it to cover up the crime coolly and calculatedly?"

The witness said he didn't believe that.

Rawley continued: "He said he could not bear to leave her there entirely, and on *impulse* he cut off her head with the ax—he wanted to take some of her back with him?"

"Yes."

Was it an impulse, the prosecutor asked, "to cut off the head of the corpse . . . not planned but done in the spur of the moment?"

"That is what he told me."

"Did you believe it?"

"Yes . . ."

"He took with him the ax?"

"Yes."

"He took plastic bags?"

"Yes."

"To put the head in, did he not?"

"I do not know."

"He had bags, but whether he took them with him to put the head in, I do not know," Dr. Bluglass said.

In the dock, Michael handed a note to one of his lawyers: "It's a matter of coarse [sic]. When I travel I always take bags with me. I took some to Monte Carlo, Australia, USA for rubbish, dirty washing, etc."

"Supposing," Rawley said, "he had done it in order to disguise the identity of the corpse and take the head away so that if the corpse is found they still would not know who it is . . . it would have been a very cold, determined, planned course of conduct?" Couldn't this simply be a case in which an irate husband decided, out of revenge, jealousy, or any of the other motives that spring from an unhappy marriage, to get rid of a wife he no longer wanted? Wasn't everything part of the same pattern—a calculated, premeditated murder followed by a resourceful and effective cover-up by a manipulative liar.

No, Dr. Bluglass insisted.

57.

Michael did not testify in his own defense, which was his right. The final witness was Dr. Paul Bowden, who, like the two psychiatrists before him, possessed credentials placing him at the top of his profession in Great Britain. He was a Fellow of the Royal College of Psychiatrists and consultant forensic psychiatrist at Maudsley Hospital (the clinic where Michael had spent part of his youth); like Dr. Bluglass, he had appeared as an expert witness in approximately four hundred murder cases.

Dr. Bowden agreed with Dr. Bluglass. He said he believed the trigger finger that had pumped three bullets into Monika Zumsteg-Telling was guided by an invisible force over which Michael Telling had no control, a force rooted in a childhood that had left him unable to tolerate denial of his wishes. He was a man who "wanted to have things immediately or even quicker."

Starting his cross-examination, Alan Rawley inquired: "Mr. Telling is a manipulative man, is he not?"

"I believe so, yes."

Rawley quoted a passage from the report Bowden had written after interviewing Michael at Exeter Prison:

I found that the defendant was able to give a reasonable account of his
life, but the time we spent together tended to be dominated increasingly
by his attempt to get me to commit myself to the view that he did not
require a custodial remand or to be deprived of his liberty as a result of
sentencing. Mr. Telling behaved like a spoiled child in pressing very
hard, and in a petulant manner, to get his own way and if he sensed
failure he became threatening.

In addition, he was unwilling, or unable to consider his own con-
tribution to his predicament, intent only, he said, on gaining maximum
publicity for his account of Monika's shortcomings.

Under questioning by Rawley, Bowden acknowledged again that
Michael was a manipulative man, but said it didn't change his opinion.

The lawyer asked whether the witness believed Michael's claim that
he had brought his wife's head back to West Wycombe as a token of
his undying love for her.

No, Dr. Bowden said. Siding with Dr. Hamilton, not Dr. Bluglass,
he said he thought Michael had probably kept the head because he
wanted to conceal her identity and avoid arrest.

If Dr. Bluglass had accepted Michael's claim as truthful, wasn't it
possible he had manipulated and deceived the defense's psychiatrists in
other ways? Many men, Rawley continued, had difficult childhoods but went on to lead reasonably normal adult lives. Certainly all
of them didn't murder their wives. Even if the defendant had an
"abnormality of mind," wasn't it likely he still possessed sufficient will
power when he killed his wife to realize it was *wrong* and not pull the
trigger?

No, Dr. Bowden said.

There could be no doubt, Rawley pressed, "can there, that when he
killed his wife Mr. Telling knew perfectly well what he was doing?"

"I would agree with that," Bowden said.

"That he also had the ability to form a rational judgment whether he
was doing right or wrong. There can be no doubt about that, can there?"

"There is a doubt in my mind about that," Dr. Bowden said.

Elaborate, please, Rawley asked.

Bowden said that, if Michael had actually asked himself whether
shooting Monika was right or wrong before he did so, he would have
concluded it was wrong; however, the doctor doubted that Michael
had applied the question to himself.

"But the question," Rawley said, "is whether he had the *ability* to
form a rational judgment as to whether an act is right or wrong. Would

you agree with me that he had the ability? Whether he exercised it or not is perhaps a different question?"

It was possible, Bowden responded, that Michael had the ability to understand that what he was doing was wrong based on rational judgment, but "I suspect that he was in such a disturbed emotional state that the impulse would be irresistible."

"You say he was acting under an *irresistible impulse?*"

"I suggested that he was in such an abnormal state of mind that the strength of the impulse to shoot Monika would be irresistible."

"Therefore, he was acting under an irresistible impulse?"

"Probably."

But, the prosecutor argued, if the defendant knew that what he was doing was wrong, wasn't he "simply doing what he *wants* to do, come hell or high water?" Wasn't he simply refusing to heed the knowledge that what he was doing was wrong—simply *choosing* not to exercise his will power?

If so, "it follows as night follows day, I suggest, that he is not suffering in that possible situation from diminished responsibility. . . . What you have told us is in fact that you believe that he was suffering from an irresistible impulse which he simply could not resist and—possibly—that he simply *chose not* to control his actions."

Furthermore, how could Michael have been driven to kill his wife by an uncontrollable irresistible impulse when—according to Dr. Hamilton—he made the decision to do so several days before he actually did it?

"One might have the impulse to commit an act and plan it," Dr. Bowden said.

The prosecutor reminded him Michael had told Dr. Hamilton he had decided to kill Monika days before he actually did it: "If that is true, then it is as clear a case of premeditation as one can find. Do you agree?"

"If that is true, then it would appear that the defendant premeditated his crime," Dr. Bowden admitted, but added: "A person can be suffering from the most severe form of mental illness and plan a crime for months. The question of premeditation has to be considered in the context of the other information available at the time."

"Let us look at the four days," Rawley said. "Look at the few moments before he killed. He goes to get the gun: are you saying he was not able to control himself from getting that gun?"

"I am saying I suspect his feelings were such that he would have been unable to resist the feelings even if he had tried."

"To take a conscious decision to walk into another room and get the gun?" Rawley asked.

"Conscious, certainly."

"He could have controlled that conscious decision, that exercise of his will power, could he not?"

"I do not think he could," the witness declared.

"So he gets the gun. We will assume he had already loaded it with a number of cartridges."

"He told me it was loaded with a number of cartridges. . . ."

"He shoots the first shot and she goes down. Now, are you saying that he could not resist the desire?"

"Yes."

"He was unable to?"

"Yes."

"He picked up the gun, brought it up to his shoulder. Are you really saying he could not resist that?"

"That is what I am suggesting."

"Then he, having fired one shot, used the lever again to cock the gun, aims again, and fires again, and he did not have the ability to resist that act?"

"Indeed . . .," Dr. Bowden said.

When he fired a third time, he was still in the grip of an irresistible impulse?

Yes, the doctor said.

"He had a period of over four days to back down, did he not?" Rawley reminded the witness.

"He could have changed his mind," Bowden said.

"That is the point," the prosecutor said. "He did not change his mind, but he could have, could he not?"

"He could have."

"He chose not to?"

"I am saying that his strength of feeling was such that he could not, even if he tried, exercise control over his physical actions."

———————

The cross-examination ended, leaving behind a cloud of disputed, unresolved, and ambiguous questions about will power, responsibility, and self control. Rawley had scored points for the prosecution, but Bowden had stood his ground.

58.

Michael's fate was delivered to the jury—seven men and five women —shortly after ten o'clock on a sweltering Friday morning following eight days of testimony and six hours of summing up by the opposing lawyers and Mr. Justice Sheldon. In his final appeal for the prosecution, Alan Rawley urged the jurors to focus on a simple issue: when he fired three bullets into his wife, did Michael Telling possess sufficient will power to stop himself? If they asked this question, he predicted, they would answer it yes. It was not an irresistible impulse that made him pull the trigger, but the calculated act of a husband who wished to eliminate a troublesome wife he no longer wanted.

"Despite his mental abnormality, this man determined to kill his wife—he could have prevented himself from doing so if he wished, but he determined to do it some days before he killed her. He then took elaborate steps–gruesome steps—to avoid detection, which also needed determination and will power."

From the moment he killed his wife, Rawley said, the defendant lied to protect himself, and in a final act of deception, he cut off her head. He lied again and again to protect himself because "he did not want the police to realize quite how much of a smoke screen he had

285

laid down; that would not marry in with a mentally abnormal man whose responsibility was substantially impaired."

In his final plea for the defense, George Carman placed Monika in the defendant's dock once more.

For eight days, he had led the assault on the young woman whose body was lying beneath the turf of a hillside in California unable to defend herself. Now, once again, he blamed Monika for her own murder:

"If this woman had not finally taunted him, she might still be alive."

Michael's mother sat next to Alison in the front row of the gallery, a few feet from Michael, as Britain's foremost trial lawyer reviewed for a final time Michael's lonely childhood, his mother's rejection of him, and his marriage to the woman he depicted as a vixen and a shrew.

Sympathy for Michael—that's what Carman wanted from the jury.

"Michael Telling had all the money in the world—but nowhere to go and nobody to love. . . . He was the inadequate black sheep of the family. No achievements. Nothing to write home about. He didn't even have a trade. . . ." Inside him was a sickness of mind that needed "help and understanding," not "taunting and humiliation" from a cruel and faithless wife who married him only for his great wealth. Carman said it was nonsense to claim that Michael had murdered his wife in cold blood, and he ridiculed Dr. Hamilton's claim that Michael had admitted plotting her murder several days beforehand. Hamilton's testimony was "appalling, flimsy" evidence. The defendant had shot his wife because of a force over which he had no control, an impulse set off by her goading: Monika Telling died because she *goaded* him to kill her.

Carman asked for Michael's acquittal on the murder charge not simply out of compassion for him, but because it was the only true verdict: "It would not be a verdict of sympathy or compassion . . . though, heavens above, you must have felt moments of sympathy for Michael Telling, mixed with the horror of what he did. . . . He has suffered throughout his life rejection after rejection after rejection.

"Are you going to deliver a final and ultimate rejection?

"I suspect not," Carman said.

Before summing up the trial evidence, Mr. Justice Sheldon spoke briefly in behalf of the woman whose headless image had dominated the trial: "In many respects, the people affected have had no opportunity of meeting criticisms made of them. As between the defendant and his victim, she is no longer alive to give her account of the story, so far as it is material to the issues that you have to decide. You may think it prudent, therefore, to examine with the very greatest care the different statements made from time to time by the defendant before deciding whether—or to what extent—you can rely upon them. You may also think it prudent to examine carefully the evidence of other witnesses to ensure that it is not colored by partiality or prejudice to persons, or against either of the principal parties in this affair."

There was no dispute that Michael Telling had killed his wife, the judge said; it was up to the jury to determine *why* he had done it. "You have to choose, and the one overall issue that you have to decide: has the defendant proved, on the balance of probabilities, that when he killed his wife he was suffering from such abnormality of mind, as defined in the statute, as substantially impaired his mental responsibility for his act in so doing? If that is proved, then he is not guilty of murder, but guilty of manslaughter by reason of diminished responsibility. If it is not proved, then he is guilty of murder. Parliament has left it to you and you alone to decide the question, looking at the matter in a broad commonsense way, to say whether the defendant's mental responsibility for his act in killing his wife was impaired, and if so, whether it was substantially impaired by his abnormality of mind. . . . If Dr. Hamilton is right, the defendant has not established the defense, and the defendant will be guilty of murder. If Professor Bluglass and Dr. Bowden are right, the verdict would be, not guilty of murder, but guilty of manslaughter. It is for you, members of the jury, to say which view is correct. . . ."

As the jury began its deliberations, Britain's newspapers had already rendered their judgment. For Monika, the verdict was GUILTY. Headlines told the story. "MILLIONAIRE'S COUSIN KILLED AND BEHEADED WIFE 'AFTER SEXUAL TAUNTS,' " the *Times* reported with more restraint than its competitors. The *Daily Star* headlined a profile of Michael "SLAVE OF THE VAMP." Another tabloid blared: " 'I GUNNED DOWN HORRIBLE WIFE' "; another, "THE SAD TALE OF THE POOR LITTLE RICH BOY AND THE WICKED LADY." The *Sun* headlined a spread about Monika "I WANT YOU IN MY SEX SANDWICH." *The Daily Express* published a special section on the trial: "THE HELL OF LIFE WITH MONIKA—THE BIZARRE STORY OF MILLIONAIRE MICHAEL TELLING AND THE HEADLESS CORPSE CASE."

———

In West Wycombe, Ettie Turner shook her head in disgust. "That's not Monika," she told Alf after reading the reports from Exeter that were titillating Great Britain. I think Michael and his friends have been lying so he can get off." She reminded Alf that after Michael's arrest she had told detectives and reporters that Monika was one of the kindest and most decent young women she had ever met, not the woman depicted in the papers. But none of it had come out, nor had good things other neighbors had said about Monika.

Like the press, the police and prosecutors had said little that was favorable about Monika. They wanted to convict Michael, and it had served their purpose—as it had Michael's defense—because it gave Michael a motive to kill.

———

In San Francisco, the private detective who was hired by Michael's solicitors to investigate Monika's past in California told a reporter that what he read about her didn't square at all with what *he* had learned about her: according to his investigation, "she was an attractive and intelligent girl about as normal as you can get."

Stunned most of all were Monika's parents and friends in America.

"She was certainly not a saint," her father told a reporter, "but she was nothing like she's being painted. To put my daughter on trial like that was absolutely disgusting, to have to sit here, seeing it in the papers every day, unable to deny it, was terrible. They have taken little things and half truths and exaggerated them. It adds insult to the injury we have all suffered. She was a loving, caring girl. . . ."

Lou had recently found a job as vice-president of an industrial-relations consulting firm, and on the eve of the trial he was ordered to Missouri to settle a labor dispute. But he could not bring himself to leave Elsa alone during the trial. When he refused to go, he lost the job.

It was true, he told reporters, that Monika had become an alcoholic after she married Michael, but this was largely because of the stress she was under, trying to adjust to a difficult marriage in a new country. "As for the drugs, she may have experimented as many young people do, but I've never known her to be addicted to or under the influence of drugs." Monika's bereaved father even had to suffer the indignity of defending his daughter's sexuality to strangers: "I know my daughter had perfectly normal sexual habits. Monika was open about everything with me and her mother; she was a normal heterosexual girl. Whatever other problems they had together, Monika and Michael both told me their sex life was not a bone of contention between them; Michael said that to me, and so did my daughter. It was ludicrous to say he was frightened of her—at the end, she feared for her life at his hands. . . . My wife and I had reservations to go to Britain for the trial, but a police inspector there discouraged her, saying it would just bring us heartache. If I had known what was going to be said, I would have been there to stand up for her."

When a reporter told Elsa that Michael claimed he had killed Monika because she was an alcoholic and promiscuous, she said: "Where did the court get all this information about my daughter?" Then she answered the question herself: "From a man who has been a chronic liar all his life and from his friends. They crucified her. The Vesteys used my daughter to help Michael deal with his problems and after he killed her, they do *this* to her. The defense has spent twice as much to blacken her name as the prosecution did to convict him."

When the reporter left, Elsa, in tears, said to Lou he had told her that Michael's lawyers claimed he killed her because of an "irresistible impulse." She repeated that she wished desperately they had gone to England to speak up for Monika.

"Elsa, the last thing in the world that occurred to me was that I should go to Michael's trial in England to prepare a defense for Monika."

Then he thought of Michael and New Year's Eve and the red tag Elsa found in the trash. "It wasn't an *impulse*. It was premeditated murder—I think I know exactly what happened."

59.

Santa Rosa,
New Year's Eve

It was on New Year's Eve morning—less than three months before Monika was murdered—when Elsa found the small red tag. Cleaning the house, she spotted it among the ribbons and other debris left over from Christmas. She read it twice and showed it to Lou.

"Where there's smoke, there's fire," she said.

It was a safety warning—the kind attached by gun manufacturers to new firearms.

"Monika is terrified Michael is going to buy another gun," Elsa said. "She's deathly afraid."

In Reno, two days before Christmas, Monika had told Elsa she had decided to go back to England and give Michael one more chance, because it was her responsibility, despite his threats and lies. She said she had warned him that, if he ever hit her again or bought another gun, she'd report him to the police. It was the one thing she had over him: if the police learned he had bought another gun, he would have to go to prison and serve the sentence he had narrowly escaped the year before. There was nothing Michael feared more than going to jail, she said. Once, when he was a child, one of his nannies, after he had thrown all her clothes and furniture out a window because she was

290

taking a new job, had reported him to the police, and he had never gotten over a fear of jail. He had promised to behave himself, Monika said, and never buy another gun.

It was during that trip to Reno, extended by a sudden Sierra snowstorm, that Elsa understood for the first time the depth of Monika's obsession with Michael.

Later, when it was too late to matter, she looked back on the trip and wondered: Why do women put up with marriages like Monika's? What convinces them they can change a man? What motivates their campaigns to control and reconfigure a man they regard as inadequate?

Monika had accepted and excused and forgiven so much: Michael's lies, his deceptions, tantrums, and threats. Even after he had chased her outdoors into the snow with a gun at her head, she believed she could change him. Then Elsa remembered the abuse and humiliation *she* had tolerated during the worst years of Lou's drinking. Like Monika, she had denied to herself that he had a problem and always managed to find excuses for him. She had also tried to change Lou. But in the end, she realized she couldn't do it: Lou had changed, but he had done it himself. Only after admitting to himself that he had hit bottom did he stop drinking; only then, with A.A.'s help, did he learn how to accept himself. It was impossible to change someone who did not want to change. She knew that now. Monika had never learned it.

Alcoholics Anonymous called women like Elsa "enablers"—tormented but loyal wives of alcoholics who, despite every reason not to, took on the problems of troubled men and sometimes even enjoyed their martyrdom. Perhaps Lou's weakness had even made her feel strong in a perverse way: it had put her on top. Maybe, in trying to fix Michael, Monika had been trying to feel better about herself in the same way. "Enabler" was the word A.A. used long before the pop psychologists of the eighties coined a new word—"codependent"—that meant the same thing: someone obsessed with changing another's behavior, for whom another's well-being was more important than his or her own—someone, like Monika, who thought she could make a silk purse out of a sow's ear.

For Monika, love had first become an obsession, then a disease.

After Elsa found the red firearm-safety tag, she urged Lou to suggest a bike ride to Michael. Once they had gone, she went to the guest room and searched his luggage and the dresser drawer he was using. She couldn't find the gun, but in a waste basket she found a small box; it was an empty container for a gun-cleaning kit.

When the men returned, Michael said he was going to take a shower, and Elsa told Lou what she had found. The only place she hadn't looked for the gun was the saddlebag on the motorcycle he had been riding. While Michael was in the shower, she went to the garage and unfastened the saddlebag, burrowed into it, and pulled out a snub-nosed Colt Python magnum and four boxes of steel-jacketed bullets.

"Maybe we shouldn't say anything about it and just report him to Customs, so he's arrested at the airport," she said. "It would teach him." But then she said: "No—we can't do that. Monika would lose it if he was arrested and she found out about the gun."

When Michael came out of the shower, Lou was waiting outside the bathroom with the gun in his hands.

"I'm glad you caught me out," Michael said.

"Where did you get it?" Lou asked.

Michael said that a member of the Perkins family had bought it for him and he picked it up when he went to San Francisco two days before Christmas. As if to prove everything was legal, he produced a receipt dated December 23, 1982: "Sold to Michael Telling; One Colt Python V28233/H7656937." It was signed by Michael and a member of the Perkins family of Harley dealers.

Michael said he was still upset over the British law that prevented him from buying a gun. The law, he implied, was not meant to cover someone in his position.

"Michael, if they had caught you with that gun, they'd have put you in jail," Lou said. "You just barely missed going to jail a year ago."

Michael agreed it was a mistake, and became contrite. He handed the receipt to Lou, imploring him not to tell Monika. He said he had promised her he wouldn't buy any more guns; if she knew, she'd leave him.

Lou and Elsa talked it over and decided not to tell Monika: Lou had the gun—no harm had been done—there was no danger to Monika. Lou promised Michael he wouldn't mention it to her. "I loved the guy and wanted the relationship to work," he said years later. "I think it was because I could see a lot of myself in Michael—his self-doubt, his lack of self-esteem, his attempt to get it by riding motorcycles. I knew he was wrapped up in a fantasy world of Harleys and guns and uniforms and soldiers of fortune, and so I thought I understood it. I chalked it up to something else he needed to fill his vacuum of self-esteem. It all seemed to fit into place. Elsa and I discussed it and we agreed: 'Let's not tell her. They seem to be getting along better now; why upset her?' That, in retrospect, was an awful dumb decision, but that's how we felt."

After Michael and Monika returned to England, Lou telephoned the man who had bought the gun and said he now had it. This surprised the motorcycle dealer: he said he had thought Michael needed it for his work.

"He is in the British intelligence service, isn't he?"

During the next three months, while Monika reported by telephone that she and Michael were continuing to work on their problems, Lou and Elsa nearly forgot the gun. But when she told them, in early March, that Michael had cleaned out Lambourn House and left for Australia, they urged her to come home, and Lou told her about the gun. He mailed her a copy of the receipt and said: "If Michael gives you any trouble about a divorce, show this to a lawyer at your discretion—but don't show it to Michael."

On March 29—the day Monika died—the telephone rang at the Zumsteg home. It was about 10 A.M. in Santa Rosa, late afternoon in England. When Elsa recognized his voice, she said: "Hi, Michael, how are you doing?"

"I'm okay," he responded coldly.

"How's Monika?"

"She's fine. Is Lou there?"

When Lou picked up the phone, his greeting to Michael was enthusiastic, reflecting his love for his son-in-law. But Michael cut him off: "You lied to me. You promised you wouldn't say anything to Monika about the gun. You *promised* me."

Before Lou could defend himself, Michael continued: "I trusted you, and you broke your promise. That's it. You'll never hear from me again."

He hung up without another word.

It was the last time Lou or Elsa ever spoke to Michael.

Later, when they could think clearly enough to fit the pieces together, they realized what must have happened: Michael had murdered Monika to silence her.

Despite her promise, she must have told him that she knew about the gun and that, if he didn't keep his promise and return to St. Andrew's, she would use it against him—and he might have to go to prison.

Indeed, a few days before she died, Monika had told Ettie Turner about the receipt. She said Michael was returning from Australia and they were going to meet in London to discuss a reconciliation. She also said she had a receipt that proved he had bought a gun in America, violating his probation; if he didn't keep his promise and resume his medical treatment, she could use it against him. She told Cheryl Richardson the same thing.

Perhaps Michael had learned about the incriminating receipt even before he left for Australia, and it was why he returned so quickly with a gun: according to his half-sister, he was very fearful Monika would be waiting for him at Heathrow with policemen before he left for Sydney.

What *is* certain is that he returned from Australia only a few days later with the smuggled rifle he used to kill her. It was unlikely Monika knew about the rifle: if she did, she would have fled Lambourn House, because of her deathly fear of guns, or carried out her threat to call the police—instead of trying to convince him to re-enter St. Andrew's.

At Michael's trial, Joe Stennings said that, on the day before Monika's dental surgery, she had complained repeatedly to Michael, "You bought a fucking gun." Stennings also said that, after Michael dropped her off at the hospital, he saw him frantically emptying trash cans at Lambourn House searching for a mysterious piece of paper. Whether Michael ever found Monika's copy of the receipt is unknown.

When Stennings repeated Monika's remark about a "fucking gun" at the trial, those in the court assumed she had been referring to the rifle Michael had bought in Australia. More likely, she was referring to the pistol he had bought at Christmas—the gun she knew was safely in California—and she did not know that hidden in Lambourn House was the loaded carbine that would take her life.

Twice following the discovery of Monika's body, Lou met with lawyers in California and signed affidavits describing the events on New Year's Eve. He sent them, together with copies of the receipt, to the police in Exeter. But neither of his statements was introduced at Michael's trial: the police and the prosecution apparently decided these were not relevant to their case, which was based on the premise that Michael Telling had killed his wife because she was a shrew.

"Michael must have started backing out of his agreement to go to the hospital," Elsa told Lou, "and Monika must have said, 'Look what I've got, I'm going to use it against you,' and he killed her. 'Irresistible impulse,' my foot. He was terrified of going to jail. He killed Monika for one reason: to save himself."

60.

At the end of murder trials in England, it was a tradition among policemen, reporters, and court clerks to wager a few bob on how long it would take jurors to determine the fate of the man or woman in the dock. Detective Inspector Jeff Henthorne bet that Michael Telling's jury would be out no more than two hours and forty-five minutes. It returned its verdict in two hours and thirty-six minutes, winning him almost £20. The verdict:

"Not guilty of murder, but guilty of manslaughter by reason of diminished responsibility."

The decision brought relieved gasps from several working-class women in their twenties who had been regulars at the trial, using their every opportunity to catch the eye of the millionaire in the dock.

Standing to hear the verdict, Michael—a beneficiary of the best legal defense money could buy—looked relieved. He closed his eyes and bowed his head. Tears glistened in the eyes of his mother and several jurors.

The jurors had rejected the prosecution's claim—and the testimony of Dr. John Hamilton—that the murder of Monika Elizabeth Zumsteg-Telling was cold-blooded and premeditated and a product of malice aforethought. Instead, they had accepted Michael's contention, supported by two other psychiatrists, that he killed her because she provoked him into it and he was overtaken by an impulse that told him to extinguish her life.

Michael had won.

Or, had he?

Before the judge passed sentence, George Carman asked mercy for Michael. "He instructed me he would wish to express to Your Lordship his own appreciation of the terrible thing he has done in the taking away of the life of his own wife, whom he loved so dearly."

In dealing with a manslaughter conviction, Mr. Justice Sheldon had broad latitude: he could release Michael on probation, send him to jail for a fixed length of time, or give him a life sentence whose ultimate duration would subsequently be determined by penal experts in the Home Office. For months, Michael had been pressing his lawyers to see to it that he spent *no* time in jail. Before the trial, he had told a fellow inmate that he would be acquitted of murder, spend no more than a year in prison, then leave in a Rolls Royce. After that, he was going to America, or perhaps Australia.

"Michael Henry Maxwell Telling," Mr. Justice Sheldon said, "the jury have found you guilty of manslaughter by reason of diminished responsibility. There was ample evidence upon which they could do so, including, in particular, the evidence of Professor Bluglass and Dr. Bowden. Accordingly, just as I accept the jury's verdict, so I must have regard to their evidence in considering sentence. In my opinion, it would be unpleasant and unkind for me once again to repeat the evidence as to your past, present, and likely future mental state. Suffice it to say that it must clearly be the case that you have matured very little from the profoundly disturbed little boy that you were in your early life, with little or no greater ability now, as then, to control your emotions and your impulses, and that the prognosis for the future is bleak. That is the evidence which the jury must have accepted, and it is therefore evidence upon which I must now act.

"In those circumstances, I am satisfied there can be no alternative to passing a sentence, as I do, of life imprisonment, thus leaving it to those responsible for your custody to decide whether, and if so, when, it would be safe and proper to permit your release."

Michael winced. He bit his lip and stared at the floor in disbelief. His lawyers glanced at each other without apparent surprise.

Outside the court, they told Michael he might be free in five years. Although he was upset about the sentence, his lawyers told reporters, he felt vindicated—as did the members of his family—because the jury had not branded him a murderer. The family honor, they implied, had been saved.

When Detective Superintendent Brian Rundle heard the verdict, he offered his theory concerning the trial: "We had a doctor who said it was premeditated. They had a professor who said it wasn't. It came down to a doctor versus a professor, and the professor—in the eyes of the jury—had more standing."

A reporter asked Detective Inspector Jeff Henthorne for his opinion of Michael. "He's a little boy in a man's body—and not a very nice little boy at that. When he wants something from you, he's as nice as pie, very eager to please, but if you refuse him, he turns all sulky and spiteful and arrogant. Basically, he's got a massive inferiority complex. He doesn't like himself—and therefore other people—very much at all. . . ."

———

After Michael was lead out of the courtroom by his guards, he asked for his usual restaurant lunch and customary half-bottle of claret. But a guard said: "You're a prisoner now, no longer on remand, and such privileges are no longer available to you."

One of the first things Michael did was write a letter to Cheryl and Richard:

> Everyone says the verdict was the right one, but at the cost of destroying Monika all over again. . . .
>
> I and most people think that the sentence was wrong, unfair, unjust and heartless to say the least. I do not need to be locked up. I need to get back to the outside world and family and friends. . . . Hopefully, an appeal will be successful.

———

In his summation of the evidence, Mr. Justice Sheldon had told the jurors they were dealing with a "bizarre story," although, "in essence, the story amounts to a variation of a not unknown theme—of an ill-matched couple—both of them, in Professor Bluglass's view, 'very disturbed' people whose love—in Dr. Bowden's view—alternated with intense hatred."

Perhaps he could have added that they were a couple programmed by the past to live as they did. Like the seamless strands of a cable, each generation of a family is linked to the generations that come before it. In a continuous thread, the past reaches out to shape the future, as it did for Michael and Monika. If Wordsworth was right and "the child is father of the man," both were emotionally crippled children who grew into emotionally crippled adults.

As a child, she had learned to cope with the mayhem, violence, and abuse in her home by taking charge and trying to make her father stop drinking. As an adult, she still felt a need to control others and to fix troubled men. Like a moth to a flame, she was drawn irresistibly to Michael.

Emotionally insecure, deprived of parental love and hobbled by low self-esteem, Michael for the first time in his life found a woman who valued him. But she wanted to change him. He wanted her unconditional and uncritical love. Instead, he was judged and found wanting. In the war of words in Lambourn House, he was outgunned, and so he went to Australia and bought a hunting rifle and silenced her.

———————

After its excesses during Britain's most celebrated murder trial since the Yorkshire Ripper case, Fleet Street found new diversions to entertain its readers, unrepentant even after a few voices rose to condemn its sordid performance:

"One of the hazards of being murdered nowadays," *The Spectator* observed, "is that, at the subsequent trial, your character is likely to be posthumously assassinated by the defense in an attempt to get a lighter sentence for the killer. With hanging abolished, the chances are that, if the victim's reputation is sufficiently blackened in court, the convicted murderer or manslaughterer will serve only a short time in prison and may even get a suspended sentence. The trial which followed the killing of Mrs. Monika Telling was a particularly bad example of this decline in our judicial standards. . . . It should not be necessary for parents of a slaughtered girl to stand up for her at the trial. . . . Fleet Street has behaved exceedingly badly over this case, but so has the law itself." Expressing the same view, another London magazine, *Time Out*, declared: "Monika Telling will go down in history as 'the headless corpse,' the woman whose 'bisexual love life led to her brutal killing.' A fairer and more compassionate verdict would describe her as a double victim—of her husband and the gutter press. . . ."

There was little criticism, however, of the Homicide Act of 1957, which had enabled Michael to preserve his family's honor and avoid a murder conviction. In America, however, the uproar over the acquittal of John Hinckley, Jr., for attempting to kill President Ronald Reagan persuaded legislatures in more than half the states and Congress to restrict the rights of murderers to claim they had killed because of diminished capacity. During a review of the insanity defense touched off by that case, a panel of the American Bar Association noted that since the 1950s psychiatrists had claimed that they were able to determine whether an accused killer killed with malice aforethought or had been seized by an uncontrollable urge.

> Yet, experience confirms that there is still no accurate scientific basis for measuring one's capacity for self control or for calibrating the impairment of such capacity. There is, in short, no objective basis for distinguishing between the offenders who were undeterrable and those who were merely undeterred, between the impulse that was irresistible and the impulse not resisted, or between substantial impairment of capacity and some lesser impairment. . . . The question is unanswerable or, at best, can be answered only by "moral" [and not medical] guesses. In our opinion, to even ask the . . . question invites fabricated expert claims, undermines the equal administration of the penal law and compromises the laws' deterrent effect.

The American Psychiatric Association took a similar position. Calling for a return to the M'Naghten standard for determining the sanity of murderers, it said: "The line between an 'irresistible impulse' and an impulse not resisted is probably no sharper than between daylight and dusk. . . ."

———

Not long after Michael's trial, Brian Rundle and later, Jeff Henthorne, the biggest case of their careers behind them, retired from the Devon and Cornwall Constabulary, Rundle to become director of security for a department store in Plymouth, Henthorne to spend more time on the golf links.

The lawyers in the widely followed case continued, in their silken gowns, to polish their reputations as formidable advocates, and the psychiatrists who had stood behind them appeared often as experts on the mental capacity of accused murderers. When Dr. John Hamilton died of cancer in 1990 at the age of forty-six, the *Times*, in a laudatory obituary, said: "He will be remembered . . . with respect by his colleagues as being a good clinician who gave first rate opinions. . . . Hamilton was always on the side of the underdog. . . ."

After the trial, Michael's mother returned to Australia, and his first wife, Alison, told friends she intended to go there, too.

Security agents hired by Michael's family kept Lambourn House under guard while trustees of the Vestey Settlement tried to sell the infamous country house. After several months, a mother of four children, unaware of its past, placed a down payment on the property, but in the village she discovered its macabre history and withdrew her offer. Even after the trustees renamed Lambourn "Hill View Cottage" and cut the price repeatedly, it took them more than two years to sell Monika's dream house. In time, the new owner renamed it again: "Lamburn House."

Still feeling a sense of obligation to Michael, Cheryl and Richard Richardson continued to visit and correspond with him for several years, but the friendship ultimately ended in a dispute over Michael's insistence that they be his go-between in a romance with a woman whom they did not like.

The Vestey family reclaimed the privacy it revered so much, and if its name appeared in the papers at all, it was in the social pages or the polo reports. But in the early nineties, the family experienced a new embarrassment: The business empire founded in the stockyards of Chicago by William and Edmund Vestey began to encounter economic headwinds. Too much borrowing and unwise investments, a recession, and what some critics called a failure to adapt more successfully to the era when Britons were increasingly buying meat from supermarkets instead of their local Dewhurst shop, produced a mountain of debt that forced the family to sell off some of its holdings. "Lord Spam" and his cousin Edmund retired from active management of the company and were succeeded by Edmund's eldest son. In the press, observers blamed the decline of the House of Vestey in part on a failure of the new generation to run the family's global empire with the same single-minded sense of commitment to business as their ancestors: the new generation, it was proposed, was more interested in polo and hunting than in making money.

After Michael's release from prison, his solicitors said, he would again become a full-fledged beneficiary of the Vestey Settlement, but until then, his spending would be limited to £104 a year—the maximum allowed residents of Her Majesty's prisons.

Abandonment to Broadmoor had been Michael's biggest fear—once you go there, he said, you never get out—but he avoided the former lunatic asylum and was shuttled, through the years, between various jails in Britain's overcrowded penal system, from desolate Wormwood Scrubs in London to Maidstone in the Kent countryside—not far from Pinehurst, the boarding school he had tried to burn down at the age of nine, and Tunbridge Wells, where he had taken Monika to live.

In letters from prison, he occasionally said he still loved Monika. He complained that he was sane and said it was impossible to get by on £104 a year. His dream that his family would free him with an appeal never materialized.

Prisoners sentenced to life in Great Britain serve an average of ten or eleven years, so he had hopes of being freed in the nineties. His dream then, he said, was to go to Australia—where he hoped people had never heard about the Headless Corpse Case—or to America, where he wanted to buy another Harley-Davidson.

———

In Santa Rosa, Lou and Elsa often visited Monika's grave in the hills above the city, hoping in vain to ease the grief and guilt they felt over introducing her to Michael. But, along with their guilt and grief, they carried happy images of the warm and beautiful woman they had produced, the woman who always tried to see the best in people, the daughter who was full of optimism that she could fix the world, the daughter they loved, the daughter who had written them a few weeks before she died:

Dear Mom and Dad:
    Our winter is mild this year, but just the same requires 'thermal' underwear! I'm busy trying to get weed killers laid down before the weeds get out of control again. I've planted some nice shrubs & trees since you were here. I'll send photos when they bloom in summer. . . .

As soon as I get the house in order I think I'll go out and look for some work. I'm still selling antiques twice a month, but I'd like something a bit more challenging.

Michael is back to his old tricks, but promises he'll try harder. I'm still trying to get him to ask help from his 'Higher Power,' as I've been helped. He promises, but you know Michael. I still think there's a lot of good in him if he'll try to bring it out. I think I'm still needed here and I'm trying to help him. That's the commitment I took on. . . .

Love, Monika

Acknowledgments

I am indebted to many people on both sides of the Atlantic for help during the research and editing of *Irresistible Impulse*. It is difficult to express fully the extent of my gratitude and respect for Alice Mayhew of Simon & Schuster, the editor of this, my fourth book under her stewardship. The care and intensity she applies to her work, her sound instincts, sensitivity and intelligence, and the standards she imposes on authors makes me understand why she is valued as our country's preeminent editor of nonfiction books, a friend and editorial ally especially to journalists. At Simon & Schuster, I am also indebted to Eric Steel, who made substantial and important contributions to the manuscript; to Richard E. Snyder, Charles Hayward and Eric Rayman; Felice Javit, George Hodgman; Natalie Goldstein; Frank and Eve Metz; Victoria Meyer; Lydia Buechler, Marcia Peterson, and Terry Zaroff, an especially skilled and astute copy editor.

Samantha Hynes Zelinsky, Monika's best friend, patiently helped me reconstruct the story of her life in California, as did Isabella and Edward Zumsteg. In England, many people gave generously of their time, especially Maureen Busby, Brian Rundle and Jeffrey Henthorne of the Devon and Cornwall Constabulary. Cheryl and Richard Richardson not only spent many hours recollecting experiences with

Michael and Monika but made available their voluminous correspondence from Michael. Among Monika's friends in England, I am especially grateful to Ettie Turner and Betsy Ligon and several of her associates in Alcoholics Anonymous, who spoke to me behind the organization's traditional cloak of anonymity. Several British journalists gave generously of their time, including Jonathan Goodman; Bob Perrin, formerly of the *Bucks Free Press*, and in particular, Phillip Knightley of the *Sunday Times* of London, whose articles and subsequent book, *The Vestey Affair*, were the source of much of the history of Michael's family in Chapter 13. Works by E. Spencer Shew helped me understand the British legal system. To Thomas Maeder, author of *Crime and Madness: The Origins and Evolution of the Insanity Defense*, I am indebted for much of the history of the insanity defense in Chapter 50. Others to whom I owe thanks are Christine Freedman, Inspectors James Sullivan and Larry Homenick of the United States Marshals Service, my friend Jonathan Coleman, my agent, George Diskant, and, most of all, my wife, Sandra, whose love, support, and friendship overshadow everything else in my life.

Finally, my deepest thanks to Lou and Elsa Zumsteg, who generously opened their hearts and lives to me and, often with great pain, helped me understand the events of a past they would sooner forget. Although Monika's life ended, theirs went on, as has their pain.

Robert Lindsey

About the Author

Robert Lindsey, who was born in 1935 in Glendale, California, was for twenty years a reporter and correspondent for *The New York Times*. His first book, *The Falcon and the Snowman*, won the Edgar Allan Poe award in 1980. His most recent work, *A Gathering of Saints*, won the Gold Dagger Award of the Crime Writers Association of Great Britain in 1989. He is married and lives in Carmel, California.